THE RACIST MURDER
OF STEPHEN LAWRENCE

THE RACIST MURDER OF STEPHEN LAWRENCE

Media Performance and Public Transformation

Simon Cottle

Westport, Connecticut
London

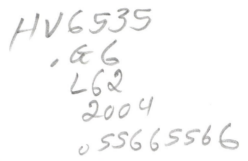

Library of Congress Cataloging-in-Publication Data

Cottle, Simon, 1956–
    The racist murder of Stephen Lawrence : media performance and public
transformation / Simon Cottle.
        p. cm.
    Includes bibliographical references and index.
    ISBN 0–275–97941–5 (alk. paper)
    1. Lawrence, Stephen, 1974–1993. 2. Murder—Press coverage—England—London.
3. Hate crimes—Press coverage—England—London. 4. Murder—Investigation—Press
coverage—England—London. 5. Murder in mass media. 6. Race relations in mass
media. 7. London (England)—Race relations. I. Title.
HV6535.G6L62 2004
364.152'3'09421—dc22   2004050968

British Library Cataloguing-in-Publication Data is available.

Library of Congress Catalog Card Number: 2004050968
ISBN: 0–275–97941–5

First published in 2004

Praeger Publishers, 88 Post Road West, Westport, CT 06881
An imprint of Greenwood Publishing Group, Inc.
www.praeger.com

(∞)™

Printed in the United States of America

The paper used in this book complies with the
Permanent Paper Standard issued by the National
Information Standards Organization (Z39.48–1984).

10 9 8 7 6 5 4 3 2 1

Copyright Acknowledgements

The author would like to thank the following for permission to reproduce their material in
this book: *Guardian*, *Observer*, *Independent*, *Daily Mail*, *Voice*, Reuters, the Photo News
Service Limited, The Times/News International Syndication, ITN News, the BBC, Channel
Four, Peter Lee-Wright, Trevor Phillips, Mark Honigsbaum and the Institute of Race Relations.

For Stephen Lawrence, not the public symbol who continues to illuminate the shameful racist secrets of British society, but the young man that most of us never knew and who was yet to be.

Contents

Tables and Figures

Preface

The research for this book was undertaken over a number of years and in two different countries. Along the way I have benefitted enormously from the generous support of colleagues, friends and different institutions. Without their help this book would not have seen the light of day. I would like to thank David Timms, Assistant Director at Bath Spa University College, for continuing to support academic research, this project included, when other institutional priorities seemed to be in the ascendant. Julian Matthews, colleague and friend at Bath, generously offered critical insights and enthusiasm in equal measure, and William Lee kindly worked as a research assistant expertly collecting data in the early stages of research. Commentary on the original book proposal by Stuart Allan and others was greatly appreciated and here I sincerely thank Elisabetta Linton, former U.S. commissioning editor at Praeger Publishers and Greenwood Press for believing in this study when UK publishers deferred on grounds of 'markets', 'texts' and current 'trends'. Mike Best, former editor, and Nicole Sylvester, librarian, both at the *Voice*, generously supported this project with time, photocopies and back issues notwithstanding other pressing commitments. The book was written when based at the University of Melbourne, Australia, and here I thank Melbourne University, the Faculty of Arts and especially my new colleagues in the Media and Communications Program for being so supportive in the final stages of research. I would also like to make special mention of Mugdha Rai, research assistant, for her practical help, intelligent insights and efficiency on this project. Mugdha has expertly recovered long-lost media materials, extended the range of data collected, written appendices and generally helped to prepare the manuscript for publication. Her help has been invaluable. Sam Cottle, my son, also kindly helped to prepare some of the data.

This book and its argument are indebted to the ideas of a number of social theorists. Here I would simply like to acknowledge, notwithstanding their marginalisation within current academic fashions, the continuing intellectual gifts found in the writings of Émile Durkheim and Victor Turner, as well as the writings of Jeffrey Alexander who has done the most to apply these to the study of contemporary mediatised public crises. I alone take responsibility for the final book and any discerned shortcomings.

Simon Cottle
Melbourne, 2004

One

Thesis

Stephen Lawrence, an eighteen-year-old black student, was murdered in an unprovoked racist attack as he was making his way home with his friend Duwayne Brooks on the evening of 22 April 1993. They were waiting at a bus stop in southeast London at around 10.30 PM when a group of white youths spotted them and charged across the road shouting, 'What, what Nigger?' Duwayne managed to run away, but Stephen hesitated. He was surrounded and subjected to a hail of blows, including two savage knife thrusts. He staggered a short distance before eventually succumbing to his mortal wounds on the pavement in a pool of blood. The attack occurred in Eltham, an area well known to harbour organised racists and wider racist sentiments. The headquarters of the British National Party—a right-wing racist, fascist organisation—was located nearby, and two racist murders had recently been committed in the vicinity. Monitoring reports indicated that incidents of racial harassment and abuse in this area were some of the highest in the country.

There have been unforgivable racist murders in Britain both before and since this crime, and annual incidents of racial attack and harassment continue to be recorded in the many thousands. But the case of Stephen Lawrence proved to be different. Over time the name of Stephen Lawrence became a potent symbol and catalyst for change. The murder, followed by the Lawrence family's pursuit of justice, prompted widespread reexamination of questions of (in)justice, cultural identity and continuing racism in British society, and it eventually initiated processes of institutional reflexivity, including government policies targeting institutional racism within some of Britain's most powerful organisations of state and civil society.

Stephen's parents, Doreen and Neville Lawrence, and their legal team doggedly pursued justice for their son over many years, notwithstanding an appalling catalogue of institutional failures and obstacles, professional insensitivities and personal setbacks. Their fight for justice focused on the pursuit of Stephen's known killers and their evasion from due processes of law. Across the years and with growing media exposure, however, the Stephen Lawrence case became much, much more. It became a 'mediatised public crisis' challenging the British system of (in)justice as perceived and experienced by Britain's minority communities and a litmus test of the extent to which wider British society was prepared to move beyond the anachronistic practices of the past, acknowledge and counter institutional racism, and embrace cultural diversity. The case thereby progressively served to focus national attention on deep-seated issues of 'race', racism and British identity and as it did so embroiled powerful institutions (police, judiciary, government) and prominent public figures (Metropolitan Police Commissioner Sir Paul Condon, Home Secretary Jack Straw, Leader of the Labour Party Tony Blair, Public Inquiry Chair Sir William Macpherson, Leader of the Opposition William Hague and many notable others). These pillars of the establishment were ritually obliged to manage their public responses to a growing sense of injustice and rising pressure for change, and were compelled to do so in the full glare of the media.

As a mediatised public crisis, the case of Stephen Lawrence extended politically outwards and culturally downwards. It caught up within its ambit powerful institutions of state and society and penetrated the normally subterranean soil of collective solidarities and cultural identities. It reached into the bowels of state and society, where no institution or powerful figure was seemingly immune from public scrutiny and criticism. Mediatised, the Stephen Lawrence case helped to expose the 'profane' reality of racist violence and inequality in contemporary British society and also served, in some quarters, to promote 'sacred' solidarities that aspired to a future society without racism. Mediatised, the case served to reenergise core and contested values of civil society and focused, at least for some, future visions of a more inclusive multiethnic, multicultural society. Mediatised, the name of Stephen Lawrence became, and has remained to this day, a potent symbol for the injustices experienced by and perpetrated against Britain's minority communities.

The case of Stephen Lawrence, then, was not confined to the criminal justice system, its various police investigations, committal and trial proceedings and courts, or even the high-profile public inquiry that was finally authorised by the home secretary, which took place some five years after the murder. It was principally enacted within the nation's media (and some international media, too) since it was there that the symbolic and moral charge of the case became generalised and extended outwards to different publics in society, galvanising emotions and feelings, and canalising differing political outlooks and projects. The media didn't simply report the Stephen Lawrence case; they actively performed it. How exactly they did so goes to the heart of current debate about the media's relationship to wider structures and processes of power, and it also raises fundamental questions about the media's commitment to multiethnic, multicultural British society. It is these concerns that form the basis for this book.

The media story of Stephen Lawrence is of historical importance and may even, in retrospect, be seen as a watershed in the shifting contours of 'race', racism and ethnicity as British society and culture struggles belatedly, and often in contradictory ways, to accommodate diversity and difference. The case is clearly important in such terms, but it also prompts us to rethink and retheorise our understanding of contemporary media and the mediatisation of public crises. Too often media communication researchers, who hold to relatively fixed or predetermined ideas about media power and its determinations and locations, overlook or undertheorise the multiple roles enacted, the cultural complexities expressed and the political contingencies that unfold through media conflict reporting. The case of Stephen Lawrence helps to reveal how in fact a differentiated media is capable of acting in concert while performing different roles and constituting different publics through the deployment of powerful appeals, ritual and symbols, as well as reasoned arguments and accounts mediated within the prevailing communicative forms of journalism. To understand the transformative potential of media performance as well as the media's involvement in reproducing the conservative structures of the present, we need to attend to the expressive possibilities of symbols and form, the dynamics and contingencies that inhere within both politics and narrative and the strategic interventions of involved interests and identities.

The Racist Murder of Stephen Lawrence: Media Performance and Public Transformation, then, sets out to examine the complex ways in which the mediatised public crisis of the Stephen Lawrence case energised processes of institutional and cultural reflexivity and change. As such, it opens up new insights into the role of media in transformative processes and challenges us to rethink not only the nature of media but also its impact within civil society and on culture and polity more generally. This book is both a case study of an important mediatised public crisis—the Stephen Lawrence story as it unfolded in and through the British (and international) media and how it reconstituted the institutional and cultural fields of 'race' and racism in British society—and a theoretical attempt to make sense of this and other exceptional news events that periodically break through routine media conventions and unleash social pressures for change. The book thereby brings media and communications theory into dialogue with the empirical details of the Stephen Lawrence case and, in so doing, refines a conceptual and theoretical framework of 'mediatised public crises' whilst also illuminating the trajectory and determinants of this historically momentous case.

PLAN OF THE BOOK

Following this brief overview of the book's central thesis, Chapter 2, 'Events', first contextualises the Stephen Lawrence story in relation to the contested and changing field of 'race', racism and identity in Britain and then outlines the basic events in the public story of the Stephen Lawrence case as it unfolded over a period of ten years. This background context and public story provide the beginning of our own 'story', the attempt to better understand how the media contributed to and played an essential role in publicly enacting the Stephen Lawrence case into a mediatised public crisis. Chapter 3, 'Theory', next identifies relevant positions of theory and, through critical engagement with these, develops an approach to mediatised ritual in general and the exploration of mediatised public crises in particular, both of which are here analytically defined. With the basic elements of the Stephen Lawrence story outlined and a theoretical framework in place, Chapter 4, 'Mapping', begins to document the phenomenal outpouring of the UK media in respect to the Stephen Lawrence case and its exponential growth over the period 1993–2003, and establishes how the case became generalised to diverse readerships, via mainstream and minority, elite and popular newspapers. This is then followed by five chapters each of which explores in more qualitative and detailed ways how this mediatised public crisis was enacted by different media across five developmental phases, and how they canalised the crisis to different publics and summoned solidarities. Chapters 5, 'Breach', 6, 'Crisis', 7, 'Redress', 8, 'Reintegration/Schism', and 9, 'Ebbing/Revivification', therefore, all attend to the developmental dynamics, forms and performative appeals of different media and how these publicly worked to constitute the Stephen Lawrence case as a major and potentially transformative moment for British society. Finally, Chapter 10, 'Conclusion', brings together the principal findings and key arguments of the study as a whole and underlines the central thesis interwoven throughout the preceding chapters, namely, the continuing importance of mediatised rituals in contemporary life and society and the value of attending to such exceptional media phenomena through the theoretical and conceptual prism developed in the course of this study, that of 'mediatised public crises'.

Two

Events

The Stephen Lawrence case was played out in a particular social context and at a particular historical moment. If we are to understand how and why the public story of Stephen Lawrence registered with such impact and became the exceptional mediatised phenomenon that it did, we will first need to situate it in relation to the contested field of British 'race' and racism and how this was configured, and being reconfigured, across this period. This chapter also sets out the basic events and developments in the Stephen Lawrence case as they unfolded across the ten-year period following his murder. This public story is our starting point, not the end point of the analysis that follows. Closely interwoven with the known story of the Stephen Lawrence case, its various institutional developments and revelations, is another story of course: the story of how the media enacted this to wider and particularised publics and how, in so doing, the Stephen Lawrence case became both a potent symbol and powerful catalyst for change. At the heart of this media story reside important insights into the performative nature of the media and its cultural power, and these will be addressed throughout the remainder of this book.

The story of the Stephen Lawrence case was principally played out, then, in two different arenas: the criminal justice system and the mass media. It was by these institutional means that the story publicly unfolded through time, assumed narrative form and progressively won widespread public interest. These institutions work according to their own temporal rhythms and logics, and, in consequence, significant details and developments in the Stephen Lawrence case often only became known long after the events themselves had taken place—sometimes after many years. Indeed, it was the temporally delayed nature of some of these public revelations as much as their shocking nature that served to propel the story forward and generate culturally cathartic or transformative effects. In the criminal justice system the Stephen Lawrence case was played out in a complex of arenas and interlinked processes. This comprised no less than two police inquiries, two internal police reviews, the actions or inactions of the crown prosecution service, committal and trial proceedings and a private prosecution, a coroner's inquest and, eventually, a full public inquiry authorised by the home secretary of the day. Each of these addressed the murder of Stephen Lawrence and sought to redress the failings of other parts of the criminal justice system.

The other narrative was performed by the media, which, though dependent on and occasionally directly intervening in the first, reworked and extended these same materials into a story that culturally reverberated throughout society and polity. The media's narrative and its relationship to the criminal justice system, as we shall see, were far from simply parasitic or just working in parallel. And, like the institutions of the criminal justice system, the media also exhibited its own internal differences. Through time, for example, important sections of the media began to push beneath the successive failures of the criminal justice system to expose deeper, more systemic problems of racism in the police force, the criminal justice system, and society at large; in so doing, these media outlets performatively summoned a moral solidarity that enveloped the story and which served to publicly shame authorities into action. Other sections of the media, however, though also caught up within this 'moral mood' and calling for justice in the name of Stephen Lawrence, could only go so far in their criticisms of the police or in their acknowledgement of deeper issues of 'race' and racism; and here a more particularised public was summoned into being, one based on traditional nostrums of British identity and an abiding confidence in Britain's central institutions positioned at the front line of maintaining law and order.

Before we can attend to the complex ways in which the media enacted the Stephen Lawrence story, summoned collective solidarities and unleashed powerful forces of change, it is first necessary to briefly situate the Stephen Lawrence case in relation to the surrounding and contested field of 'race' and racism in Britain and outline the known events of the case.

BRITISH 'RACE RELATIONS': INEQUALITIES AND IDENTITIES

Historically racism, in discourse and practice, has assumed different forms within the social formations of British society, its power structures and belief systems. Whether 'legitimising' the inhumanity of slavery, colonial expansion and economic exploitation; insinuated within Enlightenment science and the formulation of racial typologies; or enacted as racialised politics and immigration acts designed to exclude former British subjects, all these types of racism are entwined in British society, its politics and culture—and have variously been struggled against (Fryer 1984; Malik 1996). With respect to extreme racist violence, British society produced a catalogue of racist murders across the twentieth century. Most notorious, perhaps, are the lynch mobs who ran amok in Liverpool and Cardiff in 1919, but there has been continuing racist violence and killings by far-right organisations and other racists ever since. The Institute of Race Relations (IRR) has recorded 124 killings with a racial motivation in England, Scotland and Wales across the period 1970–2003, and documents 50 racially motivated murders (both known and/or suspected) from 1991 to 2002 (IRR 2001, 2002a, 2003). In 2000–2001, police recorded 25,100 racially aggravated offences in England and Wales, of which 12,455 were racially aggravated harassment, 4,711 were racially aggravated common assault, and 3,176 were racially aggravated wounding (IRR 2002b). The London Metropolitan Police recorded on average 5,000 reported racist incidents per year across 1994–1998, a figure that has more than doubled in more recent years. In 2000–2001, 53,090 racist incidents were recorded by the police in England and Wales, a figure that we know from the British Crime Survey is likely to be an underrepresentation of the actual figure (Commission for Racial Equality 1999; IRR 2002b).

In the 1990s, notwithstanding its preferred public image as a successful multicultural society, Britain produced appalling acts of racist violence (see Appendix 1). It also generated damning indices of inequality and discrimination—whether in fields of employment, housing, immigration, health, education or criminal justice (Blackstone et al. 1998; Skellington and Morris 1992). In 1993, the year that Stephen Lawrence was murdered, nearly twenty years after the first Race Relations Act (1976) and 45 years after the SS *Empire Windrush* disembarked the first West Indian migrants coming to Britain in the postwar period, Britain's multiethnic society fell far short from the ideal of a successful multicultural society. A combination of structural and institutional processes as well as blatant racism in housing and employment had led to urban concentrations of minority ethnic communities in major cities and run-down inner city areas (Rex and Moore 1967; Rex and Tomlinson 1979; Skellington and Morris 1992, 44–49; Smith 1989). Discriminatory and heavy-handed policing practices in many of these deprived urban locales sparked widespread urban unrest across the 1980s (Benyon 1984; Benyon and Solomos 1987; Cashmore and McLaughlin 1991; IRR 1987), and led to Lord Scarman's report on the Brixton disorders of 1981 (Scarman 1984). *The Scarman Report* concluded that policing practices had contributed to these disorders and that some individual police officers were racist; it therefore recommended, in the context of high inner city unemployment and in their dealings with black youths particularly, that 'the police adjust their policies and operations so as to handle these difficulties with imagination as well as firmness'. Significantly, Lord Scarman's report fell short of acknowledging 'institutional racism' as part of the problem (Scarman 1984, 15).

The urban unrest that had broken out across Britain's inner cities, and which had placed 'race' on public and media agendas (Benyon and Solomos 1987; Cottle 1992, 1993; Tumber 1982), took place against the backdrop of industrial decline, rising unemployment and the ruthless experiment in free-market policies of the Thatcher government. Deregulation and free-market policies had produced growing social dislocation and polarisation, and the Conservative government had responded with tough law-and-order measures (Hall 1988). However, across this same period, powerful countercurrents also flowed and marked the 'irresistible rise' of multiracial Britain (Phillips and Phillips 1998). Assimilationist models of race relations and essentialist thinking about 'race' started to be questioned, and a new focus on racism and antiracist forms of engagement informed local politics as well as black and Asian community struggles. The common sense category of 'race' (and thereby 'race relations' also) was criticised as a spurious biological concept that 'racialised' vulnerable social groups and rendered them vulnerable to exploitation (Miles 1982; Miles and Torres 1999; Solomos and Back 1996). The 'new racism' of the right, an integral part of Margaret Thatcher's populism and ideological reworking of British nationalism and electoral appeal, was also challenged as the latest expression of racist thinking and cultural intolerance towards others (Solomos et al. 1982). Across the 1970s and 1980s, ideas of multiculturalism had begun to celebrate cultural difference and the display of ethnic minority cultures and traditions, and these became an established part of the educational and wider cultural sensibility of Britain, though often in some tension with antiracist politics and under assault from new right doctrines.

More recently, ideas and debates about cultural identity and difference have come to the fore. Here ethnicity has been theorised in terms of fluid, internally contested and cross-cutting discursive 'subject positions,' which challenge primordial ideas of ethnicity and tradition and point to the end of 'the essential black subject' as a unified political focus (Brah 1996; Hall 1988, 1999; Yuval-Davis 1999). These 'new ethnicities' are theorised in relation to globalising processes of cultural translation rather than local tradition; postcolonial hybridity and cultural syncretism rather than antiracist politics; and the cultural routes of diaspora rather than the imagined roots of origin (Bhabha 1990; Clifford 1997; Gilroy 1987). Through an interrogation of identity construction at the margins, we can also better understand the normally invisible processes of white ethnicity enunciated from the centre of the British state, society and culture (Julien and Mercer 1988). These academic ideas, based on poststructuralist arguments and a metalinguistic theorisation of the fragmentation and play of the social, have proved extraordinarily influential within the academe and some black arts. They are not without their critics however.

The new 'cultural politics of difference', say its critics, is incapable of providing the grounds for building an emancipatory politics based on solidarity rather than infinite deferral and difference (Malik 1996; Rojek 2003; Sivanandan 1990; Turner and Rojek 2001). The 'politics of recognition', or the pursuit by minorities to find public acknowledgement and cultural representation, tends to displace the 'politics of redistribution' that demands to be grounded on the collective pursuit of equality and shared human rights. Questions of identity can become condensed in the interior processes of individual identity formation rather than related to exterior structures of inequality and collective struggle.

These debates are today often played out at the level of high-octane theory within university seminars, but they also register within the shifting contours of public discourse and representation that inform contested ideas of 'race', multiculturalism and national identity and which periodically become refracted through particular issues and media events. White backlash culture (Gabriel 2000), as well as expressions of multicultural society as a normative ideal (Parekh 1998, 2000), crash and collide in the field of British 'race', racism and ethnicity, a field that is simultaneously marked in the media sphere by continuity, contradiction and change (Cottle 2000, 2004; Law 2002; Malik 2002). Today, it seems, the 'multicultural question' refuses to go away, and this nebulous and contested term remains a common, if often ill-defined, conceptualisation of the historically changing field of British race relations (Hall 2000; Parekh 1998, 2000).

The mediatised public crisis that eventually developed out of the racist murder of Stephen Lawrence proved to be an important moment in this changing cultural-politics of 'race' in British society, which helped to shift the centre of gravity of public debate away from the complacent, often racist assumptions, exclusionary politics and representational silences of the past towards a more self-conscious, socially inclusive and possibly more compassionate view of multiethnic Britain and its future. As such, it helped to expose the myth of civil society as a place of equal opportunity, cultural tolerance and racial justice and, in so doing, summoned identities and solidarities that sought to better ground the normative claims of universalism embedded within this 'utopian civil society discourse' (Alexander and Jacobs 1998, 28). While it would be wrong to suggest that the Stephen Lawrence case single-handedly and irrevocably moved the field of British race relations—both affectively and politically—in a progressive direction or did so without giving rise to contradictory forces and white backlash culture, it would also be a gross oversight to theoretically underestimate the momentous push that the case has given to progressive forces of change. Before we examine the role performed by the media in all this, however, we first need to set out the known facts of the Stephen Lawrence story.

THE STEPHEN LAWRENCE STORY

To talk of the Stephen Lawrence 'story' is to concede that we are involved with an act of narration, which involves a narrator and the imposition of structure, arrangement, emphasis and much else besides. Though we are here concerned simply with the known events and principal developments of the case over a ten-year period, it is clear that these do not always speak for themselves. While the events outlined took place at specified times, in certain places and involved named individuals, the interpretation and meaning that has subsequently been placed on these has often been subject to heated dispute. Such is hardly surprising given that the case of Stephen Lawrence involved a murder trial where the prime suspects denied responsibility and where prominent individuals and institutions in the criminal justice system sought to publicly defend their actions (and inactions) against the charge of incompetence and institutional racism. Needless to say, this study does not pretend, nor does it set out, to reveal the 'truth' about the individuals who killed Stephen Lawrence—the available evidence in the public domain is widely known and appears to be overwhelming. Our story, rather, is concerned with the collective dynamics of how, through time, the media progressively intervened in this case and imbued it with transformative potential and effects that reverberated throughout society.

To this end, and distilled from available published accounts of the case, the following provides a descriptive summary of the principal events and developments that comprise the Stephen Lawrence story (a detailed chronology can also be found in Appendix 2).[1]

Murder

In 1993 Stephen Lawrence was an eighteen-year-old student pursuing his exams so that he could go on to study architecture, his chosen profession. Stephen was the son of Doreen and Neville Lawrence, who immigrated to Britain from the Caribbean when both were children. Doreen Lawrence was forty years old and had enrolled for a university degree, and Neville Lawrence was fifty. Both were hard-working and religious and believed in self-advancement through education. Neville Lawrence had previously worked as a plasterer and decorator but was now finding it difficult to find work, despite having undertaken various training courses. They lived in Plumstead in southeast London. By all accounts Stephen Lawrence was an amiable and popular young man, a good athlete and not unduly concerned about issues of 'race' and racism. On the day of the murder, he had gone to college and met his friend Duwayne Brooks; the two also met up later that evening at Stephen's uncle's house. At a little before 10.00 PM, they set off on the three-mile journey home that involved two bus rides. Stephen was expected home at 10.30. Whilst waiting near a bus stop in Well Hall Road in Eltham, a group of five or six white youths ran across the street towards them. One shouted out, 'What, what Nigger?' Duwayne Brooks called to his friend to run and took off, but Stephen hesitated. He was surrounded by the youths; one pulled a knife from his trousers and, with an upraised arm, brought his knife down into Stephen's upper chest. He was stabbed twice, perhaps by the same person or possibly two of the attacking group. It was over in seconds. Stephen fell to the ground but managed to get up, and the attacking youths ran off. After a short while, Stephen staggered and collapsed onto the pavement.

Duwayne was frightened and probably in shock. He tried to make an emergency call and stop motorists to take his friend to the nearest hospital, which was less than a mile away. One car slowed to a halt but then sped away. A couple on their way home from a local prayer meeting walked by, but they too seemed reluctant to help. Then an off-duty police constable and his wife drove by and attended to Stephen, with the help of the passing couple. Police arrived first, followed by an ambulance at 10.54. A witness on a passing bus, who had seen the incident and happened to know the Lawrences, went to their house to tell them what had happened. Doreen and Neville went to look for their son and then went to the hospital. There they waited outside the resuscitation room, but it was hopeless. Stephen Lawrence had lost too much blood, his veins had collapsed and he could not be revived. He had probably died not long after he had been stabbed, a little after 10.40 PM.

Locality

The borough of Eltham was notorious for racist violence, a fact that both Duwayne Brooks and Stephen Lawrence knew and which had informed their decision to catch buses through the area. Thirteen percent of the residents were ethnic minorities, but they were dispersed throughout the borough and so had little sense of communal security. Unemployment, and especially male unemployment, was high, as were other indices of poverty. Recorded levels of racial harassment were estimated to be one of the highest in the country. Eight racially motivated murders had occurred in London in the two years before the murder of Stephen Lawrence, including that of Rolan Adams in 1991, a black fifteen-year-old, who had been stabbed in the throat by a twelve-strong gang shouting 'nigger' in the Greenwich area; and in July 1992 Rohit Duggal had been killed on Well Hall Road. A local white boy, Peter Thompson, had been convicted of Duggal's murder only eight weeks before the murder of Stephen Lawrence (IRR 2002a). Racial tensions were, therefore, running high in the area and at a time when the Metropolitan Police under the new commissioner, Paul Condon, had publicly proclaimed its intent to improve the Met's relationship with local black communities.

The day after the murder, two of the investigating officers attended a meeting of the Greenwich Council Police Consultative Group in Woolwich Town Hall and heard community concerns about the increased racist attacks in the area. The Labour MP for Woolwich, John Austin-Walker, also said he would be meeting with the government minister to make sure effective action would be taken against rising racial attacks and harassment in the area, and a march was scheduled to protest against the British National Party (BNP) headquarters nearby, which was distributing racist leaflets and fomenting racial hatred in the area. A member of the Lawrence family also contacted the Anti-Racist Alliance (ARA), which offered support and a network of contacts of possible help. A debate in Parliament about creating a new offence of racial harassment had also preceded the murder of Stephen Lawrence, and this, too, was part of the political context that surrounded this latest racist murder.

Mounting Distrust

On 23 April, Neville Lawrence made a short statement at a press conference calling for witnesses to come forward. This was carried by the *Evening Standard* that Friday evening and London television news services, and the murder was also featured in brief news reports in national newspapers the next day. Neville Lawrence also phoned Nick Schoon of the *Independent,* who he had known through his work as a decorator, because he was concerned that his son's murder hadn't been reported in the press that morning (though the murder had in fact happened too late to meet the publication deadline of the morning papers).

Following their son's murder, the Lawrences became increasingly concerned that the police were not pursuing his killers as determinedly as they should, and as time moved on they became angered by the treatment they received from the police. Only one of the two assigned police liaison officers had been trained in the sensitive task of how to treat families of murder victims, and it was apparent that the Lawrences were not being kept in the picture. Moreover, the police appeared to resent the involvement of the family's supporters and their legal representative, Imran Khan, a solicitor introduced to them by the ARA. Doreen and Neville Lawrence had also heard from Stephen's friends that the police seemed intent on trying to establish that Stephen or Duwayne were in a gang, and therefore that the murder was gang-related.

In an effort to redress the deteriorating relationship between the Lawrences and the police, Detective Superintendent Brian Weeden invited them to visit the incident room at Eltham, but refused to let their solicitor, Imran Khan, attend. Detective Chief Superintendent William Ilsley later invited them again, this time with their solicitor. Before the meeting began, as she later recounted (at the inquest in 1997), Doreen Lawrence handed Ilsley a piece of paper with the names of the principal suspects on it. Ilsley took the note, but as the meeting proceeded, Doreen Lawrence watched him fold the piece of paper up into an ever-smaller lump of paper as if it was of no consequence. This seemed to typify to her the lack of seriousness with which the police were treating the case and the information that had been forwarded to them.

On 6 May, the Lawrences met African National Congress leader Nelson Mandela, who was reported as saying, 'their tragedy is our tragedy' (*Guardian*, 7 May 93). Finally, on 7 May, two weeks after the murder, the police arrested Gary Dobson and Jamie and Neil Acourt, and then David Norris two days later (and Luke Knight on 3 June). Identity parades took place on the Saturday but were poorly managed and subject to constant delays. Only two of the available three witnesses, Duwayne Brooks and Joey Shepherd, one of the bus stop witnesses, were present; the police couldn't locate on such short notice the other bus stop witness, Royston Westbrook. The three suspects were freed that night on police bail, until mid-July.

On Saturday, 8 May, a protest march over the BNP presence in the area took place, and when police blocked the route, disorder broke out. Duwayne Brooks was later arrested and charged with offences relating to the disorder, notwithstanding the relative insignificance of this offence and its possible impact on the Lawrence case. Police then banned a further joint anti-Nazi league/Indian workers association march past the BNP building on 15 May. On 18 June, 800 mourners attended Stephen Lawrence's memorial, and in July, the Lawrences flew Stephen's body to Jamaica, where he was buried. Then, on 29 July 1993, the Crown Prosecution Service (CPS) dropped murder charges against Neil Acourt and Luke Knight on the grounds that there was insufficient evidence to secure a conviction. There would be no committal proceedings and consequently no trial. This came as a bombshell to the Lawrences, who later described the decision (during the private prosecution in 1996) as 'an act as hurtful and as painful in its effect as the news that Stephen had been killed' (Cathcart 2000, 254).

In 1993, the Metropolitan Police Service commissioned an internal review, headed by Detective Chief Superintendent John Barker of the first police investigation. As an internal police review, the report was not released to the public; but it led Chief Commissioner Paul Condon to write to Imran Khan expressing his complete satisfaction with the investigation. On 13 September of the same year, the Lawrences held a torch-lit vigil in Eltham on what would have been Stephen's nineteenth birthday. On 21 December, presiding coroner Sir Montague Levine postponed the inquest into Stephen Lawrence's death on grounds of 'breaking' new evidence. This turned out to be based on hearsay, which suggested that Luke Knight had confessed to a social worker that he had been involved in the crime—a claim that could not later be verified.

The Second Police Investigation

On 15 April 1994, contrary to the advice of the CPS, the Lawrence family announced that they would mount a private prosecution against the five prime suspects—embarrassing both the Metropolitan Police Service and the CPS. On 20 April, Paul Condon authorised a meeting with the Lawrences at which Assistant Commissioner Ian Johnston showed them the findings outlined on the first page of the Barker Review, a document that was unlikely to reassure the Lawrences and which would subsequently be described as 'factually incorrect, inadequate, insensitive and thoughtless' (Macpherson 1999, sec. 46.21). The first page of the report stated: 'This has been and remains an investigation undertaken with professionalism and dedication by a team who have experienced pressures and outside influences on an unprecedented scale' (Cathcart 2000, 191).

The Met also initiated a new investigation. It was proposed that immunity could be offered to one of the suspects if they broke ranks, and a reward would also be offered for information leading to a conviction. A high-ranking police officer, Commander Perry Nove, replaced retiring Detective Superintendent Brian Weeden with an expanded team of officers, new resources and specialist support. Proactive tactics were now deployed, including making full use of the range of surveillance technologies permitted under the law. Covert film and sound recordings of the suspects' houses and a common friend's car were undertaken. And leverage would be applied if any of the suspects were caught committing new crimes to encourage them to confess about the group murder of Stephen Lawrence in exchange for personal immunity.

Criminal Proceedings and Private Prosecution

That same year the CPS insisted on pursuing Duwayne Brooks for his involvement in the 8 May Wellington march—despite the fact that he had not taken a leading or organising part in the trouble, and that hundreds were present and only six people had been charged with violent disorder. The trial finally began and was quickly aborted on 13 December, on the grounds that the prosecution should not have pursued it.

Also in 1994, Clifford Norris, the father of murder suspect David Norris and a hardened criminal suspected of intimidating witnesses, was arrested and later jailed, and Jamie Acourt was also sent to trial for knifing and nearly killing another youth in a fight in a nightclub in August that year—a charge that he later escaped on grounds of self-defence. In April 1995, a memorial service was held for Stephen, followed by the unveiling of a plaque at the site where he was attacked. On 23 August, a committal hearing took place at Belmarsh magistrates to see if Luke Knight, Neil and Jamie Acourt and David Norris should stand trial in a private prosecution. For the first time the Lawrences had access to police information about the earlier investigation, which clearly showed the flood of information that had been received shortly after the murder, naming the prime suspects within the first forty-eight hours, as well as the possible role of Clifford Norris in intimidating witnesses. The video evidence collected by the police in the second investigation also clearly showed the racist nature of the suspects and their predilection for knives and acting out knife attacks, including the use of raised arm stabbing movements.

Early in September 1995, however, charges against Jamie Acourt and David Norris were dropped on grounds of insufficient evidence; but Luke Knight and Neil Acourt were sent for trial, with Gary Dobson following in December. The trial at the Old Bailey began on 16 April 1996 and ended on the 25th. Neil Acourt, Luke Knight and Gary Dobson were cleared after identification evidence against them was ruled inadmissible. Here the status of the evidence provided by Duwayne Brooks proved to be crucial. Duwayne Brooks had picked out Neil Acourt and Luke Knight in identity parades but had told police immediately after the murder that he could only describe the man who had stabbed Stephen. The judge also heard that Duwayne Brooks allegedly told Detective Sergeant Christopher Crawley that he could only remember the men's physical descriptions and hair, but not their faces, and that he had also conferred with another witness at the time of the parades (when the police should have kept them apart). Mr Justice Curtis then ruled that Duwayne Brook's identification was not based on true recognition, was contradictory and possibly contaminated. The collapse of the trial meant that the jury did not hear important evidence presented at the earlier committal hearing. This included the video footage, shot by a secret police camera in Dobson's flat in Eltham, that demonstrated the three defendants were extreme racists accustomed to brandishing knives. Fibres taken from Stephen's hands were consistent with fibres taken from a jacket belonging to Dobson, and a 10-inch knife, suspected of being the murder weapon, was found hidden under a bed at Dobson's girlfriend's house. But, with the identification evidence squashed, the trial was not permitted to proceed, and the three suspects could now no longer be retried for the same offence under the British legal system and the so-called double jeopardy rule.

Jamie Acourt and David Norris were the only two remaining prime suspects who could still be prosecuted, though these two had previously been found to be the least likely to be successfully prosecuted on the basis of available evidence. The Lawrences decided to take their case to the Police Complaints Authority (PCA), which initiated a second review of the police investigations.

Coroner's Inquest

With the committal proceedings and trials now over, the inquest into Stephen's murder could finally take place. This opened on 10 February 1997. It was at the inquest that the Lawrences began to learn about the first police investigation and its many faults. A new communication system, the Holmes system, designed to store and render accessible incoming information in serious crimes was rendered less than effective by the lack of indexers and trained officers who could operate it. Incoming information from witnesses and the local community in the first forty-eight hours of the investigation was not acted upon, even though many sources explicitly named those whom they thought responsible, including statements about the suspects' involvement in previous knife attacks, with some witnesses even providing the suspects' addresses. This delay proved consequential as the opportunity to collect crucial forensic evidence was squandered. Detective Inspector Bullock, second in command, did not hear of two important leads naming the suspects that night, nor was Detective Superintendent Ian Crampton, the first senior investigating officer, not aware of any leads. When Crampton finally did hear about the leads the next day, he made the decision to wait before arresting the five named suspects. On that Monday, at a crucial time in the investigation, Crampton handed over the lead of the investigation to Detective Superintendent Brian Weeden. In the fortnight that followed, the police had no less than twenty-five anonymous calls, most naming the prime suspects as Neil and Jamie Acourt, Dave Norris and Gary Dobson (and also naming Dave Norris and Neil Acourt as the known attackers of Stacey Benefield who had nearly died from stab wounds some five weeks earlier).

The first police investigation, Operation Fishpool, had been incompetently handled and would later raise serious issues about institutionalised racism within the Metropolitan Police. Doreen Lawrence used the occasion of the inquest to vent her feelings about the police and their conduct. In response to a question from Sir Montague Levine, the coroner, she said:

When my son was murdered the police said my son was a criminal belonging to a gang. My son was stereotyped by the police—he was black then he must be a criminal—and they set about investigating him and us. The investigation lasted two weeks. That allowed vital evidence to be lost. . . . Our crime is living in a country where the justice system supports racist murderers against innocent people. (Cathcart 2000, 276)

While the inquest could only seek to determine cause of death, and not the criminal guilt or innocence of those involved, it nonetheless afforded an opportunity to directly question the five prime suspects. They, however, turned the coroner's court into a farce by repeatedly 'claiming privilege' or the right of silence to avoid incriminating themselves.

On 13 February, the inquest jury returned an unambiguous verdict: Stephen had been unlawfully killed 'in a completely unprovoked racist attack by five white youths' (Cathcart 2000, 285). The jury members thereby went beyond their instruction to return a verdict simply as to whether cause of death was unlawful, accidental or open, and clearly indicated who they thought were responsible.

Public Inquiry

The day after the coroner's verdict, the *Daily Mail* pictured and named on its front page the five suspects as Stephen Lawrence's 'Murderers', with the knowledge that any legal challenge to this controversial ('trial by media') move would involve the five having to publicly defend themselves against the charge. The calls for a public inquiry that followed were made by, amongst others, Sir Herman Ouseley, Chairman of the Commission for Racial Equality; Michael Howard, the home secretary, said he would consider it, though a general election was imminent. Doreen Lawrence later met the new Labour home secretary, Jack Straw, on 4 June who announced to the House of Commons on 31 July that he was about to convene a public inquiry, for which the terms of reference would be: 'To inquire into the matters arising from the death of Stephen Lawrence on 22 April 1993 to date, in order particularly to identify the lessons to be learned for the investigation and prosecution of racially motivated crimes' (Cathcart 2000, 311). The public inquiry was to be headed by Sir William Macpherson of Cluny, a retired High Court judge, and supported by the black bishop of Stepney, Right Reverend John Setamu; Chairman of the Jewish Council for Racial Equality, Dr Richard Stone; and former Deputy Chief Constable of West Yorkshire, Thomas Cook.

On 15 December 1997, the Police Complaints Authority released a 23-page summary of its detailed 400-page inquiry into the Stephen Lawrence murder investigation by the Metropolitan Police—the second police inquiry—which was submitted to the Macpherson Inquiry in 1998 in full. Carried out by Deputy Chief Constable Bob Ayling, of Kent Police, the report identified a number of serious failings in the earlier investigation: vital witnesses had been ignored; evidence linking suspects to other knife attacks had not been properly pursued; and there had existed confusion in the handling of identification evidence. The report also said that the police had lost the confidence of the Lawrence family and had claimed that they confronted a 'wall of silence', when in fact local people had come forward with valuable information. The 1993 Metropolitan Police internal review, which broadly endorsed the conduct of the police murder investigation, had also reassured senior officers about the investigations and thereby compounded earlier mistakes and hampered the possibility of successfully pursuing later inquiries. The PCA report stated, however, that there was no evidence of racist conduct by the police, corruption or collusion with the suspects or members of their families. Only one officer, it recommended, should face disciplinary charges over the Lawrence case.

The public inquiry began on 16 March 1998 and immediately faltered as the credentials of Sir William Macpherson himself were called into question by the *Observer* and were also of concern to the Lawrences. The matter was resolved with the help and assurances of Home Secretary Jack Straw. The inquiry resumed on 24 March, and additional evidence about the 'seriously flawed' nature of the initial police inquiry soon came to light, including the failure to make early arrests, properly convene identity parades and prevent witness intimidation; the failure of the police to check for forensic evidence from bags placed on Stephen Lawrence's hands after he had died; the failure of the police to use photographs to challenge Gary Dobson in an interview in which he claimed he did not know David Norris (police photographs had captured him with Norris outside of the latter's address); and the failure to stop and question the occupants of a car seen repeatedly driving past the murder scene on the night of the murder.

It also became known that a surveillance car with a police constable and civilian photographer was not dispatched to one of the named suspect's houses until late on Monday afternoon, four days after the murder. The photographer did not have time to set up his camera, however, before one of the suspects was seen leaving with clothes in a bag. The surveillance car did not follow because there was no prearranged backup or, incredibly, any contact with the Eltham police station via radio communications. The inquiry also brought to light suggestions of possible police corruption with respect to Clifford Norris. The police acknowledged that they had initially seen Duwayne Brooks as a suspect, raising suggestions of possible stereotyping. The apparent insensitivity of the police displayed towards the Lawrences was also described, including the astonishing fact that the chief investigating officer, Brian Weeden, had not met the Lawrences until one year after the murder.

Teams of barristers were involved throughout, and countless witnesses were summoned and publicly called to account. Metropolitan Police Commissioner Paul Condon complained that the inquiry was unfair to the police, and one investigating detective continued to deny that the murder was a racist killing. At first the named suspects sought leave to apply for judicial review to try to avoid giving testimony at the inquiry, but to no avail, though it was agreed by Lord Justice Simon Brown that they could not be asked directly whether they killed Stephen Lawrence. Doreen and Neville Lawrence gave testimony, as did Duwayne Brooks, and the inquiry also viewed the videotape of the suspects brandishing knives and using racist language. Police Commissioner Paul Condon sought to defend his force against the charge of institutional racism, a concept that was elaborated and discussed at length within the inquiry, but issued an apology on 17

June 1998, five years after Stephen Lawrence's death, for the failures of the Metropolitan Police. At one point, disorder broke out outside the inquiry and involved members of the black organization Nation of Islam who attended the inquiry in force but could not gain access to the small building. And on 30 June, the suspects were pelted with bottles and fruit when leaving the inquiry, following their evasive and implausible testimony. The first stage of the inquiry ended on 20 July with the Lawrences calling for the commissioner's resignation. On 29 July, the Met announced that it was setting up a special task force headed by John Grieve to tackle corruption and racism in its ranks.

The second stage of the inquiry began on 16 September, with the purpose of more generally examining the relationship between the criminal justice system and ethnic minorities throughout Britain. Paul Condon testified and personally apologised to the Lawrence family but dismissed racism claims. However, other senior colleagues, including the chief constables of Greater Manchester and deputy chief constable of West Yorkshire, acknowledged the existence of institutional racism in their forces. The inquiry included visits to Birmingham, Bradford and Bristol before ending with a public hearing in Birmingham on 13 November 1998.

The publication of the report was marred by seeming incompetence when the government was forced to obtain a High Court injunction to prevent publication of details of the report after leaked extracts appeared in the *Sunday Telegraph*. Jack Straw ordered a formal investigation into the leak. Sir Paul Condon and the Lawrences were permitted to see the report at the Home Office on 22 February 1999 before it was officially published on 24 February. The report made seventy wide-ranging and extensive recommendations designed to increase trust and confidence in policing amongst minority ethnic communities (see Appendix 4 for summary of main report recommendations). This was preceded by a damning principal conclusion about the Stephen Lawrence police investigation involving 'institutional racism':

The conclusions to be drawn from all the evidence in connection with the investigation of Stephen Lawrence's racist murder are clear. There is no doubt but that there were fundamental errors. The investigation was marred by a combination of professional incompetence, institutional racism and a failure of leadership by senior officers. A flawed Metropolitan Police Service review failed to expose these inadequacies. The second investigation could not salvage the faults of the first investigation. (Macpherson 1999, sec. 46.1)

Post–Public Inquiry

Following the publication of the Macpherson report, the Stephen Lawrence case remained in the public eye for a considerable time and continues to do so through disparate events and developments: whether to do with the criminal activities of the suspects and police investigations; the lives of the Lawrences and Duwayne Brooks; or processes of legislation and social reforms. In 2002, two of the Lawrence suspects were accused of a racist attack on an off-duty policeman, tried, subsequently convicted and jailed for eighteen months. To date the police have not laid any new charges for the murder of Stephen Lawrence. Following the Macpherson inquiry, the Lawrences have also been publicly acknowledged through various awards, including 'Media Personalities of the Year' at the Race in the Media Awards, and 'Public Figures of the Year' at the Ethnic and Multicultural Media Awards. In 2000, they announced that they had divorced, and in October of that year, the Metropolitan Police agreed to pay them £320,000 in compensation. In December 2002, the Lawrences were awarded OBEs (Order of the British Empire).

On 2 April 2001, new antiracism laws came into effect with the Race Relations (Amendment) Act, which covers all public bodies and brings them for the first time under the accountability of the Commission for Racial Equality (see Appendix 4 for major institutional reforms implemented since the Macpherson report). Ten years after the murder of Stephen Lawrence, on 22 April 2003, over 500 people gathered in Trafalgar Square for a memorial service. In May 2004 Scotland Yard announced, to the dismay of the Lawrences, that they would stop pursuing the case given the latest CPS decision that there was insufficient evidence to bring a prosecution against the known suspects. Today, however, the name of Stephen Lawrence continues to be invoked in public discussion and policy arenas concerned with 'race', racism and identity in contemporary Britain (see Postscript). This, then, is the story as publicly known and recounted about the tragic death and unforgivable murder of Stephen Lawrence.

SUMMARY

The Stephen Lawrence case, as we have seen, took place at a particular moment in the changing history of British race relations, and, in its mediatisation, it thereby entered into a contested field of public discourse and representation. This comprised discourses and debates, identities and ideas, that were contended around the meanings of 'race', racism and British identity. We have also plotted the known public story of the Stephen Lawrence case and how it unfolded across time—this, however, constitutes only the beginning of our own 'story'. The media sometimes figured as actors within this, but through time, as we will see later, they also actively 'performed' the Stephen Lawrence story and extended its emotional, political and moral charge throughout society. How are we to make sense of this? Why did the media transform the Stephen Lawrence story into a major mediatised public crisis? And how exactly did this enter into the life of society? The following chapter identifies and fashions relevant positions of media theory to help answer these questions, which are then pursued throughout the remainder of the book.

NOTE

1. The chronology of principal events and background outlined here draws on previously published accounts and media commentary. This includes Brian Cathcart's award-winning journalistic account, *The Case of Stephen Lawrence* (2000), Sir William Macpherson's official report, *The Stephen Lawrence Inquiry* (1999), as well as the daily reporting provided by such newspapers as the *Guardian* and the *Independent* across the ten-year period beginning 22 April 1993.

Three

Theory

As the mediatised Stephen Lawrence case grew into an emotionally charged and potentially transformative moment in British race relations, so it became apparent that this was something that should not be happening. Or, rather, that it should be happening, needed to happen, but that it would not have been predicted, nor could it be adequately explained, by widely held theoretical expectations. This media story, contrary to received theoretical wisdom, was not for the most part elite driven; it broke through news thresholds and short-term attention spans; it threatened to unseat prominent dignitaries and poured opprobrium on 'pillars of the establishment' and some of society's most hallowed institutions; and it also instigated processes of cultural reflexivity, parliamentary legislation and widespread institutional reforms. Not only this, it also managed to bring to the surface normally subterranean issues of 'race', racism and injustice, placing these at the centre of public debate, as well as within the horizons of popular culture. How could this be? How did this come about?

A number of evident features seemed to place the mediatised story of Stephen Lawrence at odds with current theoretical thinking and expectations. These can be summarily stated before we move on to deepen these features theoretically in the rest of the chapter and provide a framework for use in this study. First, the mediatised portrayal of the Stephen Lawrence case assumed a highly ritualised and expressive form. Through its representations, the media appeared to embody and express powerful collective feelings and emotions while it delivered information and accounts. In this way, the media portrayal appealed to collective solidarities, identities and outlooks. It was this ritual dimension, defined more analytically below, which served to charge and vivify public sentiments around normative views of justice and civil society, and it did this as much by the display of emotive signs, symbols and ritual performance as by the delivery of information, rationalistic accounts and legalistic arguments. The cultural charge of the Stephen Lawrence case, moreover, was embedded within both the 'serious' broadsheet newspapers and mainstream television news and current affairs programmes as much as their more popular cousins, the tabloid newspapers and populist forms of television. The 'ritual' dimension of the Stephen Lawrence representation, then, problematises current media theories that remain wedded to overly rationalistic views of the news media functioning, say, as a 'public sphere' of information exchange, rational debate and opinion formation. Clearly we need to attend further to theoretical ideas on ritual and the expressive capability of media if we are to better understand how the mediatised story of Stephen Lawrence delivered such cultural punch.

Second, this was a story that 'moved' through time, both temporally and affectively. The case of Stephen Lawrence refused to go away; it unfolded over a period of many years—the timeframe of this study is 1993–2003—and it continues to inform public debate and discussion to this day. The long-term trajectory of the Stephen Lawrence story, therefore, cannot be meaningfully captured in terms of a one-time spectacular story or as a form of 'media event'; nor can it simply be taken as a succession of disaggregated events or updates. The Stephen Lawrence narrative unfolded diachronically, gathering momentum as well as potentially explosive effects as it went. Here institutional developments, damning revelations and political contingencies as much as the dramatic structure of the narrative propelled the story forward from one moment, one phase, to the next. It is here that much of the charge of the Stephen Lawrence story was felt and this too demands closer analysis. As we have already noted, 'time' was not confined to the chronological succession of events in real time, but was constituted within and through the institutional routines and rhythms of the criminal justice system and the mass media. It was these dynamics that helped to give the Stephen Lawrence case its narrative structure as well as its enhanced capacity to build public solidarities and unleash pressures for change. The dynamics of the story, therefore, challenge relatively ahistorical accounts of media-society relations, as well as prevailing views of the institutionalised relationships of power often assumed to explain their interaction. The dynamic nature of this mediatised story, as well as its transformative capacity, consequently invites further theoretical reflection and raises interrelated considerations of media and power.

Third, this story seems to challenge ideas about elite-dominated news production and representations. If dominant sources and elite power—traditionally a key explanation for privileged news access and the successful imposition of 'primary definitions' on news events—were at work in this case, at least it was apparent that they were not completely controlling the media narrative. Powerful processes of symbolisation were also at work and moving the story forwards. Dominant state institutions and elites increasingly had to struggle for public legitimacy within the mediatised field populated not only by elite actors but also by a profusion of signs and symbols, at the heart of which was the symbol of Stephen Lawrence himself. As symbol, Stephen Lawrence breathed life into the struggles conducted in his name. The symbolic aura that became attached to Stephen Lawrence was also extended by Doreen and Neville Lawrence, two 'ordinary' people, affording them unusual cultural powers in their dealings with institutional authorities and elites. It was they who publicly took possession of the moral high ground in their quest for justice. Within the media spotlight, then, cultural symbolic power often appeared to successfully challenge the strategic power of institutionalised interests. This begs further reflection on the sufficiency of theories of news access and media source power that maintain that the news media are institutionally and structurally dependent, and that the nature of their representations is thereby determined. When set loose within the mediatised field of contending interests, we also need to consider the cultural power of symbols and symbolism as agents of change.

Finally, the media portrayal of the Stephen Lawrence case also demonstrates the performative dimension of media representation and enactment, and how this, too, became a powerful agent within the unfolding story. It is the contention here that the media did indeed 'perform' the Stephen Lawrence story, that is, that they purposefully propelled the story forward on the public stage and generalised the case to a wider readership or audience while deliberately canalising it in respect of particularised solidarities invoked in and through the rhetorical embodiment of different 'publics'. It was by these performative means that dispersed readers and audiences could temporarily coalesce into publics and recognise themselves as part of a higher collectivity sharing sentiments about the injustices of the case and hopes for a better future. This move from the indicative to subjunctive mode of reporting, from the reporting of the here and now to the prompting of normatively informed evaluation and future-oriented imagining, involved the media in performative action. Or, to put it more sharply, the media engaged in the purposeful construction of representations with attitude, with ambition. So here we need to attend to questions of mediatized power in respect of the performative capacity of the media, as well as its differential forms and expressions in sustaining particularised solidarities in and through media public sphere(s). The media 'performed' the story of Stephen Lawrence and as such were powerful protagonists in both enabling it 'to mean' as well as 'to move'—diachronically, developmentally, emotionally—through time. In this performative respect, then, they were doing far more than simply reporting the Stephen Lawrence case from a position outside of the main frame of action; they were inside the frame and often reconfiguring it as they moved it forward. Ideas of media performance and performativity, closely aligned to ideas of ritual, therefore, also prompt further theoretical reflection and discussion.

Together, these dimensions of the Stephen Lawrence media story—ritual, dynamics, symbolism and performativity—challenge us to rethink our understanding of certain mediatised conflicts and the roles that media, and news media in particular, are capable of playing. They also render problematic the blanket findings and generalised pessimism recounted in countless studies of the mass media and its representations of 'race', racism and minority ethnicity across the years (Cottle 2000, 7–15). The Stephen Lawrence case, in fact, demonstrates that not all media must always and necessarily reproduce unthinking stereotypes or rehearse the same conflict-driven news agendas. In the case of Stephen Lawrence, powerful sections of the mainstream media became emboldened through his role as public cipher to expose the inequalities and iniquities of 'race' and racism and, further, to promote forces of cultural reflexivity and political and social change. The media became actively caught up within the transformative energies that they themselves had actively performed and helped to unleash.

These opening observations prompt further reflection and development if we are to build a theoretical framework that can help map the complexities and dynamics of the mediatised Stephen Lawrence case. Having situated the study theoretically we will then be in a stronger position to explain the exceptional nature of the case and better account for its eruption and transformative capacity within culture, polity and society.

RITUAL SUSPICIONS

To begin, however, we first need to address some deep-seated suspicions that inform much contemporary media scholarship about 'ritual'. Paddy Scannell has observed:

A resistance to rituals has a history as old as enlightenment opinion: it is a complex dislike of public life as theatre, a fear (perhaps resentment) of the politics of the spectacle. (Scannell 2001, 700)

Three fundamental suspicions in particular deserve comment: that ritual is: 1) essentially arational (and irrational) and therefore ideologically obfuscatory and/or politically dangerous; 2) an anachronism confined to the maintenance of predemocratic 'cults' and that ritual meaning today is eviscerated by modern mass media; and 3) rendered socially irrelevant by the increasingly blasé attitude found within contemporary cosmopolitan, postmodern societies.

Jürgen Habermas's treatise on the historical rise and modern demise of the 'public sphere' gives full vent to rationalist concerns over the 'refeudalization' of modern forms of mediated publicness where the powerful once again parade their influence before a communicatively emasculated audience (Habermas 1989; Peters 1993). Habermas's treatise provides a foundational critique of the media and its contemporary propensity towards ritual display and spectacle. But his view of deliberation and opinion formation, discussed further below, is overly rationalistic and thereby fails to acknowledge the role of emotions, symbols and sentiments within communicative encounters, as well as their contribution to human understanding and democratic advance. Symbols, emotion, rhetoric and performance are constitutive of human communication (and communicative action), and these remain available for ritual expression across time and place.

Walter Benjamin's work on art in the age of mechanical reproduction has also proved influential in propagating suspicion of rituals. Benjamin argues that ritual has historically served to bolster the power of 'cults'. He also observes how modern mass media contribute to 'the liquidation of the traditional value of the cultural heritage' (1977, 223), which 'emancipates the work of art from its parasitical dependence on ritual' (226). Ritual, in this account, then, has no place in democratic politics and in any case is undermined by modern means of reproduction that contribute to the loss of 'aura'.

This view rightly, I think, invites careful consideration of the means of communication and how they mediate in time and place and thereby transform meanings, but it also risks essentialist thinking in two major respects. First, in relation to 'mediums' as technologies of communication, which are thought, inherently, to exert specific communicative impacts; and, second, in respect to 'ritual' that is conceived as inevitably bound up with conservative, predemocratic traditions. The different mediums and genres of today's media in fact demonstrate that they are capable of performing various roles and, given their embedded position within the contexts and flow of contemporary society, so, too, can they sustain different identities and relations to social power. Historically and across cultures we can also note how ritual assumes diverse forms and has served different political ends (Kertzer 1988). Ritual need not, then, always be assumed to be confined to 'traditional' ceremonies or the maintenance of hegemonic power. When enacted within a vortex of historical change, ritual can in fact serve democratising impulses as much as forces of conservatism.

Some currents of contemporary social theory also challenge the idea and practice of ritual for being out of step with the postmodern condition of media-saturated society. Essentially, this argues that ritual has become irrelevant to the easily distracted gaze of viewers and readers who, surrounded by an incessant but always transitory kaleidoscope of mediated signs, remain oblivious to anything other than their surface effects. Today's media create a 'bombardment of signs' that lead to 'semiotic excess', it is said, which proves incapable of penetrating to, or sustaining, deeper 'solidarities' (Baudrillard 1983). Keith Tester has argued in the context of televised images of human suffering, for example, how 'increased visibility to the gaze seems to go hand in hand with increasing invisibility from the point of view of the responsibility of moral solidarity' and 'media significance means moral insignificance' (1994, 130). Again, we appear to be confronted by essentialist thinking about television approached as 'medium', as well as in respect of processes of reception that are curiously desocialised. Audiences, in this account, seemingly bring no preceding identities or wider social commitments to the encounter with specific television images, and yet these are known to inform reception, generate felt obligations and, on occasion, even prompt a preparedness to engage with 'the serious life'. Mediacentrism as much as medium essentialism, therefore, are apt to underestimate the processual and social dynamics involved in audience reception and they short-circuit consideration of how media audiences can, on occasion, become constituted as 'publics'. To better understand the power of contemporary ritual and the part played by media within this, we can usefully revisit, and then rework, seminal ideas from Émile Durkheim—a sociologist whose ideas too often are overlooked or misunderstood.

RITUAL, CEREMONY AND COLLECTIVE EFFERVESCENCE

The later writings of Émile Durkheim continue to provide profound insights into the nature of society and how society generates a collective sense of itself. In particular, Durkheim's reflections on the idea of society as the soul of religion provides a key to unlock the potency of ritual as a means of generating a collective sense of a higher (sacred) power—whether religious or collective/moral. In *The Elementary Forms of Religious Life* (1912), Durkheim outlines his arguments for the social nature (and origins) of religion, the distinctions between the sacred and the profane which this gives rise to and the role of symbols and rituals in sustaining social solidarity.

If religion has given birth to all that is essential in society, it is because the idea of society is the soul of religion.

Religious forces are therefore human forces, moral forces. It is true that since collective sentiments become conscious of themselves only by fixing themselves upon external objects, they have not been able to form without adopting some of their characteristics from other things: they have thus acquired a sort of physical nature; in this way they have come to mix themselves with the life of the material world, and then have considered themselves capable of explaining what passes there. In reality, the essential elements of which these collective sentiments are made have been borrowed by the understanding. It ordinarily seems that they should have a human character only when they are conceived under human forms; but even the most impersonal and the most anonymous are nothing else than objectified sentiments. (Durkheim 1912, 466–67)

Durkheim's later sociology invites an understanding of the power of ritual and how public ceremonies—whether religious or secular—serve to revitalise collective sentiments that constitute a sense of higher (sacred) purpose. On such occasions, according to Durkheim, individual egoistic motivations that ordinarily inform interactions within the mundane world of everyday life give way to a higher form of collective belonging or moral solidarity. At such moments, intense feelings of 'effervescence' may be experienced, based on a sense of collective belonging and transcending the limited capacities of ordinary life.

For our definition of the sacred is that it is something added to and above the real: now the ideal answers to this same definition; we cannot explain one without explaining the other. In fact, we have seen that if collective life awakens religious thought on reaching a certain degree of intensity, it is because it brings about a state of effervescence which changes the conditions of psychic energy. Vital energies are over excited, passions more active, sensations stronger; there are even some which are produced only at this moment. . . . In order to account for the very particular impressions which he receives, (man) attributes to the things with which he is in most direct contact properties which they have not, exceptional powers and virtues which the objects of everyday experiences do not possess. In a word, above the real world where his profane life passes he has placed another which, in one sense, does not exist except in thought, but to which he attributes a higher sort of dignity than to the first. Thus from a double point of view it is an ideal world. (Durkheim 1912, 469–70)

Understandably, Durkheim identifies public ceremonies and assemblies as key venues for the periodic moral remaking or revitalisation of collectivity and 'society'.

[S]ociety cannot make its influence felt unless it is in action, and it is not in action unless the individuals who compose it are assembled together and act in common. It is by common action that it takes consciousness of itself and realises its position; it is before all else an active co-operation. The collective ideas and sentiments are even possible only owing to these exterior movements which symbolize them, as we have established. Then it is action which dominates the religious life, because of the mere fact that it is society which is its source. (Durkheim 1912: 465–66)

These passages include much that is profound, as well as much that demands careful reflection and development. Durkheim's ontology of 'society', for example, has rightly been criticised on a number of grounds (see, for example, Coser 1977; Emirbayer 2003; Giddens 1971; Lukes 1973, 1975; Thompson 1988). Major criticisms include its hypostatisation of society as *sui generis*, that is, as having its own separate essence or being; its totalising view of collective solidarity; its dualistic thinking about the 'real' and the 'ideal'; and the seemingly impermeable bifurcation of the world into the 'sacred' and 'profane'. Its physiological sounding interpretation of 'effervescence' also sounds strange to contemporary ears, though here we may want to acknowledge that societies and cultures, as well as collectivities and individuals, are indeed periodically caught up in intensified group feelings, and that these often become unleashed in response to a resonant symbolic object or event.

To avoid Durkheim's universalising, totalising and seemingly ahistorical claims about the nature of 'society', however, we would do better to situate our analysis in respect to a particular society or constellation of social relations at a particular moment in time and, importantly, to see these as structured and invariably conflicted (Kertzer 1988; Lukes 1975). So we need to carefully deploy Durkheim's insights into the integrative force of rituals and also ground these with respect to particular groups, publics and projects. It also follows that the organizing force of rituals need not always be assumed to be consensual nor uniformly inflected (Chaney 1986), much less coextensive with a singular collectivity resident within national borders (Kellner 2003; Tomlinson 1997). But, equally, we should not lose sight of the powerful insights that Durkheim's later writings have bequeathed to us. These include his fundamental understanding of ritual as 'society in action' and as a potent means by which solidarity (and 'sacred' sense of higher moral purpose) can be periodically secured and/or reaffirmed. These ideas continue to have explanatory purchase when trying to fathom the force of mediated rituals and also the state of 'effervescence' that can result through mass mediated events. Durkheim's original theorisation of the 'sacred' force of ritual and symbols and how these crystallise and energise collective sentiments and solidarities remains to this day invaluable for understanding mediatised rituals as well as their transformative capacity.

In the field of media communication scholarship, the depth of Durkheim's original insights and theorisation is often lost. When distinguishing between a transmission model and a ritual model, two paradigmatic orientations in the field, James Carey famously observed:

> A ritual view of communication is not directed towards the extension of messages in space, but the maintenance of society in time (even if some find this maintenance characterised by domination, and therefore illegitimate); not the act of imparting information or influence but the creation, representation, and celebration of shared even if illusory beliefs. If a transmission view of communication centres on the extension of messages across geography for purposes of control, a ritual view centres on the sacred ceremony that draws persons together in fellowship and commonality. (Carey 1989, 43)

Carey's formulation maps competing approaches within the field of media communication study, but his formulation, and the dualism that underpins it, perpetuates a common and delimited understanding of ritual. This positions ritual as necessarily consensual in nature, oriented to binding societies through time, and as integrative through sacred ceremonies (see Shils and Young 1956). This view finds support in a surface reading of Durkheim, but a deeper reading allows for a more variegated range of ritual expressions, as well as the involvement of conflicted parties and, in consequence, less than consensual or certain outcomes (Alexander 1988; Emirbayer 2003). A neo-Durkheimian reading of ritual as 'society in action', but which also has the capacity to build particularised solidarities or publics through the creation of sacred symbols and mobilization of collective sentiments, provides the foundation for a more temporally dynamic and politically contested view of ritual and one that may even permit on occasion transformative possibilities. Today, 'society in action' is often enacted in and through the media sphere.

MEDIATISED RITUALS

Mediatised rituals, as we shall see, can assume diverse forms and expressions. Here I will define 'mediatised rituals', in encompassing terms, as follows:

Mediatised rituals are those exceptional and performative media phenomena that serve to sustain and/or mobilise collective sentiments and solidarities on the basis of symbolisation and a subjunctive orientation to what should or ought to be.

This definition will be grounded and elaborated upon further below. But here we can note how mediatised rituals may variously draw upon or make use of institutionalised ceremonies or rituals staged elsewhere, or they may not. And they may also be dependent on and be directed by social authorities and institutions outside of the media sphere, or they may not. When reporting on institutional rituals or ceremonies elsewhere, however, to classify as a mediatised ritual, the media will be doing something more than simply reporting such occasions; they will be actively enacting it in a subjunctive mode—that is, invoking and sustaining through symbolisation collective sentiments and solidarities about how society should or ought to be (typically through future-oriented imagining). This definition, then, makes no prescriptions about whether mediatised rituals are essentially consensual or hegemonic, include contending views and conflicting interests, or whether they are potentially binding or disruptive—or even transformative. These are essentially empirical questions that cannot be theoretically or conceptually prescribed in advance.

The types of media events that can be described as mediatised rituals are also, by definition, 'exceptional'; that is, they are salient or obtrude in terms of high-level media exposure and media performativity across media outlets in space and/or time. There is much, of course, that is habitual and ritualised in media presentation and everyday media consumption (Becker 1995; Couldry 2003; Larsen and Tufte 2003; Rothenbuhler 1998; Silverstone 1994), but this is not the stuff of those exceptional, symbol-laden, performative, subjunctively oriented and media-enacted mediatised rituals that elicit publics and which concern us here. Anthropological approaches to ritual often seek to establish the nature of media ritual in relation to the spatial-temporal arrangements and/or phenomenology of media consumption in everyday life as well as specificities of medium approached as form, but these thereby often lose purchase on the political contexts and powered nature of exceptional media phenomena and how these relate to the wider play of power (and uncertain outcomes) of contending social relations and forces of change. While the everyday is without doubt the terrain for the enactment of power, we cannot afford to lose sight of exceptional rituals that periodically crash through routine media conventions and seemingly galvanise sentiments and solidarities directed at 'higher' collective projects and which, by definition, speak to collective life beyond the mundane world of everyday consumption practices.

Within the field of media communications research, five theoretical approaches have engaged with this class of exceptional media phenomena: moral panics, celebrated media events, contested media events, media scandals, and mediatised public crises. Each serves to address a subclass of mediatised ritual, and each thereby helps to refine our understanding of the potent ways in which mediatised ritual is deeply implicated in the enactments of contemporary societies, its solidarities and identities and potentially divisive issues.

Mediatised Ritual 1: Moral Panics

Stanley Cohen opened his classic study of moral panics with the following memorable words:

Societies appear to be subject, every now and then, to periods of moral panic. A condition, episode, person or group of persons emerges to become defined as a threat to societal values and interests; its nature is presented in a stylised and stereotypical fashion by the mass media; the moral barricades are manned by editors, bishops, politicians and other right thinking people; socially accredited experts pronounce their diagnoses and solutions; ways of coping are evolved or (more often) resorted to; the condition then disappears, submerges or deteriorates and becomes more visible. . . . Sometimes the panic passes over and is forgotten, except in folklore and collective memory; at other times it has more serious and long-lasting repercussions and might produce such changes as those in legal and social policy or even in the way society conceives itself. (Cohen 1972, 9)

Cohen did not frame his celebrated analysis in terms of mediatised ritual, but he could well have done. The premise of the theory of moral panics is, of course, the idea of 'society in action', the mobilisation of collective fears and anxieties amplified and sensationalised through the media and focused in relation to a symbolic other, a folk devil, that ultimately serves processes of societal control through the policing of collective moral boundaries. In many respects, this is classic Durkheimian sociology of deviance. Ritualised media performances are rehearsed, and the collective assertion of consensual societal values is enacted in opposition to the media's depicted threat. Moral panic theory, notwithstanding mounting criticisms and refinements over the thirty years or so since its publication (see Critcher 2003; Goode and Ben-Yehuda 1994; McRobbie 1994; Media International Australia 1997; Thompson 1998), continues to help focus analytical attention on an exceptional class of media reporting. Specifically, it provides a dynamic model of media-society interaction and how periodic moral panics seemingly serve to focus and build collective solidarities, often set against a backdrop of historical change and in relation to a social field structured in dominance.

Today we may want to take issue with, or refine, the theory of moral panics on a number of conceptual, theoretical, empirical and epistemological grounds. Conceptually the idea of moral panic appears to be in danger of losing its analytical precision when appropriated by the media and applied indiscriminately to any and all mediatised phenomena that happen to embody public concerns. Some public concerns, those incalculable but potentially catastrophic 'manufactured uncertainties' of 'risk society', for example, may be all too real (Beck 1992; Thompson 1998). The theory's original informing view of a dominant societal culture, and positioning of moral panics as invariably elite-driven and functional for social order, can also be questioned on historical and empirical grounds. Historically, as later theorists have documented, moral panics have assumed diverse forms and can serve different functions and interests (Goode and Ben-Yehuda 1994; cf. Hall et al. 1978). In today's globally dynamic and increasingly mediatised societies, notions of a uniform societal control culture also begin to creak under evident cultural heterogeneity and social differentiation and, at the same time, 'folk devils' have often learnt to 'fight back' in both mainstream and alternative media (McRobbie 1994). So too can ideas of moral panics as relatively exceptional or discreet phenomena be questioned in a mediatised world where cultural discourses intermingle and become overlaid and infused with each other (Watney 1987), and where 'normal' as much as 'exceptional' media representations discursively constitute the nature of the 'real' without recourse to a presumed objectivist benchmark outside of the realm of representation (Fiske 1994; Watney 1987).

Even so, the theory of moral panics continues to have purchase on a class of periodic, exceptional media phenomena, and it reminds us of the capability of media (affectively and cognitively), and in interaction with other social institutions, to invoke and police moral solidarities through the circulation of collective representations. As such, the theory remains theoretically relevant to this day and, in terms of our encompassing definition of mediatised ritual above, clearly represents an identifiable and important subclass of this.

Mediatised Ritual 2: Celebratory Media Events

The original ideas of Durkheim also resonate strongly in the recent theorisation of a different class of mediatised rituals, so-called media events. Here the seminal study is *Media Events: The Live Broadcasting of History,* by Daniel Dayan and Elihu Katz (1994). This sets out to theorise 'the high holidays of mass communication', the defining features of which are described as follows: they are interruptions of broadcasting routine; they are often monopolistic, that is, all channels refer to the media event; the happening is live; they are typically organised outside the media by those well within the establishment; they are preplanned and presented with reverence and ceremony; they serve to celebrate not conflict but reconciliation and establishment initiatives, and they are therefore unquestionably hegemonic; they electrify very large (TV viewing) audiences, and they integrate societies and evoke a renewal of loyalty to the society and its legitimate authority (4–9). This formulation, clearly, remains heavily indebted to Durkheim but, unlike moral panic theory, is principally concerned with ceremonial or celebratory occasions of state and government and the ritualised affirmation of, and integrative appeals to, national collectivity. This is so, notwithstanding the authors' identification of three genre types of 'media events': contests, or epic contests of politics and sports (for example, the Senate Watergate hearings, the World Cup, the Olympics); conquests, or so-called charismatic missions (for example, the moon landing, President Anwar el-Sadat's visit to Israel); and coronations, or the rites of passage of the great (for example, the coronation of Elizabeth II, the wedding of Prince Charles or the funeral of Princess Diana).

Each of these, including contests, are fundamentally taken as serving to reconcile, rather than challenge or transform, the political status quo and thereby buttress hegemonic interests and reaffirm the establishment. Mediatised rituals, as suggested earlier, however, can assume diverse and often less consensual forms. Some media events, for example, can prove to be more conflicted than consensual, more politically uncertain than hegemonic, more differentiated than monopolistic, and more disruptive than integrative, as well as of longer duration and more media propelled than Katz and Dayan's special case of media events would seem to allow.

Mediatised Ritual 3: Conflicted Media Events

The term 'media event', unhelpfully perhaps, has also been used to describe such phenomena as the U.S. mediatised O.J. Simpson case, the Los Angeles riots, and the Dan Quayle-Murphy Brown debate (see Fiske 1994;

Hunt 1999). In such cases, it appears that the exceptional media interest granted to these suffices as a definition of a media event, with the added qualification that such cases also appear to tap into deep-seated conflicts that normally remain subterranean. 'Media events', according to John Fiske, 'are sites of maximum visibility and maximum turbulence' (1994, 7), and it is this that principally gives them their electrifying charge. Contrary to Dayan and Katz's formulation, then, this class of conflicted media events appears to be singled out precisely because it involves deep conflictive undercurrents, whether of race, class or gender. Influenced by the ideas of the Italian theoretician Antonio Gramsci, studies here recognize how a contest for cultural hegemony is often played out in and through such media events and their public representations.

> The Simpson case is most assuredly about more than just the murders and the trial outcomes. . . . [C]eremonial elements indeed pervaded the case and the public's re-action to it. But the case also tapped into enduring societal conflicts, into the strug-gles between counter-hegemonic projects for change and hegemonic projects for maintenance of the status quo. And much to the chagrin of authorities, 'reconcili-ation' was not always the outcome celebrated. (Hunt 1999, 43)

John Fiske also sees a cultural struggle over meaning at the centre of media events given the latter's embedded social antagonisms. But he also moves towards a postmodern view that theorizes these same representations as 'hyperreal' where the distinction between 'events' in the world and 'media events' becomes less certain, or important.

> The term *media event* is an indication that in a postmodern world we can no longer rely on a stable relationship or clear distinction between a 'real' event and its me-diated representation. Consequently, we can no longer work with the idea that the 'real' is more important, significant, or even 'true' than the representation. A media event, then, is not a mere representation of what happened, but it has its own re-ality, which gathers up into itself the reality of the event that may or may not have preceded it. (Fiske 1994, 2)

This position usefully reminds us of the way that, for most of us, the media remain the only means we have of accessing the events referenced, as well as the way in which important aspects of such hypervisual media specta-cles often originate within the media itself. It also has the virtue of placing social antagonisms at the heart of media events, which are seen as grant-ing them their electrifying charge. However, when used in this way, the term fails to analytically capture and discriminate between very different cases of media events, both consensual and conflicted, and it also fails to address the longer-term dynamics of such mediatised phenomena.

These same criticisms can also be put to recent work on 'media specta-cles' by Douglas Kellner (2003), which, building on Guy Debord's (1983) 'society as spectacle' thesis, argues that media spectacle is becoming one of the organising principles of the economy, polity, society and everyday life. Kellner's work has the distinct virtue of seeking to ground and theorize media spectacle in relation to contemporary forces of globalisation, technological revolution and the restructuring of capitalism. But, notwithstanding his criticisms of Debord's work for providing a 'rather generalized and abstract notion of spectacle', his inclusion of such very different media spectacles as sports events, celebrities, musical extravaganzas, political scandals, 'Terror War' and TV series such as *The X-Files, Buffy, The Vampire Slayer* and *Big Brother,* as well as major Hollywood blockbusters and the release of the *Harry Potter* children's novels, leads, it has to be said, to a similar, totalising impression. Discussions of media events and media spectacle, it seems, too often suffer from lack of analytical precision and tend towards a presumed explanatory self-sufficiency often located at the level of the cultural. Here the focus on the play of social power within high-profile media events/spectacles is underdeveloped and short-circuits the sociological examination of exactly how power is enacted and contested through time and informs media visualisation and narrative progression. Hypervisualisation, as much as routine media visualisation, remains no less indebted to the world of contending interests and social forces condensed in the moment of production (Cottle 2003b). And furthermore, contrary to Debord, we should not underestimate the continuing communicative capacity of words, talk and print-based media to engage audiences in today's so-called 'society of spectacle'.

Whether approached as essentially consensual (Dayan and Katz), conflicted (Hunt, Fiske) or spectacular (Kellner), the discussion of media events, then, too easily grants to the media phenomenon self-sufficiency, and the concept appears to be inherently ill-equipped to pursue developmental features of media representations over the longer term. Indeed, given the long duration, contingencies and dynamics of some media events, even to name them as such is to perpetuate a misnomer. The category 'media events', like that of 'moral panics', all too easily suffers conceptual inflation and loses analytical bite when applied too widely and too indiscriminately to different types of exceptional media phenomena. Media events, whether construed in essentially celebratory, conflicted or spectacular ways, can often be happily subsumed under our overarching category of mediatised ritual, in that these can qualify as exceptional, symbol-laden media performed and subjunctively oriented phenomena that sustain and/or mobilise collective sentiments and solidarities. But for a better grasp of the temporal, narrative and social dynamics of mediatised rituals, we must look elsewhere.

Mediatised Ritual 4: Media Scandals

Recently, a different class of events has been subject to scholarly interest, that of mediatised scandals. These, almost by definition, suggest a more dynamic and interactive role of media in such processes: scandals rarely, of course, simply present themselves, whether in the media or outside them, but depend on revelations and claims that are then followed up by further disclosures or counterclaims, often building to a climax through time and occasioning some form of socially and morally approved sanction or institutional response. But what is a media scandal? James Lull and Stephen Hinerman usefully define it as follows:

Scandal serves as a term to delineate a breach in moral conduct and authority. *A media scandal occurs when private acts that disgrace or offend the idealized, dominant morality of a social community are made public and narrativized by the media, producing a range of effects from ideological and cultural retrenchment to disruption and change.* (1997, 3; emphasis in original)

This formulation clearly positions media scandals under our covering definition of mediatised ritual. As with moral panic theory, it too is centrally preoccupied with sustaining collective moral boundaries when these are thought to have been transgressed. Here, however, the maintenance and repair mechanisms enacted are typically focussed in relation to transgressing individuals and associated institutions, and it is in relation to these that idealised collective norms of behaviour and conduct are publicly and symbolically policed (and often vicariously enjoyed). Through this mediatised performance, collective solidarity is invoked, and the media stage becomes populated by voices and views that summon into being an imagined community. The latter is now based, however, on a negatively inflected 'subjunctive' view in which opprobrious criticism and public censure implicitly calls forth an idealized sense of what public, private and moral behaviour should be. Interestingly, this definition makes no prescriptive statement about the exact effects of media scandal since these may variously prove to be integrative or disruptive, hegemonic or transformative in outcome. They may also be theorised as collectively contributing to the 'crisis of public communications' and the demise of politics as a publicly legitimised sphere of activity. Media scandals according to the same authors can also be classified as types according to whether they involve prominent individuals in public institutions; stars and celebrities; or ordinary people who have engaged in transgressive, sometimes heinous acts and behaviour (Lull and Hinerman 1997, 19–25). They all, however, serve to personify moral codes and behaviours for public and private consumption and the cultivation of public and private responses.

John Thompson usefully historicises the increased prevalence of political scandals in modern times and accounts for this in terms of the following: the increased visibility of political leaders; changing technologies of communication and surveillance; a changing culture of journalism; a changing political culture; and growing legalisation of political life (Thompson 2000, 108). He thereby helps to ground the analysis of media scandals in wider

processes of historical transformation, mediated publicness and contemporary media culture (cf. Kellner 2003). Media scandals tend to be highly
symbolic 'affairs'—both figuratively and literally—involving public performance and ritual displays designed to salvage tainted institutional and/or
personal reputations, credibility, trust and legitimacy. As such, they are essentially struggles of symbolic power. They also have a dynamic quality
that unfolds through time, and which may often involve further infractions
of 'cover up' and public retractions that can often prove equally, if not
more, damaging than the original infraction and its disclosure.

> Mediated scandals are not only stretched out in time: they also display a sequen-
> tial structure in the sense that one phase of the scandal is typically followed by an-
> other, although this sequential pattern is by no means rigid or fixed. . . . [I]f one is
> situated in the midst of a mediated scandal and watching (or participating in) its
> development in real time, it is extremely difficult to predict how it will unfold.
> (Thompson 2000, 72–73)

Thompson classifies political scandals as mediated events, though he is
clearly attuned to their dynamic and sequential nature and extends their
temporal reach well beyond, for example, that of Dayan and Katz's ceremonial formulation of media events. Political scandals, he observes, often
move through four phases: first, in the prescandal phase, an original breach
of norms or moral codes takes place (or is alleged to have taken place);
second, the scandal phase proper is based on public disclosure and claims
and counterclaims; third is the culmination phase or dénouement, when the
scandal is finally brought to a head, sometimes through a dramatically
staged event, such as a trial or a public hearing; and, fourth, in the final
phase of aftermath, commentary and criticism may continue to circulate,
but the high drama has passed (Thompson 2000, 74–77).

Here, then, the theorisation of media scandals begins to periodize the
movement of these exceptional media phenomena through time and thereby
takes us deeper into the dynamics of the phenomenon as well as into an
appreciation of the contingencies of outcome dependent on how the symbolic struggle over power is waged, won or lost in each of its various phases.
Media scandals, clearly, can be positioned as a further subclass of mediatised ritual in that they invoke and/or reaffirm moral boundaries and idealised collective norms of behaviour through a mediatised, often
performative (evaluative), response to perceived transgression and the enactment of public censure. Media scandals can also be seen as a subclass
of 'mediatised public crisis', our last class of mediatised ritual, which theoretically moves to encompass a much wider range of public crises.

Mediatised Ritual 5: Mediatised Public Crises

Finally, a number of further studies have charted the dynamics of media
conflicts as they have unfolded through time and which, like Thompson's

study, have sought to analyse these conflicts in respect to their discerned sequential phases and progression (Alexander 1988; Alexander and Jacobs 1998; Elliott 1980; Ettema 1990; Jacobs 2000; Wagner-Pacifici 1986). These authors have often deployed the formative ideas of 'social drama' developed by the anthropologist Victor Turner (1969, 1974, 1981, 1982), a schema that usefully helps to map how mediatised public crises are enacted over time and involve a sequential dramatic structure:

In previous studies I have used the notion of a social drama as a device for describing and analysing episodes that manifest social conflict. At its simplest, the drama consists of a four-stage model, proceeding from breach of some social relationship regarded as crucial in the relevant social group, which provides not only its setting but many of its goals, through a phase of rapidly mounting crisis in the direction of the group's major dichotomous cleavage, to the application of legal or ritual means of redress or reconciliation between the conflicting parties which compose the action set. The final stage is either the public and symbolic expression of reconciliation or else of irremediable schism. The first stage is often signalized by the overt, public breach of some norm or rule governing the key relationship which has been transformed from amity to opposition. Now there are a number of variations possible with regard to the sequence of the phases and to the weight accorded to them. (Turner 1974, 78–79)

Turner's schema of social dramas when applied by others to mediatised phenomena has helped to capture something of the temporal dynamics and transformative impacts of these phenomena. It also encourages a more nuanced understanding of the contingencies of power and how these are enacted through time and in relation to the moments, and possibilities, of an unfolding social drama. James Ettema, for example, in a case study of the mediatized 'Cokely affair', a U.S. conflict focusing on race and alleged corruption, observes that his exploration

illustrates a definition of mass-mediated ritual as something more conceptually complex and more politically volatile than the transmission of mythic tales to mass audiences. Following Turner, the affair may be seen as a progression of rituals organised within the social drama paradigm. And following Elliott, that progression of rituals may also be seen to have been enacted within and through the press by other institutions of social power. Indeed, the progression was a veritable catalogue of the means available to contemporary social institutions for the ritual cleansing of civic pollution. . . . [T]he affair also suggests that the social drama is an important cultural resource both for waging and for narrating politics. (1990: 477–78)

Turner's ideas of social drama are apposite to this particular mediatised conflict that also reveals a politically dynamic view of the institutional processes enacted through time and via the press. To what extent, following the ideas of Philip Elliott, these remain principally dependent on outside institutions and power-holders will be considered further below.

The work of Jeffrey Alexander and Ronald Jacobs, perhaps more than any other, provides a sophisticated theorisation of mediatised public crises. It incorporates a sense of narrative progression, the contested nature of mediatised public crises and the expression of surrounding interests, as well as the contingencies and opportunities that ritualised dramas and performances can unleash. It also fits within our more encompassing definition of mediatised ritual with its identification of exceptional, symbolic, performative and subjunctive features.

Celebratory media events of the type discussed by Dayan and Katz tend to narrow the distance between the indicative and the subjunctive, thereby legitimating the powers and authorities outside the civil sphere. Mediatized public crises, on the other hand, tend to increase the distance between the indicative and the subjunctive, thereby giving to civil society its greatest power for social change. In these situations, the media create public narratives that emphasise not only the tragic distance between is and ought but the possibility of historically overcoming it. Such narratives prescribe struggles to make 'real' institutional relationships more consistent with the normative standards of the utopian civil society discourse. (Alexander and Jacobs 1998, 28)

This model of mediatised public crisis captures the way in which mediatised rituals often involve contending forces of state and civil society, played out over time, with potentially transformative effects. This, then, is a theoretical model that deserves serious consideration, and further empirical exploration.

To return to our earlier formal definition of mediatised ritual, it is now clear that the five cases of exceptional media phenomena discussed—moral panics, celebratory and conflicted media events, media scandals and mediatised public crises—all exhibit defining analytical features and therefore conform to our overarching category of mediatised ritual. If we are to better understand the force and appeal of such media phenomena, we must acknowledge the involvement of mediatised ritual within and across contemporary societies and how this serves to sustain and/or mobilise collective sentiments and (pluralised) solidarities within structured fields of dominance, difference and inequality. We also need to recognize how different mediatised rituals can assume different expressions in terms of whether they are event focused or involve longer-term dynamics; are essentially consensual or conflicted in nature; and whether they principally serve integrative or disruptive purposes and outcomes. Table 3.1 summarises the general theoretical thrust of each of our five classes of mediatised ritual in such ideal-typical terms.

As discussed mediatised rituals can assume different forms of expression and exhibit differing relations to time, social structures and political processes, as well as commonalities of 'ritual' form and appeal. This must be borne in mind when analysing particular cases of mediatised ritual, given

Table 3.1
Mediatised Rituals: A Typology

	Event Focus	Story Dynamic	Consensual	Conflicted	Integrative	Disruptive
Moral Panics (Cohen 1972)		X		X	X	
Celebratory Media Events (Dayan and Katz 1994)	X		X		X	
Conflicted Media Events (Fiske 1994; Hunt 1999)	X			X		X
Media Scandals (Lull and Hinerman 1997; Thompson 2000)		X		X		X
Mediatised Public Crises (Alexander and Jacobs 1998)		X		X		X

their differentiated nature and capacities. The previous discussion of ritual and dynamics also prompts further reflection on the nature of symbolic power and media performance within and across a differentiated news media as well as the constitution and participation of differentiated publics within this.

ON SYMBOLIC AND STRATEGIC POWER

The study of mediatised rituals invites a closer look at theoretical views about the media's involvement with strategic and symbolic power. Given the centrality and communicative force of symbols identified by Durkheim, and practically all authors interested in ritual since, we might anticipate that symbols and symbolism will have heightened affect in mediatised rituals. Following Turner, who observed how symbols are the 'molecules' of ritual (1969, 14), we can also predict that mediatised rituals provide for a more complex interplay between elites and non-elites when the latter, for example, can mobilise powerful symbols challenging the strategic power and routinised media interventions of dominant institutions.

Mediatised rituals, as we have seen, are highly symbolic affairs. As Durkheim states, 'Without symbols social sentiments could have only a precarious existence' (1912, 265). If ritual and symbolism in classic Durkheimian terms, then, serve to construct collective solidarity and build social order, it is not difficult to see how these same processes could be interpreted from a critical vantage point as legitimising social power and authority. Here the flipside of collective values and consensus is revealed as dominant control and ideological legitimation (Lukes 1975). Philip Elliott, in an influential contribution to the field of media and ritual study, deliberately sought to return the analysis of mediatised rituals to questions of social structure and their control by dominant interests and institutions (see also Chaney 1986). He regarded 'press rites' as one of the means by which the connection between media and dominant social institutions was enacted:

Press rites are those stories which the press as a whole unite in treating as important. They are stories which reflect on the stability of the social system by showing it under threat, overcoming threat or working in a united consensual way. . . . They share the same formal grammar of treatment and development. In that development considerable emphasis is put on the symbolic significance or interpretation of the events. . . . Part of the development involves reference to Bagehot's 'dignified' and 'efficient' leaders of society for comment. (Elliott 1980, 143)

Formulated in such terms, Elliott's views lend support to established media communication theories of elite access, whether conceived in terms of a 'hierarchy of credibility' (Becker 1967), 'hierarchy of structured access' (Glasgow University Media Group 1976, 1980) or 'primary definers' (Hall et al. 1978); indeed, Elliott's earlier work on Northern Ireland prefigured the influential theses of primary definition (Elliott 1977). These theories have today become widely accepted within the field of media communications study and continue to help explain the systematic and routine patterning of elite access to the news media and the privileged opportunity granted therein to define and pontificate on newsworthy events. A more detailed discussion of this literature can be found elsewhere (Cottle 2003a, 3–24). But here we can note, once again, that ritual need not always, necessarily and invariably be structurally determined and under the exclusive control of powerful institutions and elites (which is not to suggest a liberal pluralist alternative). Likewise, the role of symbols within mediatised rituals may not always work in the service of powerful institutional interests and authorities and may even perform a more powerful role than often assumed by these models of strategic access. As Jeffrey Alexander has observed:

The social experiences which constitute intense and awesome symbols . . . are not necessarily harmonious and thoroughly integrating. They may be subject to intensely competitive processes, to individuation and reflexivity, and they may integrate some parts of society rather than the whole. (1988, 190)

This returns us to the complex dynamics unfolding through time as well as the conflicted nature of many mediatised rituals—characteristics that can permit and sometimes demand symbolic public displays by elites designed to counter challenges to their right to public office and ward off the molten lava of moral pollution that can flow dangerously on such occasions (Alexander 1988). Once moral opprobrium is publicly set in motion, bodies can become stigmatised, reputations can be destroyed and citizens can become 'expelled into a guild of the guilty' (Carey 1998, 45). In this respect, Turner's anthropological ideas on 'ritual humility' and rituals of 'status elevation' and 'status reversal' may also prove of relevance to the analysis of mediatised rituals (Turner 1969, 1982).

To be clear, mediatised rituals and the struggles played out on the media stage cannot be viewed in terms of an opposition between strategic and symbolic power, where the former is seen to be the monopoly of institutional interests, and the latter the preserve of the organisationally non-aligned or resource poor. Both, in fact, are likely to mobilise forms of strategic and symbolic power. But the point here is that these resources and capacities are more often than not unevenly distributed within and across fields of contention. When enacted in and through mediatised rituals, however, there are good grounds to suggest that the symbolic power attached to 'challenger' groups, rather than 'authorities', can sometimes counter this structural and routine imbalance of power (Cottle 2003a; Wolfsfeld 1997, 2003). From the foregoing, we need to be attuned to the likelihood that symbols and symbolic processes will have heightened salience and affect in mediatised rituals and, moreover, that these may afford challenger groups additional cultural power.

PERFORMATIVE MEDIA, PARTICULARISED SOLIDARITIES, PUBLIC SPHERES

Our formal definition of mediatised ritual has deliberately made reference to the 'performative' nature of media involvement and the media's active involvement in sustaining and/or mobilising collective sentiments and solidarities. Implicit to our definition, therefore, is also a view of media as constituting, normatively speaking, a public sphere. A few words on each are therefore necessary.

Performative Media

Attending to the performative nature of the media is crucial if we are to understand how mediatised rituals can produce heightened affects among audiences and thereby build solidarities, or 'publics', and contribute to wider collective processes. Ideas of performance and performativity can be traced to diverse fields (Carlson 1996), including linguistics and the study of language (Austin 1975; Bakhtin, 1986; Searle 1969), symbolic interactionist sociology (Goffman 1959, 1974), anthropology and ethnography (Geertz 1992; Hughes-Freeland 1998; Rostas 1998; Schieffelin 1998; Turner 1969, 1974, 1982), and gender and identity studies (Butler 1990). Each moves beyond the referential or 'constantive' (Austin 1975) level of communication to reveal how words, social encounters, culture and identity are respectively performed and enacted and are thereby doing something. Moreover, this performative doing is necessarily conducted with an awareness of, and relationship to, an audience (Bakhtin 1986; Hymes 1975).

Studies of ritual and performativity give rise to issues of agency and intentionality, creativity and constraint, as well as the participatory nature of spectatorship (Hughes-Freeland 1998). In the context of this study of media performance, with its theoretical stance towards mediatised ritual, ideas of performance and performativity invite analysis of the ways in which media purposefully deploy symbolisation and sentiments, sources and accounts, and rhetorically embody particularised solidarities that serve to constitute and (subjunctively) galvanise identities and social action. Ideas of performance and performativity need not, however, be presumed to be confined to identity performance conceived in terms of the simultaneous display and enactment of self and seemingly divorced from wider, extradiscursive, forms of social engagement.[1] The study of media representation and social ritual, for example, provides the basis for returning ideas of identity performance and performativity to the social world as well as the collective forces that contend within it. Again the work of Victor Turner is instructive in these respects. Eschewing a functionalist reading of ritual as relatively 'flat', or simply as 'expressive' of the social order, Turner conceives of ritual as complexly layered and composed of social performances capable of both responding to, and in part serving to secure, change:

I like to think of ritual essentially as *performance*, as *enactment* and not primarily as rules or rubrics. The rules frame the ritual process, but the ritual process transcends its frame. . . . Without taking liminality into account, ritual becomes indistinguishable from 'ceremony', 'formality'. . . . [T]he liminal phase is the essential, anti-secular component in true ritual, whether it be labelled 'religious' or 'magical'. Ceremony indicates, ritual transforms. (1981, 155–56)

Public performances in Turner's schema are thereby displays of ritual caught up within the spontaneous outpouring of creative energy, ideas and feelings that the performances can sometimes invoke. Turner sees this as an expression of 'communitas', which serves to create a 'liminal' space and time outside of the normal structures and quotidian routines of society, and in which often inhere unusual powers:

Communitas breaks in through the interstices of structure, in liminality; at the edges of structure, in marginality; and from beneath structure, in inferiority. It is almost everywhere held to be 'sacred' or 'holy', possibly because it transgresses or dissolves the norms that govern structured and institutionalised relationships and is accompanied by experiences of unprecedented potency. The process of 'leveling' and 'stripping' . . . often appear to flood their subjects with affect. (1969, 128)

Ideas of liminality and communitas here provide further sensitising concepts but these cannot simply be taken on face value. Turner's positing of history as an incessant succession of alternating 'structure' and 'communitas' (Turner 1969, 203) can be questioned in relation to the relatively closed and 'simple' societies subject to his anthropological gaze, and it most definitely can be criticised in the context of complexly structured, fractured, multiethnic and mediatised societies. Turner himself later preferred to use the term 'liminoid' to refer to the more specific or localised forms of 'liminality' that tend to be generated in complexly structured societies (Turner 1982, 53–56), though his ideas about social dramas and liminality continue, he suggests, to apply across time and societies.

Particularised Solidarities

If we are to move beyond Durkheim's views of public ceremonies and rituals as organically binding, towards an appreciation of how exactly mediatised rituals work performatively to energise different 'social solidarities'—many of which are structurally and discursively positioned in contention—so we have to pluralise our view of social solidarity or 'imagined community' and further acknowledge that mediatised rituals are destined to have differential effects on different participants. We also need to acknowledge what I shall term here as the 'the ritual paradox'. Ritual, it has often been observed (Elliott 1980; Rothenbuhler 1998), depends on the willing involvement of participants. Closely following Durkheim, Rothenbuhler emphasises just this point in his definition of ritual as 'the voluntary performance of appropriately patterned behaviour to symbolically effect or participate in the serious life' (1998, 27). The paradox of ritual, then, is that it only 'works' when we want it to, that is, when we volunteer something of ourselves, such as our collective identities, sentiments and aspirations. This is not to say that the role of media performance is thereby diminished or rendered impotent, since it is often only through media performance and performativity that ritual comes into being. But we can say that ritual only comes alive empirically, emotionally, subjunctively, when actively experienced by audiences who are prepared to 'participate' within its symbolic meaning for them and accept the imagined solidarities (or 'social imaginary') that it offers. We can therefore make a necessary conceptual distinction between 'text' and 'performance' in that the former fails to capture the relational and experiential nature of performativity (Chaney 1993, 4). Edward Schieffelin, a social anthropologist, elaborates the conceptual distinction nicely:

The character of performance as accomplishment, together with its interactive quality and element of risk, make it easy to differentiate it from the notion of 'text'. . . . To be sure, performances share some qualities with texts. They have beginnings, middles and ends, they have internal structure, may refer to themselves etc. But it is precisely the performativity of performance for which there is no analogue in text. Unlike text, performances are ephemeral. They create their effects then they are gone—leaving their reverberations (fresh insights, reconstituted selves, new statuses, altered realities) behind them. Performances are a living social activity, by necessity assertive, strategic and not fully predictable. While they refer to the past and plunge towards the future, they exist only in the present. Texts are changeless and enduring. (1998, 198–99)

The media 'texts' subject to analysis in the remainder of this study—principally mainstream and minority newspapers and, to a lesser extent, television news, current affairs and documentary programmes and internet sites—bear more than just traces of performative work. The 'texts' demonstrate how it is possible to imbue them with immediacy, urgency and life. Even so, in the context of mediatised ritual, performativity is not confined to the performances of media producers alone but also includes the 'spectators' who actively enter into ('commit themselves to') the proceedings and who identify themselves and their sentiments within them (Ryfe 2001), if only in fleeting or momentary ways (Dayan 2001).

Mediatised ritual, then, is not necessarily coincident with the widest possible collectivity approached in undifferentiated terms. For it to 'work', emotional and intellectual investment is required from all those concerned (producers, performers and participating audiences). Given the sociological reality of complexly structured societies characterised by conflicting interests and identities, we need to be sensitively attuned to how particular media address and 'perform' mediatised rituals in respect of differentiated 'publics'. This calls for close engagement with the performativity of different media outlets within their media ecology and how this serves to embody and elicit particularised 'publics'. Philip Elliott states:

In short, while some press rites are run by the press itself, others are run by other social institutions, but developed and given their peculiar form by press presentation. . . . Not only does the press relay social ritual, it may also act as an instigator. (1980: 163–64)

Today there are many possible roles performed by the news media within mediatised rituals, whether instigator, conductor, narrator, mediator, advocate, campaigner or champion, just as there are diverse roles performed by the news media in situations of conflict more generally (Wolfsfeld 1997, 2003). These can also change through time (Bennett 1990; Butler 1995; Hallin 1986), be mediated differently through various programme forms (Cottle 2002, 2005; Elliott et al. 1986) and may also demonstrate varying degrees of reflexivity in respect to their own media 'doing' or performance.

Public Sphere(s)

To refer to particularised 'publics' performatively embodied within and across media representations problematises the notion of the public sphere, defined by Habermas as that space in which public opinion is formed on the basis of universal access and deliberative engagement leading to *consensus* (1989, 1996). Some mediatised rituals, given the oppositions involved and their conflicted nature, may be far from consensus forming. Notions of performativity also render problematic overly rationalistic accounts of democratic processes and public will formation. Affective, emotional and symbolic appeals are an inextricable part of mediatised rituals and lend them much of their affect (and effects). Emotions display a 'deep sociality' and are constitutive of social life; they cannot therefore be presumed to be outside of the play of discourse and human understanding. In the words of Nick Crossly, 'emotions form part of our point of view on the world; we do not just have them, we exist in and by way of them' (1998: 27–28). The role of emotions within social life is today receiving increased recognition (Bendelow and Williams 1998; Collins 2003; Crossly 1998; Emirbayer 2003; Meštrović 1998: 96–108; Sewell 2003) but has yet to be meaningfully deployed in analyses of the media.

In the field of journalism studies, analyses of popular and tabloid news forms have begun to pursue the emotional, symbolic and affective dimensions of communication (Barkin and Gurevitch 1987; Bird 1990; Campbell 1987; Cottle 1993; Dahlgren and Sparks 1992; Langer 1997). But such insights are less often pursued in respect to so-called serious journalism, though this, too, can perform in expressive and emotional ways. Recent studies of mediatised trauma reach the same conclusion (Edkin 2003; Zelizer and Allan 2002). It is for this reason that I have used Durkheim's term 'sentiments' throughout this discussion because it helps to capture something of the coexistence of emotional and cognitive, affective and rational aspects of beliefs, which are invariably involved in the performative appeals to social solidarity. Too often studies of news journalism approached through the theoretical prism of Habermas's 'public sphere' methodologically reinforce rationalist and cognitivist pretensions and, in consequence, fail to interrogate or appreciate the affective and emotional resonance of both the materials analysed and their performative role in both the constitution of wider public discourse and summoned 'publics'.

Habermas's original formulation of the public sphere has generated considerable debate, which often breaks down into two fundamental camps. The first, based on Enlightenment premises, argues for the necessity of rational, consensual debate in which universal reason and deliberation are able to prevail; the second moves towards post-Enlightenment premises and argues for public sphere(s) conceptualised in more radical, relativist and expressive ways, where differences are publicly acknowledged and played out, but where consensus may neither be attainable nor socially positive (Curran 1991; Dahlgren 1995; Elliott 1986; Fraser 1992; Garnham 1986; Hallin 1994; Livingstone and Lunt 1993; McGuigan 2000; Thompson 1995). While the former camp tends to approach the media public sphere in terms of its capability to marshal 'public knowledge' and address substantive 'issues', the latter tends towards explorations of how media disseminate meanings in 'popular culture' and everyday life and how this serves to sustain different 'identities'. These oppositions are often too harshly drawn.

Similar dualisms often inform the study of different journalism forms, which have been approached in terms of analytic-expressive, rational-emotional, propositional-aesthetic modes of communication (Corner 1995; Dahlgren 1995), objectivist and subjectivist news epistemologies (Cottle 1993), 'transmission' and 'ritual' models (Carey 1989), 'public knowledge' and 'popular culture' problematics of audience reception (Corner 1991) or 'dialogue' and 'dissemination' approaches to communication (Peters 1999). Again, however, the study of mediatised ritual will suggest that these dualisms don't do justice to the complex nature of expressive cultural forms. In today's differentiated journalism ecology, such communicative dimensions interpenetrate and, in their specificity, help to define the competing types of news and grant them their characteristic form and, often, communicative force. When seeking to understand how mediatised rituals become powerfully enacted and serve to focus both public attention and feelings on deep social issues and to summon solidarities and identities— doing so in symbolically meaningful, affective and deliberative ways—less dichotomised thinking is clearly necessary.

SUMMARY

Mediatised rituals are a constitutive part of contemporary society and can serve to sustain and, periodically, mobilise collective sentiments and solidarities. Based on Durkheim's original insights into 'society as the soul of religion' and the importance of ritual in securing solidarity (1912, 466–67), this chapter has moved to develop a view of ritual performance and processes in more dynamic, differentiated and sometimes disruptive terms. These ideas have been expanded and also empirically grounded in respect to studies of five identified classes of mediatised ritual. Attending to theories of moral panics, media events (consensual and conflicted), media scandals and mediatised public crises, each was found to exhibit shared characteristics of mediatized ritual. This was analytically defined as 'those exceptional and performative media phenomena that serve to sustain and/or mobilise collective sentiments and solidarities on the basis of symbolisation and a subjunctive orientation to what should or ought to be'. This definition helps sensitise the research to important and evident characteristics of such phenomena—ritual, dynamics, symbolism, performativity—mediatised characteristics that also rhetorically embody group sentiments and particularised solidarities in respect to 'higher' collective concerns ('the serious life') enacted in and through today's media public sphere(s). Together these theoretical coordinates and associated concepts provide a framework of use for both the exploration and explanation of the Stephen Lawrence case as it unfolded over the ten-year period 1993–2003 and turned into a mediatised public crisis with far-reaching consequences and effects.

This study, then, is principally concerned with the cultural dynamics informing and animating the media's collective representations of the Stephen Lawrence story as they became publicly narrativised across time. This is not to suggest that the public story of Stephen Lawrence story was not also informed by sociological considerations of production and the strategic interventions and public relations activities of various sources, including those of the Lawrences and their campaign for justice; but it is to say, following the ideas of Victor Turner and others, that in this case the media appeared to increasingly follow a cultural logic and narrative that conditioned source access and performances as well as the practices and forms of routine journalism itself.[2]

NOTES

1. The following statement, for example, both in its reference to the ideas of Friedrich Nietzsche and in its own theorisation of gender identity performance, is representative of this delimited understanding of performativity and thereby fails to interrogate the ways in which representations, or 'expressions', do, in fact, instantiate something, and emanate from a 'substance' that lies outside of their own performative enactment. This 'substance', better described as a constellation of social forces or 'society', exerts its own constraints and determinacy. Gender, for example, is a social construct but becomes historicised and institutionalised into social structures and relationships that cannot usefully be captured by, confined to, or politically challenged with exclusive reference to performative enactment alone:

The challenge for rethinking gender categories outside of the metaphysics of substance will have to consider the relevance of Nietzsche's claim in *On the Genealogy of Morals* that 'there is no "being" behind doing, effecting, becoming; "the doer" is merely a fiction added to the deed—the deed is everything.' In an application that Nietzsche himself would not have anticipated or condoned, we might state as a corollary: There is no gender identity behind the expressions of gender; that identity is performatively constituted by the very 'expressions' that are said to be its results. (Butler 1990, 25)

Ideas of performance and performativity cannot evade the theoretical necessity to engage with preceding ontological realities of 'the social', nor their enactment and mediation within collective and institutional means and arenas, including the media.

2. For a study of media organisation and production and its impact on the reporting of 'race', see Cottle 1993, and for a recent discussion of approaches to media organisation and production, see Cottle 2003b. Studies of source interventions and strategies and their relation to cultural dynamics are reviewed and included in Cottle 2003a and Manning 2001. Schlesinger and Tumber (1994) also provide a detailed discussion of source activity in respect to the media and the criminal justice system.

Four

Mapping

My hypothesis, based on repeated observations of such processual units in a range of sociocultural systems and on my reading in ethnography and history, is that social dramas, 'dramas of living', as Kenneth Burke calls them, can be aptly studied as having four phases. These I label breach, crisis, redress, and either reintegration or recognition of schism.

Victor Turner, 'Social Dramas and Stories about Them' (1981, 145)

This chapter maps the broad media contours of the media story of Stephen Lawrence as it grew over the course of ten years to become a mediatised public crisis that reverberates to this day within British society and culture. As we shall see, the media produced a massive outpouring of reportage and expressive commentary across this period, and it was this that 'generalised' (Alexander 1988) the Stephen Lawrence story to wider publics throughout society. How the media performed and 'canalised' (Alexander 1988) this public elaboration in relation to particularised publics and solidarities, and did so in symbolically resonant as well as discursively aligned ways across successive phases of its public enactment, receives more qualitative discussion in the chapters that follow. Sustained and massive media exposure can in itself be taken as an indication of media performativity of course, but we will need to move beyond the broad content analytic findings reported here if we are to recover exactly how this was enacted in and through the forms, symbols and emotional appeals of its media representation. For the moment, though, we focus on the broad parameters of press representation and how the mediatised public crisis of Stephen Lawrence was generalised to wider publics.

The study is based on an extensive sample of United Kingdom newspapers and a comprehensive analysis of their output across the ten-year period April 1993–May 2003.[1] All newspaper items that either referenced the name of Stephen Lawrence or principally focussed on the Stephen Lawrence case were selected for analysis, and newspapers (including their weekend issues) were chosen to cover the full spectrum of press political partisanship as well as market positioning and readership socioeconomic characteristics. The sample includes (with average circulation figures across the ten year period following in parentheses) 'elite' mainstream liberal and left-of-centre newspapers the *Guardian* (398,106) and its Sunday sister, *Observer* (450,435), and the *Independent* (253,070); elite conservative newspapers *Financial Times* (373,325) and upper middle-market *Times* (676,188); middle-market conservative and social democratic tabloids *Daily Mail* and *Mail on Sunday* (2,195,647) and *Daily Mirror* and *Sunday Mirror* (2,331,341); and right-wing populist and 'down-market' tabloids the *Sun* (3,745,842) and *News of the World* (4,319,477) (note: full circulation figures for all papers, 1993–2003, are provided in Appendix 3). The study also includes a comprehensive analysis of Britain's most successful popular black weekly newspaper, the *Voice* (42,391), as well as regional newspapers from Scotland, the *Scotsman*, the *Herald* and *Daily Record*, and Northern Ireland's *Belfast Telegraph*. In addition, the analysis consulted a wide range of international newspapers to determine how far the Stephen Lawrence case travelled, geopolitically as well as socially and culturally.[2] Television news, current affairs and documentary programmes broadcast in Britain, particularly at the height of the Stephen Lawrence case, were also retrieved for analysis, and newspaper and mainstream television internet news sites, as well as those produced by supporters of the Lawrence family and British racist organisations, were also consulted.

UK PRESS GENERALISATION

Table 4.1 documents that our sample of the British press produced nearly 7,000 news items referencing or principally focused on the Stephen Lawrence story across the research period, a phenomenal amount of outpouring by any standard. The 'elite' liberal/left-of-centre newspapers the *Guardian/Observer* and the *Independent* together produced over 2,500 separate items; middle-market papers the *Times* and *Daily Mail*, and the social-democratic *Daily Mirror* each produced nearly 1,000 items, two to four times as many articles as any other newspaper. Given that the tabloids have lesser available space than the broadsheets, the output of the *Daily Mail* and *Daily Mirror* is all the more remarkable, as is that of the *Voice*, which produces only one newspaper a week but nearly matched the total of the daily *Sun* and, across the early years of the story, produced more items per year than all other newspapers apart from the *Guardian/Observer*. At the story's height, some newspapers were producing over 100 Stephen Lawrence items

Table 4.1
UK Newspapers: Press Contours

Newspapers	1993 (n)	1993 (%)	1994 (n)	1994 (%)	1995 (n)	1995 (%)	1996 (n)	1996 (%)	1997 (n)	1997 (%)	1998 (n)	1998 (%)	1999 (n)	1999 (%)	2000 (n)	2000 (%)	2001 (n)	2001 (%)	2002 (n)	2002 (%)	2003 (n)*	2003 (%)*	Total (n)	Total (%)
Guardian/Observer	25	21.2	5	18.5	23	24.0	14	23.3	68	20.3	212	21.6	495	19.4	169	13.4	147	21.1	155	22.9	54	29.0	1367	19.6
Independent	21	17.8	5	18.5	16	16.7	11	18.3	50	14.9	222	22.6	425	16.7	233	18.5	106	15.2	105	15.5	17	9.1	1211	17.3
Daily Mail	17	14.4	1	3.7	6	6.3	3	5.0	83	24.8	125	12.7	289	11.3	217	17.2	107	15.4	84	12.4	27	14.5	959	13.7
Times	16	13.6	3	11.1	13	13.5	10	16.7	41	12.2	122	12.4	336	13.2	171	13.6	104	14.9	99	14.6	26	14.0	941	13.5
Daily Mirror	7	5.9	1	3.7	5	5.2	3	5.0	23	6.9	86	8.8	304	11.9	117	9.3	56	8.0	78	11.5	20	10.8	700	10.0
Sun	1	0.8	0	0.0	3	3.1	3	5.0	13	3.9	53	5.4	135	5.3	69	5.5	22	3.2	46	6.8	10	5.4	355	5.1
Voice	23	19.5	10	37.0	19	19.8	12	20.0	28	8.4	66	6.7	78	3.1	27	2.1	15	2.2	13	1.9	16	8.6	307	4.4
Financial Times	2	1.7	0	0.0	2	2.1	1	1.7	7	2.1	20	2.0	71	2.8	29	2.3	13	1.9	10	1.5	1	0.5	156	2.2
News of the World	1	0.8	0	0.0	0	0.0	0	0.0	1	0.3	3	0.3	24	0.9	11	0.9	9	1.3	11	1.6	3	1.6	63	0.9
Scotsman	1	0.8	1	3.7	1	1.0	0	0.0	8	2.4	29	3.0	153	6.0	72	5.7	47	6.7	29	4.3	6	3.2	347	5.0
Herald	4	3.4	1	3.7	7	7.3	3	5.0	12	3.6	20	2.0	124	4.9	81	6.4	36	5.2	18	2.7	3	1.6	309	4.4
Daily Record	0	0.0	0	0.0	1	1.0	0	0.0	1	0.3	21	2.1	92	3.6	39	3.1	23	3.3	17	2.5	2	1.1	196	2.8
Belfast Telegraph	0	0.0	0	0.0	0	0.0	0	0.0	0	0.0	3	0.3	26	1.0	23	1.8	12	1.7	13	1.9	1	0.5	78	1.1
Total	118	100.0	27	100.0	96	100.0	60	100.0	335	100.0	982	100.0	2552	100.0	1258	100.0	697	100.0	678	100.0	186	100.0	6989	100.0

*In this table and all subsequent data, figures for 2003 refer only to the period from January to April.

per month, with three or more separate items often featured in a single day's issue. These figures, then, are remarkable and point to the exceptional nature of this mediatised story, a story that evidently captured news agendas across elite and popular news outlets and marketplaces, as well as different newspaper political partisanships. In this way, UK newspapers generalised the story of Stephen Lawrence to readerships across political and socioeconomic spectrums. It was also played out across a considerable period of time, discussed next.

The Mediatised Public Crisis of Stephen Lawrence

Figure 4.1 maps the combined output of UK newspapers displayed in four monthly intervals across the ten-year period. As we can plainly see from the number of articles produced across this period, the Stephen Lawrence story took many years to grow into the exceptional mediatised public crisis that it became. From relatively low-level reporting across 1993 to 1996, the story found new momentum in 1997 and progressively grew into a massive outpouring in 1999 before subsiding in peaks and troughs from 2000 to 2003, though still maintaining a high level of media exposure in these 'post-redress' phases. Interestingly, all newspapers replicated this overall pattern of generalisation, whether elite/left-of-centre, popular right-wing, or minority weekly as demonstrated in Figure 4.2, which deliberately focuses on three such representative newspapers.

The discernible pattern of press generalisation mapped in Figures 4.1 and 4.2 follows those major events and developments in the Stephen Lawrence case outlined in Chapter 2, and which can now also be seen to constitute the principal phases of Turner's suggested schema. The 'breach' phase broadly encompasses the period following Stephen Lawrence's murder in April 1993 to the decision by the Crown Prosecution Service not to prosecute in July of that same year; a period of mounting 'crisis' follows with the failures of committal hearings (1995), private prosecution (1996), and then the coroner's inquest (1997) that precipitated the announcement by the new Labour government of the public inquiry to be held the following year (1998); this then led to the major phase of institutional and ritual 're-dress' that included the public inquiry (1998) and the publication of the Macpherson report (1999); a discernible period of 'reintegration/schism' followed from April 1999 to the end of 2000, which included the enactment of legislative reforms following Macpherson's seventy recommendations; and finally, a further 'ebbing/revivification' stage follows, which begins to map the long-term developments in the post-Macpherson period from 2001 up to and including the ten-year anniversary of Stephen Lawrence's death in April 2003. This final phase is one that still continues. Ebbing/revivification, which supplements Turner's proposed schema, will be elaborated on later, but here we can note that it addresses the much

Figure 4.1
The Mediatised Public Crisis of Stephen Lawrence (1993–2003)

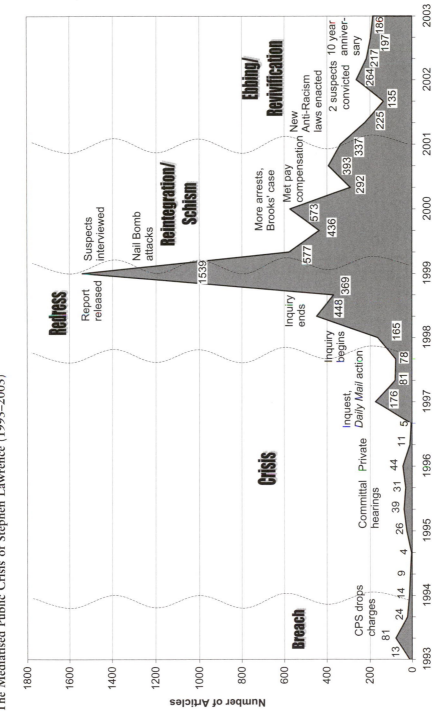

Figure 4.2
The Mediatised Public Crisis of Stephen Lawrence: Press Generalisation (*Guardian, Daily Mail* and the *Voice*, 1993–2003)

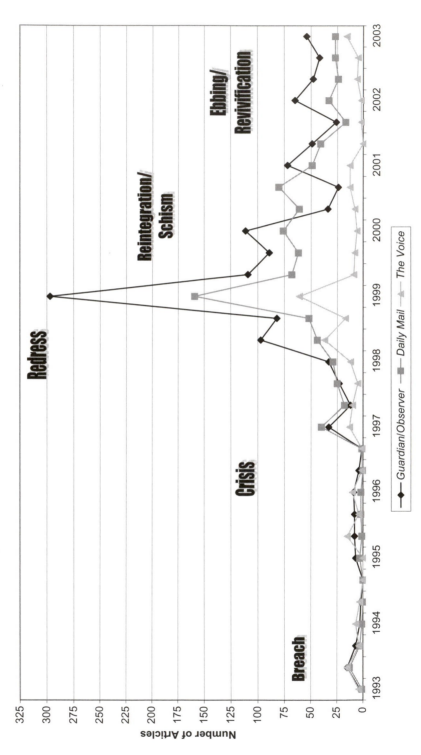

longer-term dynamics of mediatised public crises as they become established as a historical point of reference, depositing residues and traces that become etched into the practices of the present and possibilities for the future.

Even from this broad mapping, it is apparent that Victor Turner's schema clearly finds empirical support in this case study of UK press representation. However, as Turner was aware, 'there are a number of variations possible with regard to the sequence of the phases and the weight accorded to them' (1974, 79), so we will need to examine carefully the extent to which this schema really does map the dynamics and successive phases of the Stephen Lawrence case. Historical and social developments rarely conform to neat analytical schemas, and complex social structures and dynamics of change may not always be captured best in either/or terms of reconciliation or schism, continuity or change, or, if it comes to that, reform or revolution.

From Private Tragedy to Public Troubles

As documented above, the UK press produced massive media outpouring across this period, generalising the case to different publics addressed within mainstream and minority newspapers. Further important dimensions to press generalisation can also be discerned and quantitatively documented. Notwithstanding its dependency upon the institutions and processes of the criminal justice system, the press in fact moved to broaden the nature of its reporting of the Stephen Lawrence story. It did this by progressively extending its frame of reference to encompass wider social and cultural concerns raised by the case. News articles, features and commentary, for example, often reflected on the wider issues implicit to the Stephen Lawrence case, whether those of 'race', racism and inequality in fields of education, housing, health, policing, law and justice, or debates concerning cultural diversity, multiculturalism and British identity.

The findings presented in Figure 4.3 simply document how the massive outpouring of press reporting and commentary often followed the principal institutional developments outlined earlier (i.e., police inquiries, committal and trial proceedings, coroner's inquiry, public inquiry, parliamentary legislation and reforms), and how, also, the media increasingly extended its frame of reference across time to encompass wider social and cultural issues. In this way, the press generalised the resonance of the Stephen Lawrence case to much wider social, political and cultural terrains, and conflicted issues and contending identities.

As we can see, press items that are principally defined in relation to institutional developments and processes generally assume the dominant form of press coverage, but we can also clearly observe how the Stephen Lawrence case became generalised to wider social and cultural issues and

Figure 4.3
UK Press Generalisation: Institutional and Social/Cultural Frames

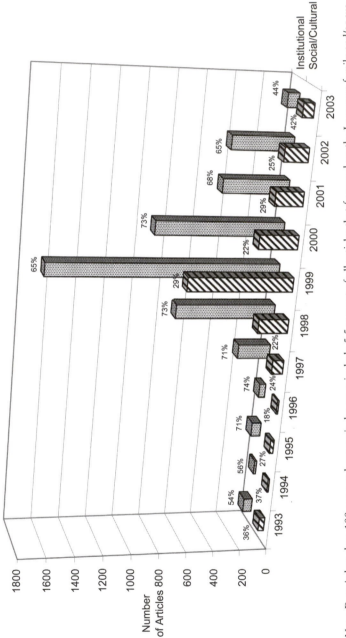

Note: Data is less than 100 percent because it does not include 5.5 percent of all articles that focussed on the Lawrence family and/or suspects' families.

in considerable measure across time. In 1999, for example, the year the public inquiry findings were published, a staggering 600 articles were produced addressing wider social/cultural themes and issues, and at least a quarter of all Stephen Lawrence-related coverage each year took this form. In the first quarter of 2003, the tenth anniversary of Stephen Lawrence's murder, no less than 42 percent of all press items addressed wider social and cultural issues raised by the case. These figures, then, help to document how the press moved beyond routine reporting and possible dependency on institutional developments and opened up opportunities for reflection and reflexivity towards the wider and deeper social and cultural issues raised by the case.

A systematic analysis of the principal themes of all newspaper items referencing Stephen Lawrence across the ten-year period produces some key findings in this regard (see Table 4.2). Themes of police/policing and police racism considerably outnumbered the number of items reporting the specifics of the Stephen Lawrence police/crime inquiry. Similarly, if we examine the percentages of items primarily focussing on legal/court proceedings in respect to the Stephen Lawrence case and those addressing wider issues of law/(in)justice, we also note a clear pattern across the period whereby the latter assumes prominent public exposure. A focus on racism in other fields also finds increasing prominence across the same period and, if combined with that of police racism, constitutes the single most prominent theme within the sample as a whole. Items about racist attacks also grew significantly over this period as a main focus. These findings, then, are suggestive of an 'opening up' of important social issues and concerns to wider public exposure across this period in ways akin perhaps to earlier observations on the changing media parameters of 'legitimate controversy' (Hallin 1986), political 'indexing' (Bennett 1990) and the state's 'aperture of consensus' (Butler 1995) that variously open up, or close down, public debate and discussion in times of war and political conflict.

At the level of principal themes, these findings nonetheless remain both discursively and symbolically blunt. We do not know, for example, how the papers inflected these themes ideologically or in ways sympathetic to their informing political outlooks and imagined readerships. But we can say, thematically at least, that the press generalised the Stephen Lawrence case to wider and important social and political concerns. The particularity of the racist murder of Stephen Lawrence, the developments associated with the police investigation and the forms of legal redress (and failures) in this case, were all extended and generalised to wider and potentially disruptive public concerns. Specifically, these addressed the growing number of racist attacks and murder in British society, police racism and the failures of the criminal justice system, and racism and injustice more broadly conceived in respect to British institutions and society.

Table 4.2
UK Press Generalisation: From Private Tragedy to Public Troubles

Themes (%)	1993	1994	1995	1996	1997	1998	1999	2000	2001	2002	2003	Total
Police/Crime Proceedings	23.8	22.2	8.4	0.0	2.7	1.2	2.8	8.7	6.5	2.2	0.0	4.3
Police/Policing	0.8	0.0	1.0	5.0	6.0	7.0	14.1	21.3	16.1	19.4	15.6	14.2
Police Racism	0.8	0.0	1.0	1.7	0.6	9.4	8.3	8.3	3.7	4.0	7.0	6.9
Ethnic Minority Police Recruiting	0.0	0.0	0.0	0.0	0.0	1.2	1.3	0.9	1.0	1.2	0.5	1.0
Legal/Court Proceedings	12.8	7.4	54.2	53.2	13.7	1.3	4.7	2.1	3.0	4.9	1.1	5.2
Law/Justice	2.6	11.1	6.3	10.0	14.6	5.2	5.8	6.6	11.9	15.8	9.7	8.0
Racist Attack(s)	14.4	29.7	1.0	5.0	4.7	2.8	6.4	7.3	6.7	4.7	2.7	5.9
Anti-Racism Protests/Demo	21.2	7.4	7.3	1.7	0.9	3.3	0.6	0.8	1.3	0.9	0.0	1.6
Asylum seekers/Refugees	0.8	0.0	0.0	0.0	0.0	0.0	0.3	0.6	1.7	0.3	0.5	0.5
Racism in Other Fields	0.8	3.7	5.2	1.7	6.0	3.5	10.5	9.6	13.9	11.3	10.2	9.2
Far Right/Racists	1.7	0.0	0.0	1.7	0.6	0.7	1.5	1.0	1.3	0.9	2.7	1.2
Multiculturalism/British Identity	0.8	0.0	3.1	1.7	3.6	2.1	1.9	2.6	1.4	1.3	4.8	2.1
Culture/Arts	0.8	0.0	1.0	0.0	0.6	3.8	4.0	3.7	6.2	5.8	5.9	4.0
Public Inquiry	0.0	0.0	0.0	0.0	15.2	44.1	10.3	3.6	5.2	1.6	1.6	12.1
Politics/Elections	4.2	0.0	2.1	1.7	6.0	1.9	8.1	9.8	7.2	1.9	0.5	6.3
Other Media	0.8	0.0	0.0	0.0	15.5	5.6	8.9	4.8	3.3	6.2	12.4	6.9
Prominent Person Statement	2.6	7.4	5.2	0.0	4.2	2.0	0.9	1.8	1.0	0.9	1.1	1.5
Lawrence Family/Rites	11.1	7.4	4.2	8.3	2.1	2.7	3.1	3.0	3.7	5.3	12.9	3.7
Suspects/Family	0.0	0.0	0.0	6.6	2.1	1.8	5.4	2.0	2.2	9.9	9.7	4.2
Other	0.0	3.7	0.0	1.7	0.9	0.4	1.1	1.5	2.7	1.5	1.1	1.2
Total	100.0	100.0	100.0	100.0	100.0	100.0	100.0	100.0	100.0	100.0	100.0	100.0

The mediatised treatment of the Stephen Lawrence case evidently extended beyond the personal tragedy of an individual murder and the inadequate response of the criminal justice system to become a public challenge signalling public troubles of racism and injustice at the heart of British society. C. Wright Mills famously set forth his understanding of the sociological imagination some time ago in terms of the dialectical relationship between 'private troubles' and 'public issues' (1975). He argued that the lived realities, 'the private troubles', of daily life and cultural milieu both express and provide the basis for collective engagement with pressing 'public issues', and thereby constitute a dialectic of historical change (Mills 1975). Today we may want to press a little harder into the ideological constitution of categories of the 'private' and 'public' (Walby 1991), especially when these are played out in relation to new forms of 'mediatized publicness' (Thompson 1995). Nor can we trivialise murder as private trouble, or overrationalise public issues by failing to attend to their affective dimensions or powered processes of public definition. Even so, these preliminary findings suggest that the Stephen Lawrence case is a socially consequential illustration of Mills's fundamental thesis. In this case, a vicious racist attack and family tragedy, emanating from surrounding social forces and contexts, eventually galvanised wider reflexivity and collective forces for change.

From the thematic findings already documented in Table 4.2, it is clear that the press played an important role in generalising the private tragedy that violently befell the Lawrence family to deeper public troubles of racism and injustice embedded within British society and its key institutions. The media may also have then gone on to perform an indispensable role in preparing the basis on which struggles could be waged 'to make "real" institutional relationships more consistent with the normative standards of the utopian civil society discourse' (Alexander and Jacobs 1998, 28).

From Sign to Symbol

The fact that the name of Stephen Lawrence became increasingly invoked in press items not principally concerned with the case across the ten-year period, and particularly following the public inquiry, further demonstrates how the Stephen Lawrence affair became established and generalised as a key point of reference within the wider field of mediatised discourse (see Figure 4.4). The name of Stephen Lawrence, formerly reported as a 'sign' of racist murder, that is, as a signifier connoting the particularity of the murder and its aftermath, through sustained media representation became a potent 'symbol' both encapsulating and speaking to much wider concerns and collective feelings. Once symbol, the name of Stephen Lawrence appeared in press items not necessarily concerned with the case at all, but which thereby found an established and resonant frame of reference in-

Figure 4.4
UK Press Generalisation: From Sign to Symbol

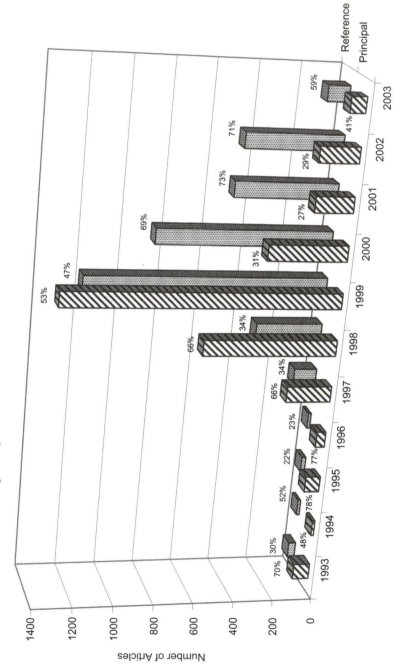

voked through his name. This transmutation of 'Stephen Lawrence' from sign to symbol also, therefore, informed processes of press generalisation. Quantitatively this can be documented by comparing the numbers of press items that are principally about the Stephen Lawrence case—that is, items that are focussed on this particular case and its developments—with those that simply reference his name but are primarily about other issues, whether 'race' and racism, criminal justice and law, or questions of identity.

From Dissemination to Dialogue

The dynamics of press generalisation are not only confined to the contours of press coverage already charted with relation to the thematic, semiotic or symbolic. They also encompass the *forms* of press representation and how these variously mediatised and enacted the public crisis. It is useful to explore how different genres of journalism address their imagined audiences, doing so through conventionalised presentational formats. It is in and through the conventionalised forms of journalism that different views and voices are variously enabled (or disabled) in the public elaboration, and deliberation, of public troubles. Here we can quantitatively document, for example, how the Stephen Lawrence story was not just simply 'reported' by the British press.

Through time, and as the story moved from one successive phase to the next, so the press increasingly deployed more 'reflective' and 'reflexive' press formats—a finding that supports Victor Turner's expectations of unfolding social dramas, and the rise in 'plural reflexivity' when a group or society 'tries to scrutinize, portray, understand, and then act on itself' (1982, 75), and its tendency to make full use of the 'many genres of cultural performance' (78). This suggests that the press were doing much more than simply following the institutional definition of events. The presentational formats of newspaper journalism exhibit wide variety—in fact more so than is usually acknowledged in studies of press journalism—and in their deployment demand close scrutiny in terms of how they shape and impact the discursive elaboration of contending interests and identities. In overview terms, however, newspaper formats in the press portrayal of the Stephen Lawrence case comprised traditional *reportage* formats: news reports and news in brief; *reflective* formats that enabled further contextualisation and discussion broadening the frame of reference: features/analysis, comment/opinion, editorial, profile/interview, open space, head to head, satire and letters to the editor; and, finally, *media reflexive* formats that variously refer to media (intertextual) materials already placed in the media sphere and now recycled via diary, media review, quiz and calendar formats. It was by these communicative means, variously deployed across the years, that the Stephen Lawrence story was both publicly told, and talked about. These established press formats contributed to public processes of dissem-

ination and dialogue and, in so doing, provided representations and resources for wider public recognition and deliberation. By these means, the
issues and identities surrounding the Stephen Lawrence case became publicly defined, expressed and, often, 'felt'. The deployment of different reportage, reflective and media reflexive formats also, then, served to
generalise the Stephen Lawrence case, and together these constituted a cultural crucible in which contending ideas and issues surrounding the case
could be publicly poured and pummelled. It was also by the use of these
different formats that the press moved the public representation of the
Stephen Lawrence story from the indicative to subjunctive mode of journalism, from text to talk, and dissemination to dialogue (see Table 4.3).

As Table 4.3 documents, the percentage of reflective (and media reflexive) formats deployed by the press increased markedly across the ten-year
period as the percentage of reportage formats decreased from approxi-
mately three-quarters to a half of all formats as time went by and the mediatised public crisis grew in public prominence. This is significant in terms
of the press enactment of the Stephen Lawrence case and its public or-
chestration of contending views and voices (see Figure 4.5). The use of reflective formats increased across time but also in respect to particular
formats. It is notable, for example, that no less than 1,075 feature/analy-
ses, 733 comment/opinion pieces, 275 editorials and 292 letters to the editor featured in this massive press outpouring. We will examine how some
of these formats served to enact the Stephen Lawrence story later. But here
we can simply note that this 'communicative architecture' contributed an
important (albeit often overlooked) dimension to the mediatised Stephen
Lawrence public crisis and signals how different mediums, genres, subgen-
res and formats contribute to the mediatisation of public crises.

A NOTE ON READING METHODOLOGY

The foregoing has mapped some of the basic parameters informing
British press representation of the Stephen Lawrence case as it grew into a
major mediatized public crisis across the ten-year research period. As we
shall go on to explore, the press, and other media too, increasingly performed the Stephen Lawrence story, investing it with cultural charge, social significance and political momentum. As they did so, they actively
summoned particularised publics and identities through their rhetorical appeals and narratives, and sought to invest the story with emotional resonance and deep symbolism. This, as we shall see, was enacted through the
full panoply of available journalistic styles, forms and genres, making use
of their expressive as well as informational capacities. Media performativity, then, was conducted through the mediums and evolving forms of contemporary journalism. This performative 'doing' was enacted within and
through press headlines, linguistic structures and lexical choices, emotional

Table 4.3
UK Press Generalisation: From Dissemination to Dialogue

Formats	1993	1994	1995	1996	1997	1998	1999	2000	2001	2002	2003	Total
Reportage												
News Reports	64	14	55	37	154	542	1249	721	386	356	74	3652
News in Brief	21	7	16	1	10	32	60	45	15	11	9	227
Sub-Total	**85**	**21**	**71**	**38**	**164**	**574**	**1309**	**766**	**401**	**367**	**83**	**3879**
Reflection												
Feature/Analysis	16	4	12	12	61	146	399	155	123	112	35	1075
Comment/Opinion	4	0	5	1	46	91	261	145	74	75	31	733
Letters	6	1	1	5	12	44	150	42	14	13	4	292
Editorial	3	0	3	1	21	35	111	48	24	27	2	275
Profile/Interview	1	0	0	0	11	20	68	39	26	44	11	223
Open Space	0	1	0	0	4	5	11	3	2	1	1	28
Satirical	0	0	0	0	0	7	3	3	0	0	1	14
Head to Head	0	0	0	0	2	4	0	1	1	0	0	9
Sub-Total	**30**	**6**	**24**	**19**	**157**	**352**	**1003**	**436**	**264**	**273**	**85**	**2649**
Media Reflexivity												
Media Review	1	0	0	0	8	35	203	49	27	31	14	368
Diary	0	0	1	0	4	11	25	4	3	3	3	54
Calendar	0	0	0	1	2	5	4	0	0	4	0	16
Quiz	0	0	0	0	0	3	6	2	1	0	0	12
Sub-Total	**1**	**0**	**1**	**1**	**14**	**54**	**238**	**55**	**31**	**38**	**17**	**450**
Other	2	0	0	2	0	2	2	1	1	0	1	11
Total	**118**	**27**	**96**	**60**	**335**	**982**	**2552**	**1258**	**697**	**678**	**186**	**6989**
Formats (%)												
Reportage	72.0	77.8	74.0	63.3	49.0	58.5	51.3	60.9	57.5	54.1	44.6	55.5
Reflection	25.5	22.2	25.0	31.7	46.8	35.8	39.3	34.6	38.0	40.3	45.7	37.9
Media Reflexivity	0.8	0.0	1.0	1.7	4.2	5.5	9.3	4.4	4.4	5.6	9.2	6.4
Other	1.7	0.0	0.0	3.3	0.0	0.2	0.1	0.1	0.1	0.0	0.5	0.2
Total	**100.0**	**100.0**	**100.0**	**100.0**	**100.0**	**100.0**	**100.0**	**100.0**	**100.0**	**100.0**	**100.0**	**100.0**

Figure 4.5
UK Press Generalisation: From Dissemination to Dialogue

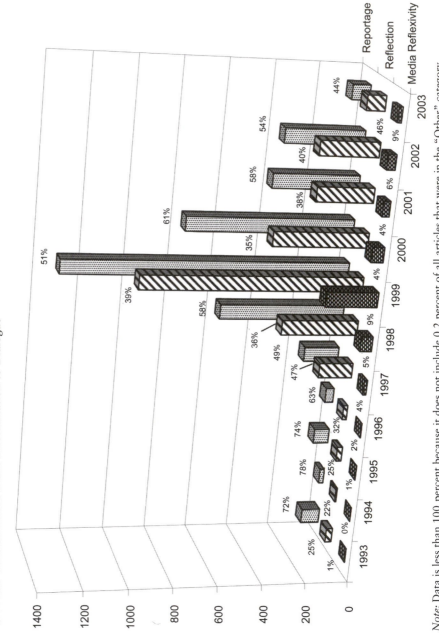

Note: Data is less than 100 percent because it does not include 0.2 percent of all articles that were in the "Other" category.

appeals and testimonies, visual images, typography, article juxtapositions, page layout and display features, occasional use of special reports, and the full array of media genres and formats, whether reportage, reflective or media reflexive, as well as different television forms of news, current affairs and documentary programmes, and internet sites.

Our analysis, necessarily, is concerned with a large sample of media output, comprising nearly 7,000 press items alone, produced over a ten-year period, as well as numerous television programmes, many of them produced at the height of the Stephen Lawrence story. Methodologically, therefore, this study grapples with a large corpus of media output and is sensitised to the performative and expressive nature of much of it. For these reasons, the reader will find that the analysis that follows reproduces many media examples, transcripts and images. These materials are positioned as an integral part of the analysis and are here used performatively again, demonstrating how they enacted the Stephen Lawrence story and invested it with symbolism and rhetorical and emotional force. These materials, then, are not merely illustrative but help to perform a key role in the analysis that follows.

Given the ambitious scope of this study with its concerns to map the dynamics and performative nature of this particular mediatised public crisis, the analysis necessarily draws on a wide range of methods and approaches. These qualitatively deepen the systematic content analytic findings reported earlier. The complexity and multidimensional nature of the media forms subject to analysis escape the ability of any one reading method to disclose exactly how they discharged their meanings. Performativity, as previously discussed in Chapter 3, is as much an active 'investment of self', as it is an invocation by the media 'to belong'. The approach adopted here, therefore, seeks to analyse but also to acknowledge and 'experience' as part of this analysis the appeals and expressiveness of the media performance enacted across the Stephen Lawrence story. Much depends, of course, on where the reader positions or aligns him- or herself in respect of the contested terrain of 'race', racism and identity, but all, apart from the most emotionally detached or politically deranged, can feel the hurt and witness the pain expressed in and through some of these media materials.

For more detailed accounts of reading methods, some of which inform this study, the reader is referred to recent developments in discourse analysis (Bell and Garrett 1998; Faircloth 1995; Van Dijk 1988, 1991, 2000); critical linguistics (Fowler et al. 1979; Fowler 1991; Hodge and Kress 1979); social semiotics (Hodge and Kress 1998); and approaches to news visuals (Cottle 1998), visual display and press front pages, and media forms (Barnhurst and Nerone 2001; Kress and Leeuwen 1996, 1998). Media performativity, as we shall see, and possibly 'feel', is enacted within and through all of these modes and forms of media communication, and the reader will need to engage with some of these materials in order to recover something of their original communicative force and experiential impact.

Limitations of space have decreed that some of these media materials can only be presented in abridged form, and where this is so, it is indicated thus: (. . .). Headlines, in either lower case or capitalized format, have been transcribed either from the original press reports or from their reproduction as loaded into the Lexis-Nexis on-line newspaper database and accessed for the purposes of this research. We are grateful to the publishers for permitting us to reproduce selected materials as originally published to ensure that their performative display and visuality is not lost from view.

SUMMARY

On the basis of the empirical measures above, the UK press publicly extended the Stephen Lawrence case over a ten-year period and massively generalised it to wider readerships and publics. They did this irrespective of their differing political partisanships, market positions or institutionalised forms as mainstream quality broadsheets, populist tabloids or minority weeklies. This massive outpouring mapped the major institutional developments in the Stephen Lawrence case and involved for the most part the agencies of the criminal justice system. But across this period, the press clearly did much more than this. Extensive and intensive media reporting progressively placed the Stephen Lawrence case on the public agenda as it grew through various, interlinked and developmental phases into a major mediatised public crisis. Quantitative findings documented in this chapter thereby buttress the argument developed in the rest of this book concerning the media's performative contribution to the development of the Stephen Lawrence story as a mediatised public crisis.

Preliminary findings, then, indicate that the Stephen Lawrence story did indeed move over time from 'private tragedy' into 'public trouble.' As the media extended its frame of reference beyond the institutional arenas and processes associated with this particular case, so it began to 'reveal "subcutaneous" levels of the social structure' (Turner 1982, 10). The Stephen Lawrence story, it seems, became both vehicle and driver for the public elaboration and generalisation of deep-seated concerns of policing, racism and injustice within British society. At the heart of this public trouble and its press elaboration was the name of Stephen Lawrence, a name that publicly migrated from sign to symbol as it progressively became infused with public sentiments centred on issues of 'race', identity and injustice. As this mediatised public crisis grew in proportion and cultural intensity, so the press also mobilised its established communicative architecture and gave—or orchestrated—vent to the play of discourses and debate, contending voices and views, surrounding the Stephen Lawrence case. This move from traditional reportage to reflective (and media reflexive) formats helped to move the coverage away from the indicative to the subjunctive mode and enact the growing public crisis in terms of both dissemination and dialogue.

With these broad quantitative underpinnings now in place, it is time to delve more deeply, more qualitatively, into the media's performative enactment of the Stephen Lawrence story across narrativised time with respect to its emotional elaboration and ritual features. It is here that we can better appreciate how the media performed and canalised the Stephen Lawrence case in respect to different publics and did so by rhetorically invoking social solidarities, which thereby invested the story with cultural charge as well as politically transformative capacities. In these ways, the generalised story of Stephen Lawrence became inflected by different ideologies and invoked identities within a contested field of discourse. Even so, as we shall see, the story helped to build a generalised and widely shared public concern over the failures of the criminal justice system based around a united abhorrence of the pollutant of racism and racist hatreds within British society. It is to this more detailed exploration of how the mediatised public crisis grew through time and unleashed such cultural and moral charge that the discussion now turns.

NOTES

Page numbers of all newspaper articles quoted or referenced in this book have been included where available from the database.

1. The research into British newspapers was based on the retrieval of all newspaper items (6,989) that referenced Stephen Lawrence across the period from April 1993 to May 2003. This was conducted by making use of the Lexis-Nexis newspaper database, a CD-Rom of *Daily Mail* and *Mail on Sunday* output across the same period, and detailed library searches of various newspaper collections. The sample collected is comprehensive.

2. In order to collect our international sample of press coverage we made use of the Lexis-Nexis newspaper database. Across the ten-year period, the contributions of international press to this database have varied. This total sample of international press reports (176), unlike the British sample, is not, therefore, proclaimed to be comprehensive, though it is likely to be broadly representative of the different ways in which the press in different countries reported on the case.

Five

Breach

Breach of regular, norm-governed social relations occurs between persons or groups within the same system of social relations. . . . [B]reach is signalized by the public, overt breach or deliberate nonfulfilment of some crucial norm regulating the intercourse of the parties . . . ('a symbolic trigger of confrontation or encounter')

Victor Turner, *Dramas, Fields, Metaphors* (1974, 38)

The momentum that would eventually propel the Stephen Lawrence case forward and distribute its charge across the institutional and cultural terrain of Britain (and even further afield, internationally) had been building before the murder in 1993. Previous racist attacks in boroughs of southeast London, as already documented in Chapter 2, included the murders of Rohit Duggal and Rolan Adams. These and other racist attacks had produced growing anger and outcry from local black communities and action groups, and calls for the closure of the British National Party's headquarters in nearby Welling. This powerfully reminds us that just as media do not operate in a social vacuum, so mediatised public crises are often dependent on preceding events and derive their charge from the surrounding social, cultural and political fields. By definition and performative enactment, mediatised public crises cannot assume the scale and intensity that they do without the media; but it is also the case that their charge is primarily located elsewhere, outside of the media sphere and within society. Cleavages of inequality, different life chances and identities all provide fertile grounds for the electrifying force of mediatised public crises, which, on reaching a heightened degree of intensity, can unearth society's subterranean fault lines and expose them to the media's public glare. This chapter examines how British media first reported on the murder of Stephen Lawrence and how this case became, in Turner's terms, publicly signalised as a 'breach' of 'norm-governed social relations'.

Did Stephen's brutal murder publicly constitute a 'breach'? In one sense the question reads as offensive. A young man had his life violently ripped from him—the ultimate breach of life. Murder in most societies is ordinarily seen as a breach of life, but this does not usually prompt a wider public crisis, because no matter how violent or unexpected it may be, an individual's murder (with the exception of elite assassinations) is not taken as an indicator of systematic or patterned behaviour that threatens the wider group. Racist murder is different. Here an individual's murder is seen as the outcome of racism, which, by definition, has its roots in underlying collective processes and structures, both past and present, and which manifests itself in discriminatory and violent practices, both individual and institutional. But whether a racist murder is widely interpreted as a 'breach' in Turner's socially dichotomising sense above will also depend in large measure on how it is responded to by the authorities and how this is perceived within the relevant groups and communities.

In contemporary British society, as in most multiethnic social democracies, the 'utopian civil society discourse' (Alexander and Jacobs 1998) now encoded in the rule of law prohibits a wide range of racist acts, and does so on the basis of widely shared (though not universal) normative values in civil society and culture. Roy Jenkins famously elaborated on this 'utopian civil society discourse' in the British context some thirty-five years ago when he stated that the national goal should be 'equal opportunity, accompanied by cultural diversity, in an atmosphere of mutual tolerance' (cited in Lester 1998, 22). This commitment to multicultural goals, however, is a relatively recent phenomenon. Prior to the first Race Relations Act in 1976, overt and direct forms of racism by landlords, employers and others were often practiced with legal impunity (Blackstone et al. 1998; Fryer 1984; Smith 1989), and it is still within living memory that racist lynchings took place in Britain, inflamed by press racism and without legal redress (Fryer 1984, 298–316). Violent racism, detailed in Chapter 2, continues to stain contemporary British society (see Appendix 1). But insofar as today's 'utopian civil society discourse' is widely and normatively shared, and believed to be enacted by the criminal justice system, so a racist murder will be perceived as a heinous and punishable crime, but it may not in itself be taken as a fundamental breach that opens a major schism within society. Much depends on the wider context of racist incidents and how racist murder is responded to by those charged with the responsibility of enforcing society's normative views and implementing its criminal justice system.

If a racist murder is seen as the latest killing in a growing number of such crimes, and if public and political recognition of this murderous phenomenon does not respond to community demands for concerted action, it can become a symbolic trigger of confrontation. The role of the media in this complex interaction can here prove crucial, both in alerting and activating power holders into redressive action, but also as a means by which threatened groups can gauge the extent of wider understanding and/or common concern about their plight (Kerner 1968). Attending to media at this juncture, therefore, provides insights into how issues of 'race' and racism are publicly conceptualised and evaluated at a particular historical moment in time and in relation to the shifting politics of 'race', racism and British identity.

The following examines how the British media first reported the Stephen Lawrence murder, as well as subsequent events that followed in close proximity, and how this began to publicly signal the Stephen Lawrence case as a 'breach' moving towards a phase of 'mounting crisis'. Initially the British press reported the case unevenly and were faltering in their interest. The campaign by the Lawrence family and their supporters to win media interest in their case won some measure of media exposure, but the nature of this coverage as we shall see challenges the idea that they managed to engineer successful publicity at this time and contradicts also the claims made later by some sections of the press that they had been responsible for moving the story forward at this early stage (Cathcart 2000). The initial press reports provide a different view. Television, for its part, largely ignored the case at this time, apart from occasional and brief news reports carried by regional news services such as *BBC News South-East*. The mainstream British press reported on the first phase of the Stephen Lawrence story in characteristic ways. Often they did so without adopting a consistent point of view or seeking to perform the case as one that demanded a collective response. This was *indicative* reporting. It was only through time and the reporting of subsequent events that the media would find the confidence and commitment to play a leading performative role that would take the reporting of the Stephen Lawrence case from the indicative to the *subjunctive* mode.

REPORTING RACIST MURDER

National television at first ignored the murder of Stephen Lawrence, though regional television news services managed to report the basic facts, as relayed by the police, the next day.

An 18-year-old boy has been stabbed to death in what police have described as a senseless racial attack. Stephen Lawrence was killed as he waited for a bus with a friend in south-east London. . . .

(*BBC News South-East*, 23.4.93)

Five British newspapers in our sample of thirteen newspapers, the *Guardian, Daily Mail, Sun, Independent,* and the *Times,* also reported the

murder of Stephen Lawrence at the first opportunity on Saturday 24 April
(papers had already gone to press on the night of 22 April) and the weekly
Voice did so on Monday 27 April. The *Financial Times, Daily Mirror* and
News of the World, as well as Scotland's *Scotsman, Herald* and *Daily
Record,* and Northern Ireland's *Belfast Telegraph* did not report it. Evidently, a racist murder in England was either too commonplace or too lack-
ing in news interest to warrant national television interest or universal press
attention from all of Britain's mainstream papers; nor did its news value
extend to Scotland or Northern Ireland.

To begin our analysis of the mediatised story of Stephen Lawrence, it is
instructive to examine these first reports in a little detail since they illustrate how, even at this early stage, press political partisanship and informing views on 'race' inflected their reporting of racist murder.

'Race' Politics and Press Idioms: Reporting Racist Murder

The mainstream British press at first covered the murder of Stephen
Lawrence in the relatively matter-of-fact terms of news reportage, albeit in-
formed by their respective press idioms and views on 'race' politics. The
Daily Mail began its report as follows:[1]

Murdered Just for Being Black

FEAR OF REPRISALS AFTER WHITE GANG KNIFE TEENAGE STUDENT

Edward Verity

A BLACK student has been stabbed to death by a gang of white youths
in what police believe was a racial attack.

Stephen Laurence [*sic*], 18, was ambushed in Eltham, South-East London, as he waited at a bus stop with a school friend after visiting his uncle.

Detectives said one of the gang of six was heard to make a racist remark before the attack at 10pm on Thursday night at the junction of Well
Hall Road and Dickson Road.

It is the third racial murder in the area in little more than two years.

Last night amid fears of reprisal attacks over the latest killing, police
appealed to residents to 'stay calm'.

Chief Superintendent John Philpott said more officers were being
drafted on to the streets in response to the incident.

He said race relations in Eltham were not significantly worse than in
some other London boroughs, but added, 'I wouldn't deny we have a racial
problem and it is not easy to deal with.' . . .

Stephen's father said he was devastated by the death of his son, a hard-working sixth former who wanted to be an architect. . . .

His head teacher, John Thurley, said, 'He was a very pleasant, popular young man of above average ability. He was determined to do well in his studies.'

The spot where Stephen died is just 200 yards from where Rohit Duggal, a 16 year-old Asian, was stabbed to death by a white youth in July last year.

In February his killer, Peter Thompson, was ordered to be detained for life by an Old Bailey judge.

In February 1991 black schoolboy Rolan Adams, 15, was stabbed to death after a clash with white youths in nearby Thamesmead. A teenager was jailed for life over the incident.

(*Daily Mail*, 24.4.93, 12)

The *Daily Mail*'s relatively lengthy news report (907 words) featured on page 12. Like many newspapers on 24 April, it misspelled the Lawrences' surname, but the framing of the report is clear enough and, as is often the case in newspaper report structures or 'schemata' (Van Dijk 1988), finds its most direct expression in headlines and lead paragraphs. Here the first headline discloses not only the fact of the murder but also proffers an explanation—MURDERED JUST FOR BEING BLACK—before immediately emphasising in bold and capitalization FEAR OF REPRISALS. This 'report', then, does more than announce the known facts of the murder; it frames the murder in terms of the possibility of further violence, violence that can only be understood in the context of racial hostilities and reaction, though the exact connection between these remains opaque and understated. It is noticeable that the *Daily Mail* declines the language of 'racism' and 'racist' and prefers to refer to 'racial attack', 'racial murder' or simply to note the Asian identity or black skin colour of recent murder victims. In doing so, it invites essentialist and simplistic thinking about racist violence as somehow endemic and/or accountable to the racial characteristics of presupposed 'races'. The term 'racial murder' simply alerts us to the involvement of different 'races' and so does not signal which, if any, 'race' may be the principal perpetrators of such acts; whereas 'racist murder', in the context of British society, is more likely to signal the known predominance of white racist violence directed at black, Asian and other minority ethnic groups.

Through such lexical choices and their informing but unstated presuppositions, the *Daily Mail* positioned itself on the contested terrain of 'race', racism and identity. It also provided an emergent, personalising view of Stephen Lawrence as a 'hard-working sixth-former who wanted to be an architect', a view that was repeated across the press and soon became established as mandatory epithets in subsequent reporting. At this point, and in conformity to the claims of objective news reporting structuring its 'straightforward' news report, the *Daily Mail*'s politics of 'race' remains implicit and undeclared, and its view of Stephen Lawrence, though humanising, is also relatively undeveloped.

The *Sun*, Britain's most popular tabloid newspaper, reported the murder in characteristically populist style, though, in comparison to the *Daily Mail*, it lexically signals a degree of ambivalence in its informing 'race' politics.

Race Murder Stabbing of Perfect Pupil

GANG ATTACK A-LEVEL BOY

Ross Kaniuk

A SCHOOLBOY with a bright future was stabbed to death by race-hate thugs—because he was black.

Stephen Lawrence, 18, an A-level student hoping to become an architect, was at a bus stop when six white youths pounced without provocation. One yob made a racist remark—then Stephen was knifed twice. . . .

His father, Neville, 51, said last night: "My family is devastated. This was the senseless murder of a decent young man."

Mr Laurence, a plasterer, said: 'Stephen was looking forward to life. He was about to take his A-levels and wanted to go to college to train as an architect. I would bring back hanging for something like this.

"I don't think the people who did this should be allowed to stay on the streets."

Stephen's distraught mum, Doreen, 46, a student teacher, was under sedation last night. . . .

Problem

Stephen's death follows the racist murders of an Asian and a 16-year-old black youth.

Murder-hunt police last night appealed for calm amid fears of reprisal attacks on whites.

Chief Superintendent John Philpott said: "We ask people to be sensible. We will not deny there is a race problem in this area but we aim to tackle it."

Hardy Dhillon, chairman of Greenwich Council for Racial Equality, said: "This is the race capital of the country.

"It is terrible. These killings must be stopped."

(*Sun*, 24.4.93, 5)

Written in the accessible, vernacular tabloid style for which the *Sun* has become famous, the murder of Stephen Lawrence is reported at relative length

(325 words). Unlike the *Daily Mail*, the *Sun* chooses to lead both in its headline and its lead paragraph with the image of the murder victim as a hardworking schoolboy. As we shall explore later, it seems unlikely that Stephen Lawrence could have become the resonant pure symbol that he later did if his public image at this early stage had been tainted by stereotypical views associating black youth with trouble and criminality.

The *Sun* leaves no doubt about its contempt for the 'race-hate thugs' and 'yob' responsible for Stephen's murder. The article also personalises and familiarises its report with reference to members of the Lawrence family and emotionally privatises the tragedy and its awful impact with reference to Stephen's father and the state of his 'distraught mum'. The *Sun*'s condemnatory stance is explicit, but at the heart of this report resides an ambiguity signaled in its RACE MURDER headline and subsequent lexicon of 'race-hate thugs', 'racist remark' and 'racist murders'. Though it appears, like the *Daily Mail*, to erroneously presuppose that 'race' is self-evidently real (rather than an ideological category historically forged and ascribed to 'others' to legitimise exploitation) and a sufficient category for the explanation of 'race murder', it also incorporates the language of 'racist murders' that demands deeper contextualisation and understanding in terms of white racism.

The *Independent*, in conformity to its liberal and left-of-centre alignment, reported the Stephen Lawrence murder with a different political inflection:

Police Appeal for Calm After Racist Murder

Nicholas Schoon and Nick Walker

POLICE appealed for calm in the London borough of Greenwich last night after the murder of a black schoolboy.

Stephen Lawrence was the third teenager from an ethnic minority to be stabbed to death in the borough in just over two years. All the killings involved groups of white youths. . . .

Stephen lived in Woolwich Common and was studying for A-levels at Blackheath Bluecoat school. He wanted to be an architect. His family and friends said yesterday that he always avoided trouble. "He wasn't into fighting one bit; he would avoid it," his father Neville said.

There had been three near-fatal racial stabbings of black people in the borough this year before Stephen's murder late on Thursday. . . .

Yesterday as Stephen's friends spoke of seeking out the killers for revenge, Chief Superintendent John Philpott of the Metropolitan Police in Plumstead said: "We would ask young people to be sensible. . . . [W]e have a racist problem in this area but we aim to tackle it." Police patrols were being stepped up, he added.

Rolan Adams was killed in nearby Thamesmead in February 1991 and buried on his 16th birthday. Stephen took part in campaigns to raise money for his family and to protest against racial attacks. In July last year, Rohit Duggal, a 16-year-old Asian, was stabbed to death in Well Hall Road—the same Eltham street where Stephen was knifed. Two youths are serving terms of life imprisonment.

The Greenwich Action Committee Against Racist Attacks and the Commission for Racial Equality yesterday called for a meeting with the Home Secretary, Kenneth Clarke, and the Metropolitan Police Commissioner, Paul Condon.

Dev Barrah, the committee's co-ordinator, said bad housing and high unemployment had made the area a breeding ground for racism. The British National Party has set up its headquarters in nearby Welling and campaigns and recruits in the area. He called for the party to be expelled. . . .

(*Independent*, 24.4.93, 4)

The *Independent*'s first report, like that of the *Daily Mail* and the *Sun*, provides a fairly detailed (473-word) report of the murder. Unlike them, however, the *Independent* explicitly signals 'racist murder' in its headline and quickly situates this in relation to previous murders in the borough of Greenwich, thereby helping to explain why the police should be appealing for calm. In contrast to the *Daily Mail*'s and, to a lesser degree, the *Sun*'s preferred lexicons of 'racial problem' and 'race hate', the named problem at the heart of this report is clearly signalled as white racism and an increasing number of racist attacks.

Revealingly, the *Independent* quotes the Chief Superintendent John Philpott as saying, 'we have a racist problem in this area but we aim to tackle it'; the *Sun* quoted the same officer as saying, 'We do not deny there is a race problem in this area but we aim to tackle it'; and the *Daily Mail* quoted him as stating, 'I wouldn't deny we have a racial problem and it is not easy to deal with'. The semantic differences of 'racist problem' (*Independent*), 'race problem' (*Sun*) and 'racial problem' (*Daily Mail*) are thereby neatly encapsulated in the direct quotations, and these serve to endorse the respective newspapers' informing 'race' politics. Given the same preceding words in these quotes, it seems likely that these were derived from the same police statement, but they have been significantly interpreted very differently and in conformity to the papers' respective outlooks on 'race' and racism.

Moreover, the *Independent*'s report not only provides further detail of two preceding racist murder victims, Rolan Adams and Rohit Duggal, but also adds an additional level of public characterisation to Stephen Lawrence. Here he is not only described as an A-level student who wanted to be an architect, but also as a member of the black community who took part in campaigns to raise money for Rolan Adams's family and 'to protest against racial attacks'—a feature that was subsequently lost from view in the wider symbolic construction of Stephen Lawrence. The *Independent* both personalises the story and politicises it in respect to the wider black community's concerns about rising racist attacks and also to named institutional power holders. A further level of contextualisation, absent in the *Daily Mail*'s and the *Sun*'s reports, grounds the report's understanding of racism and rising racist attacks with reference to the social inequalities of 'bad housing and high unemployment', as well as the activities of the British National Party in the area.

In these ways, then, the *Independent*, in contrast to the *Daily Mail* and the *Sun*, distanced itself from essentialising 'race' violence as a problem seemingly endemic to 'races' and positioned the murder within the wider and contested political field of racial inequality and racism. These differences of reporting are broadly representative of the wider field of British newspapers and their political alignments in relation to the wider politics of 'race' and racism. The *Guardian*, with its headline, GANG HUNTED AFTER BUS STOP RACE KILLING, for example, reported the murder in the terms of a crime report and provided contextual details about the rising numbers of racist attacks in the area and the Anti-Racist Alliance's call for the closure of the British National Party headquarters in nearby Welling; and in the *Times*, the article BLACK TEENAGER DIES AFTER KNIFE ATTACK BY WHITE YOUTHS provided a lengthier piece that canvassed different views including those of the British National Party, which was thereby granted the opportunity to deny that it advocated violence.

The semantic differences registered in the lexical choices, linguistic cues and thematic emphases of these different newspaper reports would later open up into clear differences of political alignment and advocacy by the British press and would do so with respect to wider issues and identities brought into public view by the Stephen Lawrence story. For the moment, though, they remained relatively understated, and the mainstream press did not, as we have seen, publicly commit to or seek to performatively enact the Stephen Lawrence case as one demanding political action and response. Not so the minority press.

The Minority *Voice*: 'We Must Protect Ourselves'

Ignored by some mainstream newspapers and reported by others in idiomatic terms, the Stephen Lawrence case was not signalled as a 'breach'. In stark contrast, Britain's most popular black weekly newspaper, the *Voice*, reported the murder from day one with an emphasis on concerns about the growing numbers of assaults on the black community, a community, moreover, which the *Voice* sought to simultaneously constitute and represent. Here the Lawrence murder became publicly signalled as part of a preexistent and widening breach opening up between the black community and Britain's political apparatus with its seeming inability to address the rising tide of white racist violence. The *Voice* devoted the bulk of its front page on Monday 27 April to the Stephen Lawrence murder under the headline MURDERED FOR BEING BLACK. The front page (665-word) report was presented alongside a picture of Stephen Lawrence sitting at home and captioned 'STEPHEN: Hounded to his death'. Unlike the *Daily Mail*'s report with almost the same headline, the *Voice* article does not raise the possibility of violent reaction to the murder, but focussed on the murder itself, the emotional reactions of Neville Lawrence, who called for the death penalty for the killers, and the connection between the rising racist violence in the area and the activities of the British National Party. The report continued on page three under the headline RACE HATE MURDER SPECIAL REPORT, where graphic descriptions of the wounds sustained by Stephen Lawrence were described and where the awful reality of racist murder was underlined by recounting how the everyday world of the Lawrences was about to irrevocably change forever when they were on their way to the hospital:

When Mr Lawrence, a 51-year-old painter-decorator, and his wife Doreen, 40, set off to the nearby Brook hospital they did not know that their son was already dead. Mr Lawrence said he thought that Stephen had been involved in 'some sort of prank.' Mrs Lawrence is too distressed to talk about what happened.

"He had many wounds on his body and that we did not see. It seems that he was hit with some sort of iron pipe, stabbed in the heart and some other wounds."

Stephen also had a horrific stab wound to his neck.

The brutal murder has shattered the close-knit family. Stephen was studying for his A-levels and had plans to become an architect.

The full effect has still to hit Stephen's sister Georgina, 11, and brother Stewart, who celebrated his 16th birthday last week.

(*Voice*, 27.4.93, 1–3)

This article deliberately seeks to bring home something of the human reality and family tragedy that lies behind headlines of murder, but it is on page three that the *Voice* assumes its most explicit performative stance (see Figure 5.1).

The *Voice*'s performative intervention, as we can see, is enacted in and through a crafted mélange of different articles and journalism styles. Five journalistic treatments are juxtaposed, which together display and evoke the known facts and feelings, hurt and hatred of racist killings in Britain. The banner headline, WE MUST PROTECT OURSELVES, rhetorically invites the reader to identify with the community under attack as well as with the newspaper that summons it into being; the simple bullet-point chronicle, KILLINGS

Figure 5.1
Voice, 27 April 1993, p. 3. © *Voice*.

RACE HATE MURDER SPECIAL REPORT

'WE MUST PROTECT OURSELVES'

The community responds to the shocking killing of Stephen Lawrence. Janet Sebastian reports

BUS STOP: *The scene of Stephen's murder.*

CAMPAIGNERS have called for Black people to mobilise and take action to defend themselves following the latest racist slaying. MP Bernie says that Stephen Lawrence's race murder must be the last.

Labour MP Bernie Grant says the Black community needs to ensure that Stephen Lawrence's murder is the last race killing it has to endure.

He said: "We will not allow our young people to go on being murdered. Every community is entitled to defend itself in law. If the police won't defend us, we must defend ourselves."

Mr Grant was backed up by angry calls from the Greenwich Action Committee Against Racial Attacks (GACARA), which has done much to highlight the racist murders in London's notorious south east region.

Dev Barrah, spokesman for GACARA, said: "This happened not more than 50 yards from where Rohit Duggal was murdered and it is the fourth racist murder in just over two years. This is the last straw.

"We have waved banners and been on too many demonstrations and this still happens. We have to reverse the fear so that ordinary, decent people can walk the streets."

The Anti-Racist Alliance

(ARA) has now renewed its call for the closure of the British National Party (BNP) office at Welling - the area in which Mr Lawrence was murdered.

An ARA spokesman said: "Racist attacks have increased by 140 per cent since the BNP moved into the area.

"The Greenwich area has become the racist murder capital of Britain. Bexley Council should use their planning powers to close down the Nazi bunker which is clearly spreading race hate among the local population."

Newham Monitoring Project (NMP) in east London was also vociferous in its condemnation of the racist murder. "A spokeswoman said: "The police and the Home Office haven't paid enough attention to these racists. So we must defend ourselves if the police won't defend our liberty."

Councillor Len Duvall, leader of Greenwich Council, urged witnesses to the attack to come forward: "Stephen is sadly one of several Black youths to be stabbed by White youths in this borough," he said.

ROLAN'S DAD SLAMS 'COMPLACENT' SOCIETY

ROLAN ADAMS: *Victim of racist thugs.*

THE BLACK community has become too complacent over racist killings, says the father of murdered schoolboy Rolan Adams.

Richard Adams, whose 15-year-old son was stabbed to death two years ago in very similar circumstances to Stephen Lawrence, was shocked but not surprised by the latest murder.

He said: "If Black people don't take hold of the reins in this situation Black boys will continue to be murdered.

"The White community don't have to do anything because it is not happening to them."

Mr Adams has led numerous demonstrations in south-east London in a bid to bring attention to race attacks, but feels that more has to be done

by the community as a whole.

"We've got to start laying down our own deterrents if the Government and the police refuse to. When the Crown Prosecution Service fail to prosecute racist murderers and take out private cases," stressed Mr Adams.

Expressing his family's sympathies to the Lawrence family, Mr Adams added: "I just feel so sorry for the family and the friend who was with Stephen at the time of the attack. I know from experience the nightmare they are going through."

Killings that shame the nation

● Panchadcharan Sahitharan - 28-year-old Tamil refugee. Died as a result of an attack by a gang on December 29, 1991. Died in hospital on January 2, 1992.

● Saddik Dada - murdered on January 23, 1992, in Manchester as a result of a machete attack by a racist gang.

● Mohammed Sarwar - beaten to death in an attack on January 26, 1992, in Manchester.

● Rohit Duggal - 16-year-old schoolboy. Died as a result of an attack on July 11, 1992, in Eltham, south London. Several members of a gang attacked him but only one was arrested.

● Ruhullah Aramesh - 24-year-old Afghan refugee.

Died as a result of a racist attack in Thornton Heath, Surrey. Died in hospital on August 2, 1992, after being attacked by a gang of up to 15 youths who were heard to shout racist abuse. Nine people were arrested. Charges against two were subsequently dropped. All others were released on bail.

● Ashiq Hussain - 20-year-old taxi driver. Died on September 1, 1992, in Birmingham as a result of attack by three White passengers.

● Khoaz Mia - 66-year-old man, died in September three weeks after a brutal beating by three White males while on his way to his mosque. One male was charged with murder.

STEPHEN'S PAL KNEW THEY FACED DEATH

STEPHEN Lawrence's companion, who escaped being killed by racist thugs, says he knew that their lives were in danger last Thursday night.

The 18-year-old, who does not want to be named because he fears for his safety, told The Voice how he escaped death but could do nothing to save his friend.

They had just got off the bus and were walking towards Stephen's home when six White boys aged between about 18 and 22 started calling out racial abuse.

The teenager told The Voice: "I just knew it was trouble and told Stephen to run. I kept shouting 'Run Stephen, run' and I started running myself. But he always thought he could work things out by talking.

"I heard him scream and looked round to see them standing around Stephen, and he dropped so I ran back and they ran away when they saw me coming. There was no time for fear as he needed my help."

The brutal race attack, which happened at 10.40pm on

Thursday April 22, left Stephen fatally injured with stab wounds to his neck and heart.

"Stephen was lying on the road. He got up and I said 'Stephen, run' and he said, 'Look at me. What's wrong?' and I just saw blood everywhere and he collapsed. I didn't realise how badly hurt he was," added the young man.

The teenager, who has been Stephen's friend for eight years, said that although Stephen was unconscious he was still breathing when the police arrived at 10.50pm. But he was dead on arrival at Brook Hospital, south-east London.

"Nothing like this has ever happened to us before and we never felt in danger in the area. They picked on us just because there were only two of us and there were so many of them," said the shocked teenager.

MURDERED FOR BEING BLACK

(Continued from page 1)

home from a short stay with his uncle in nearby Nottingham.

Up to six White youths started to hurl racial abuse at the pair who fled, not wanting to get involved in a brawl.

The gang chased the boys, who split up as they ran, and lashed out at Stephen with a long-bladed knife. He staggered for 250 yards in the direction of his home before collapsing in a pool of blood. The gang fled in the opposite direction. Stephen was dead on arrival at Brook Hospital, south-east London.

Drain

There have been too many murders in the same region and I don't think that this can go on.

"People are not going to stand and just watch their young, prosperous kids go down the drain like that any more. It's too much to ask," said Mr Lawrence.

Since the murder of Rolan

Adams in chillingly similar circumstances in February 1991, Stephen had been warned of the risks. But Mr Lawrence added that in any decent society no one's child should be a prisoner in their own home because of violent thugs.

When Mr Lawrence, a 51-year-old painter-decorator, and his wife Doreen, 40, set off to the nearby Brook Hospital they did not know that their son was already dead. Mr Lawrence said he thought that Stephen had been involved in "some sort of prank". Mrs Lawrence is too distressed to talk about what happened.

"He had many wounds on his body that we did not see. It seems that he was hit with some sort of iron pipe, stabbed in the heart and some other wounds."

Stephen also had a horrific stab wound in his neck.

The brutal murder has shattered the close-knit family. Stephen was studying for his

NEVILLE LAWRENCE: *Mourning.*

'A' levels and had plans to become an architect.

The full effect has still to hit Stephen's sister Georgina, 11, and brother Stewart, who celebrated his 16th birthday last week.

Detective Superintendent Ian Cramton, leading the investigation, said that he was treating the murder as a racially motivated attack.

"It is an outrage that two

young Black youths were on their way home and for no reason whatsoever one of them was stabbed to death."

At present the police do not acknowledge any links between the rising number of racial attacks in Greenwich and the right-wing British National Party (BNP) having established its headquarters in nearby Welling. Over the past 18 months four people have been killed in race-hate attacks.

Mr Lawrence added: "I'm angry at hearing about the presence of a group like the BNP. I don't think that people like that should be able to stay in the district. People should be allowed to get on with their lives without people like that inciting violence. They blame unemployment and every other problem on Black people.

"You cannot blame the whole of society for this. I'm not angry at anybody. I'm just angry at the person who killed my son," he said.

"Decent people should be allowed to go about their business in peace."

THAT SHAME THE NATION, chillingly bears witness to the facts of rising racist murder; the father of Rolan Adams, a previously murdered schoolboy, provides further comment and analysis under ROLAN'S DAD SLAMS 'COMPLACENT SOCIETY'; a picture captioned 'NEVILLE LAWRENCE: Mourning'; and a headlined article, STEPHEN'S PAL KNEW THEY FACED DEATH, further serve to underline the emotional reality and dire consequences of racist attacks; and angry community calls for action are made, including from Labour MP Bernie Grant and the spokesperson for the Greenwich Action Committee Against Racial Attacks (GARCARA). In this crafted configuration of descriptive, documentary, analytical and emotionally resonant articles and supporting use of images and typefaces, the *Voice* enacts—that is, 'performs'—the Stephen Lawrence story. As it does so, it envelops the murder within established collective sentiments, documented statistics, experiential accounts, political analyses and community calls for action. By these rhetorical and representational means, the *Voice* simultaneously invokes as it addresses a particularised solidarity, a black public.

This performative stance is then explicitly declared in the paper's editorial comment:

Voice

Comment

RIVERS OF BLOOD

Once again a young Black man's life has been taken for no reason other than the colour of his skin.

Eighteen-year-old Stephen Lawrence was savagely stabbed to death by odious racist thugs as he walked along the street with a friend. This is the third racist slaying of a young Black man in the area in recent years.

Black people and children are being murdered while the Government stands aside and does nothing.

It is now crucial for the community to mobilize and let the Government know that we will not be as lambs to the slaughter. It is also the responsibility of each member of the Black community to lobby their local MPs, march to Parliament and let the Government know of the discontent running through Black Britain.

Fascism is spreading across Europe, Britain's ethnic communities are under attack from racists in this country—our home. . . .

For how long will the British Government express outrage at right wing party activity in Europe yet allow Black children to be murdered on their own doorstep?

(*Voice*, 27.4.93, 8)

The ironic use of 'rivers of blood' prefacing the *Voice*'s editorial comment— an infamous phrase often cherry-picked by the British press from Enoch Powell's speech in 1968 predicting racial violence on the basis of Britain's growing black immigrant population—is here knowingly put to work in the production of a new semantic and political alignment, one that needs no introduction or explanation given the black solidarity presumed by the editor.

Unlike the mainstream press, then, copies of the first issue of the *Voice* after the murder of Stephen Lawrence went to press already committed to a cause. The paper immediately knew how to situate the Stephen Lawrence killing and did so in conformity to its imagined readership and preceding understanding of the rising number of racist murders and attacks in Britain, which it had reported on in recent years. It was this that gave the paper the confidence and the mandate to performatively enact the Stephen Lawrence case and to call for community action and political response— such was the proximity between the issues being reported and the collective interests and outlooks of the *Voice*'s actual and rhetorically embodied black readership. This wasn't a story whose import was confined to an isolated racist killing, or even to a borough of southeast London; it concerned the rise of racism and racist violence throughout Britain as a whole, and even further afield in Europe, and it demanded concerted political action and response at all levels from local communities to national government.

It would take much longer before sections of the mainstream press would find a similar confidence to publicly invoke particularised publics or seek to canalise these in respect to wider political projects. This is not to say that the mainstream press did not also seek to inscribe its own political outlooks and discourses in and through its reporting of the Stephen Lawrence story, as we have already seen, but it was not until much later that this reporting would assume the same degree of performative commitment.

FROM 'PRIVATE TRAGEDY' TO 'PUBLIC TROUBLES'

Following the first reports of the murder, a number of events kept the Lawrence killing in the news. A private meeting between Nelson Mandela and the Lawrences widely reported on 7 May lent their case symbolic gravitas. Nelson Mandela, probably the most well-known elderly statesman in the world and endowed with charismatic if not saintlike qualities by the world's media, was widely reported as saying, 'I know what it means to lose a child under such tragic circumstances. I'm deeply touched by the brutality of this murder. It's something we are all too used to in South Africa where black lives are cheap' (*Guardian*, 7.5.93, 2). On the very same day, Doreen Lawrence issued a public statement strongly criticising the police and its handling of the investigation: 'They are patronizing us. . . . They're not dealing with illiterate blacks. We're educated. It's time they woke up to our people.' She continued: 'Why is it that a leader from a foreign country shows us sympathy when our government has expressed no interest at all?' (*Guardian*, 7.5.93, 2).

The arrest and court appearances of the suspects attracted a succession of brief news reports across the mainstream press throughout the weeks of May and June 1993, reiterating as they did so the basic fact that Stephen Lawrence, a black teenager, had been killed in Eltham in April of that year. The disorder that attended an antiracist demonstration reported on 9 May led to a series of claims about political hijacking of the Lawrence case by the *Daily Mail* as well as by Marc Wadsworth, national secretary of the Anti-Racist Alliance, who was reported as saying that the organisation Militant Labour was behind the demonstration and had 'cynically exploited local feeling about racist murders' (*Independent*, 10.5.93, 6). Other newspapers then followed up on this line of political hijacking including the *Sunday Times*, PANTHERS ON THE PROWL (16.5.93), and the *Guardian*, PROTEST IS FINE, BUT WHERE'S PROGRESS? The Murder of a black youth has left political factions vying for the anti-racist banner (14.5.93). On 19 June, Stephen Lawrence's memorial attracted various press attention and involvement, including a lengthy report in the Scottish *Herald*. The *Independent*, by far the most committed liberal broadsheet at this time, ran three feature articles investigating the extent and human costs of racist violence in Britain, as did the *Guardian/Observer* which often included graphic and experiential accounts of racist attacks.

Throughout this initial phase, the name of Stephen Lawrence did not yet have the capacity to instantly signify wider issues of racist violence or social injustice but was used principally to reference the particularity of this murder and its immediate aftermath (see Table 4.2), albeit within a wider context of growing community anger. Presciently, and exceptionally for television news, BBC 2 *Newsnight*, a late-night news analysis programme, ran a rare report in which the reporter discerned how the case may in fact prove to have wider political ramifications.

The Stephen Lawrence murder inquiry is about more than finding his killers. . . . The handling of the investigation could have significant political implications too. Successfully handled, the case would boost the confidence black people have in the police; poorly judged it could seriously damage an already fragile relationship. . . .

(*Newsnight*, BBC2, 6.5.93)

With the partial exceptions of the *Independent* and the *Guardian*, mainstream press reporting was, for the most part, confined to the institutional developments in the case and did not seek to position Stephen Lawrence as a symbol in relation to wider social and cultural issues of 'race', racism and injustice (see Figure 4.3), nor did it deploy the full range of press formats available (see Table 4.3). Most press items throughout this period comprised reportage formats (news reports, news in brief) and a few occasional reflective formats (feature articles), thereby indicating the prevalence of press 'dissemination' over public 'dialogue' at this moment in the story's trajectory.

In this early phase of mainstream press reporting, then, press performativity remained for the most part undeveloped—with one partial exception. The *Daily Mail* pursued its own political agenda and one, interestingly, that was quite different from its later campaign for justice for the Lawrences. On 9 May 1993, the *Mail on Sunday* (the *Daily Mail*'s sister Sunday paper) reported briefly on the 8 May antiracist demonstration. It chose to do so in a news report under the headline 17 INJURED AS RACE PROTEST TURNS VIOLENT (*Mail on Sunday*, 9.5.93, 18). This was followed the next day by a much lengthier feature article, which, notwithstanding its wordage (1,757), failed to provide any detail, context, discussion or explanation missing from the previous 'race protest' report but instead set out to expose HOW RACE MILITANTS HI-JACKED A TRAGEDY: ACTIVISTS TURN BRUTAL KILLING OF A SCHOOLBOY INTO A POLITICAL CAUSE (*Daily Mail*, 10.5.93, 18). This was then backed up by a rare editorial, MURDER, RACE AND MANIPULATION, that concluded:

Racism is abominable. Those of the neo-nazi persuasion who preach and provoke it should be condemned. But is there not also something contemptible about professional protestors who capitalize on grief to fuel the confrontation? Such street agitators of the right and left need each other. Most of us in Britain—whatever our colour—need them like the plague.
(*Daily Mail*, 10.5.93, 6)

A further article on 12 May then followed under the headline: RACE MURDER VICTIM'S PARENTS DENOUNCE THE EXTREMISTS—FOR THE SAKE OF STEPHEN, PLEASE PUT AN END TO THIS VIOLENCE. Clearly, the *Daily Mail* had put considerable time, effort and newsprint into trying to establish that the Stephen Lawrence case was being manipulated and hijacked by 'militant' extremists. We now know that Marc Wadsworth and the Anti-Racist Alliance had been in contact with the Lawrences and that they had sought to orchestrate a campaign designed to attract the sympathies and support of the mainstream press, and Neville Lawrence had also contacted the *Independent* the day after his son's murder to ensure that the case received publicity that could help catch the killers (Cathcart 2000). The youth, ambitions and innocence of Stephen Lawrence as well as the respectability of the Lawrence family had certainly helped to counter middle England's stereotypical views of black youths and black families as problematic and had helped the press to accept the story as 'virtuous', as had the ARA's deliberate effort to downplay hard-hitting antiracist messages. But though these early efforts to secure news attention had some effect, clearly they weren't capable of shifting engrained editorial outlooks or guaranteeing sympathetic coverage, as we see in the case of the *Daily Mail*.[2]

The memorial service for Stephen Lawrence held on 19 June is a further case in point. The *Daily Mail* chose to report this in a 62-word facts-only news report under the headline MEMORIAL FOR STAB VICTIM (19.6.93, 11). This contrasted with other newspapers that reported the same event at much greater length, including the *Guardian* (587 words), the *Independent* (458 words), and the *Times* (290 words). The *Independent*'s account is perhaps worth reprinting not only because it demonstrates how some sections of the mainstream press were now beginning to publicly acknowledge the Stephen Lawrence murder case as an important story that had moral resonance for the rest of society, but also how journalists and editors were beginning to lend considerable rhetorical and emotional force to this.

Shame and Pride in a Tragic Farewell; Minister Attacks Right-wing Extremists' Campaign of Hatred as Community Mourns Black South London Teenager Stabbed to Death

Ian MacKinnon

THE 10 PALL BEARERS who carried Stephen Lawrence's elaborate gilt and wood casket at arm's length set the tone. Most who shuffled from the tiny red-brick Methodist church wore sunglasses and sported carefully-sculpted hairstyles. This was unmistakably a black affair.

Indeed, we learnt during the emotionally-charged memorial service for the 18-year-old, stabbed to death in what was said to be a racist attack, that he was proud of being black.

But when the south-east London suburb of Plumstead came to a standstill yesterday morning as the cortege traveled the mile or so from Stephen's home to Trinity church, many white faces were dotted among the 800-strong crowd which followed.

Inside the church those same faces listened to the Rev David Cruise talk of the shame of being white in the aftermath of Stephen's savage killing at an Eltham bus stop in April.

"The faith of many was shaken that night," he told the congregation. "Many of us feel ashamed to be white. But all of us of whatever colour are ashamed of what has happened in our midst when groups filled with evil and hatred can roam our streets and taunt and kill just because they do not like the colour of another person's face."

But Mr Cruise warned everyone, both inside and those standing silently outside listening on the specially-rigged sound system, that they were all equally responsible for combating racism.

"If we say we can do nothing we are in the gravest danger. We see before us developing a battle between goodness and life, and evil and death. May we all commit ourselves, black and white, to overcoming evil and death and offer to all people in this country the way of goodness and life."

Mr Cruise went on to attack the British National Party, which has headquarters in nearby Welling, for openly propagating and inciting racial hatred. It was a message that would not have been lost on the politicians among the congregation, the Conservative member for Eltham, Peter Bottomley, and the Labour MPs Dianne Abbott (Hackney North and Stoke Newington) and Paul Boateng (Brent South).

But more important than the names were the children who had come to pay their last respects. Black and white, they came from Stephen's school, Blackneath and Bluecoat, in Greenwich, and from neighbouring schools.

And finally Stephen's parents Neville and Doreen, sister Georgina, 10, and brother Stuart, 16, followed as his body was again loaded into the hearse. It is to be flown to Jamaica today to be buried on 4 July.

But Mr Lawrence warned that this would not be the end. "The racists must be told that the burial of Stephen is not the burial of our campaign for justice. It is only the beginning."

(*Independent*, 19.6.93, 3)

Stephen Lawrence's memorial, as with all memorials, was an occasion of ritual designed to summon and unleash group sentiments and sustain a common sense of purpose. Words, oratory, symbols, performances and the circulation of sentiments by these and other means serve to enact such events. But in its reporting there is clearly more going on than a straightforward rendition of the event itself. The *Independent*'s narrative, through language, rhetoric and the emplacement of voices and views, has choreographed, and in this sense orchestrated, this account of a private and community-based memorial and sought to invest it with both public resonance and political relevance. In the public play of feelings and growing community calls for action stirred by the murder of Stephen Lawrence, the *Independent*, as well as other sectors of the mainstream liberal press, was now presenting the Stephen Lawrence story as something potentially precipitous. But of what? And on what basis could this sense of anticipation be enacted? At this time, the Stephen Lawrence case still did not publicly signal 'breach', at least not so far as the mainstream press was concerned, nor could it if his murder was conceived in essentialist terms as 'race hatred' or, even, as the latest racist killing. Something else was required.

Against this backdrop of growing media interest, an event was then widely reported that would widely signal 'breach' and move the Stephen Lawrence story towards a narrative of 'mounting crisis'. The public announcement by the Crown Prosecution Service on 29 July 1993 that it was not going to prosecute the youths accused of murdering Stephen Lawrence on grounds of 'insufficient evidence' clearly breached growing media and public expectations. The *Guardian*'s report, abridged below, gives vent to the consternation of different views responding to this institutional breach and leaves little doubt about its potentially explosive consequences.

'Race Murder' Charges Dropped

Alan Travis

Fears of renewed racial violence in south-east London were raised yesterday after charges against two teenagers accused of murdering a black schoolboy, Stephen Lawrence, were dropped. . . .

Stephen Lawrence's family, who were visited by the African National Congress leader, Nelson Mandela, when he was last in London, said they were devastated by the decision. "We were constantly told by the police to trust them and that they were doing all they could. It obviously wasn't good enough. As Nelson Mandela told us, 'Black lives are cheap', said Cheryl Sloley, Stephen's aunt. . . .

Scotland Yard, whose detectives have interviewed 2,500 people, refused to comment on the CPS decision but said the murder inquiry would continue. Two teenagers arrested on May 7 remain on police bail.

The family's solicitor, Imran Khan, said he feared the decision could spark local racial unrest. "It is quite unbelievable that the police have been unable to secure the evidence required to commit these youths for trial after three months."

Peter Bottomley, Conservative MP for Eltham, said he was surprised by the decision but appealed to the local community not to take the law into its own hands, warning that only injustice would follow. He urged the Attorney-General to ask the CPS for a full explanation of their decision. "We have to trust the CPS."

But the Anti-Racist Alliance last night claimed the decision proved that "there is something rotten at the heart of the Crown Prosecution Service when it deals with racist murders" and demanded that racial violence be made a specific criminal offence.

(*Guardian*, 30.7.93, 5)

It was this event, and the play of views and expressed fears that surrounded it, which constituted, in Turner's terms, a clear 'breach' and which now served to propel the Stephen Lawrence case into a second and prolonged phase of mounting crisis.

SUMMARY

The murder of Stephen Lawrence was initially ignored by some sections of the media and reported by others in standardised ways. These first reports were written in conformity to established press idioms and preexisting political outlooks on 'race'. Even at this early juncture, however, the press had seemingly recognized the 'purity' of Stephen Lawrence, the eighteen-year-old, hard-working school student, and this moral evaluation would later lend considerable support to media enactment of the Stephen Lawrence story—despite its immoral implication that some racist murders can be taken as more heinous, more newsworthy, than others. Following the initial reports of the racist murder, the *Daily Mail* proactively pursued its conservative agenda devoting time and resources investigating 'political hi-jacking' and criticising antiracist organisations that responded to the rising numbers of racist assaults and murders. The liberal *Independent* also began to rhetorically envelop the Stephen Lawrence case and sought to summon wider sentiments about the injustice of this racist act and, by extension, rising racist violence more generally. The *Voice*, for its part, performatively enacted the case, demanding concerted political action and summoning a sense of collective black solidarity as it did so, and deployed the full range of journalistic forms and appeals at its disposal. It was not until the bombshell decision announced by the CPS not to prosecute the prime suspects, however, that a breach opened up paving the way for a period of mounting crisis that would progressively position the Stephen Lawrence as a major public concern within mainstream media discourse and wider society.

NOTES

1. For other studies of the *Sun*'s reporting on 'race' see Gordon and Rosenberg 1989; Van Dijk 1991, 2000.

2. It is also known that, following an interview with the *Daily Mail* in May 1993, Neville Lawrence spoke on the telephone to Paul Dacre, the paper's editor, who he happened to have done some work for previously. According to Brian Cathcart, this prompted the editor's interest in the case to sharpen (Cathcart 2000, 138). However, any suggestion that the *Daily Mail* then did a volte-face and followed a different and more sympathetic editorial line on the case (see, for example, 'How murder became a media event,' *Guardian*, 25.2.99) appears to be much exaggerated when we examine the *Daily Mail*'s actual output across this period.

Six

Crisis

Following breach of regular, norm-governed social relations, a phase of mounting *crisis* supervenes, during which, unless the breach can be sealed off quickly within a limited area of social interaction, there is a tendency for the breach to widen and extend until it becomes coextensive with some dominant cleavage in the widest set of relevant social relations to which the conflicting or antagonistic parties belong. . . . This second stage, *crisis,* is always one of those turning points or moments of danger and suspense, when a true state of affairs is revealed, when it is least easy to don masks or pretend that there is nothing rotten in the village. Each public crisis has what I now call liminal characteristics, since it is a threshold between more or less stable phases of the social process, but it is not a sacred limen, hedged around by taboos and thrust away from the centre of life. On the contrary, it takes up its menacing stance in the forum itself and, as it were, dares the representatives of order to grapple with it. It cannot be ignored or wished away.

Victor Turner, *Dramas, Fields, Metaphors* (1974, 38–39)

The Stephen Lawrence case now moved into a protracted phase of 'mounting crisis' that ran until 15 March 1998, the day before the opening of the public inquiry. This comprised a succession of institutional developments and setbacks, each of which constituted a further breach that poured fuel onto the glowing embers of black community anger and wider public discontent. Over time, this threatened to both scorch institutions and engulf prominent individuals charged with the responsibility of ensuring that the Stephen Lawrence case and pursuit of justice had been prosecuted with the full determination of the law. This phase of mounting crisis developed over

many years before eventually precipitating a potentially cathartic, or cataclysmic, phase of public redress. As Table 4.1 and Figures 4.1 and 4.2
mapped earlier, this period was characterised at first by relatively discontinuous media coverage before rising in peaks to the considerable outpouring that would mark the phase of publicly staged redress. Here we
examine the media's contribution to the mounting crisis that propelled the
Stephen Lawrence story forward in interaction with key protagonists and
institutions (as well as with each other), and how this began to galvanise
solidarities and canalise publics with respect to deep-seated issues of race,
racism and British identity.

To begin, we can first note the basic events that formed the basis of media
reporting across this five-year period and then introduce the analytical
themes that will help to explain the dynamics of mounting crisis. These included: the adjourned inquest into Stephen Lawrence's death (21.12.93);
the CPS's second decision not to prosecute despite new evidence (15.4.94);
the arrest of four of the prime suspects prior to the proceedings of the
Lawrences' private prosecution (22.4.95), committal hearings to judge the
sufficiency of the evidence against them (23.8.95) and the dismissal of
charges against Gary Dobson (29.8.95), Jamie Acourt (7.9.95) and David
Norris (8.9.95) due to insufficient evidence and the committal to trial of
the two remaining suspects (11.9.95). The private prosecution brought by
the Lawrences began on 16 April 1996, and collapsed on 25 April following the ruling that Duwayne Brooks's identification evidence was flawed.
The contents of covert surveillance video, showing the extreme racist attitudes of the prime suspects, was then released and widely reported. On 10
February 1997, the public inquest into Stephen Lawrence's death was reopened with public statements by Doreen Lawrence criticising the insensitivity of the police, and, on 11 February, the prime suspects stonewalled
the proceedings by 'claiming privilege'. Damning insights into the police investigation were revealed on 12 February, and on 13 February the jury returned its unprecedented verdict that Stephen Lawrence's death was an
'unlawful killing from an unprovoked attack by five white youths'. These
events prompted the *Daily Mail* on 14 February to name the five prime
suspects as 'Murderers' on its front page, and on 4 June 1997, with a new
Labour government in office, the home secretary, Jack Straw, met Doreen
Lawrence to discuss the possibility of a public inquiry. This inquiry, to be
headed by Sir William Macpherson, was formally announced on 31 July.
On 15 December, the Police Complaints Authority published part of its report into the (mis)conduct of the case, and on 13 March 1998, the PCA
announced that only one police officer would face disciplinary charges over
the Lawrence case.

Taken on their own, or even together, these events do not in themselves
necessarily constitute a crisis, whether mounting or otherwise. To be seen
and, importantly, felt as 'mounting crisis', they needed to be placed within

a narrative framework that could help establish their significance and meaning and thereby unleash their cultural and political charge. This work of constructing meaning—both cognitive and affective—was principally undertaken by the media. Here a number of discernible features acted as mainsprings propelling the story forward and pushing it deeper into the surrounding, conflicted cultural terrain. Analytically these can be identified as follows: (1) the news media's routine use of a repetitive news narrativisation that kept the Stephen Lawrence story within the public eye, established the 'known' details of the case and positioned this as an ongoing and tension-filled narrative yet to be resolved; (2) the media's transmutation of Stephen Lawrence from sign to symbol as questions of racism migrated from the particularities of this case to collective grievances and the injustices of racism in general; (3) the media's increasing willingness to act as advocates of change in respect to specific institutional reforms (and as a way of cauterising the social wound that threatened to open up around the Stephen Lawrence case); and (4), underpinning all of these the deep-seated emotions that the case gave rise to, and which the media powerfully expressed and publicly sustained. Together these helped to produce (5) a new 'emotional mood', and it was on this basis that the media felt able to (6) publicly enact a form of 'moral solidarity', which gave them license to (7) direct flows of moral opprobrium and moral approbation. These last features (5–7), emergent in the period of mounting crisis but more fully expressed in the following phase of institutionalised and judicial redress, are analysed in the next chapter. Features 1–4 acted as the mainsprings propelling both the media story and sense of public crisis forward and were essential in precipitating a period of ritual and institutional redress. Only then could liminal potentialities be created and pent-up energies for change released. The following now examines these dynamics.

A NARRATIVE OF RACIST MURDER, TOLD AND RETOLD

Following the developments of the earlier breach phase, the Stephen Lawrence story was kept in the public eye on a more mundane basis through a succession of low-key news updates and short news reports. By these means, the Stephen Lawrence story became told and retold time and again. The repetitive nature of updating news is unavoidable given the temporally discontinuous nature of news reporting, and results in a narrative structure that must rehearse time and again the known 'story'. It is in the successive flow of news reports and updating news items that the known facts, key protagonists and institutional processes are publicly signalled time and again, though often with minimal new information. These nonetheless served to publicly embed the Stephen Lawrence case as an important 'story' and narrative moving through time, and one, moreover, that promised further developments, conflicts and/or resolution. This mundane media narrative provided the grounds on which further media generalisation as well as later political canalisation could be built.

The two news reports below, one from the *Independent*, the other from television's *BBC News South-East*, are typical of the hundreds of news reports that constituted this narrative stream at this time.

Four in Court in Lawrence Case

Four teenagers appeared before Greenwich magistrates in south London charged with the murder of Stephen Lawrence after his parents launched a private prosecution. Stephen, 18, a student, was stabbed to death at a bus stop in Eltham, south-east London, in 1993.

Neil Acourt, 19, Luke Knight, 18, David Norris, 18, and a third 18-year-old who cannot be named, were remanded in custody.

(*Independent*, 25.4.95, 2)

Newsreader: The Crown Prosecution Service said new evidence on the killing of Stephen Lawrence wasn't strong enough to take the case to court. That evidence had halted an inquest in December. Stephen's family have condemned the decision and say they'll bring a private prosecution.

(*BBC News South-East,* 11.9.95)

By these means, the Stephen Lawrence case was positioned in terms of a developmental narrative, in contrast to a 'news event'. Incidentally, it is also interesting to note how even these standardised news reports chose to refer to Stephen Lawrence by his first name. This familial, personal and privatised mode of address, one rarely deployed in matter-of-fact news reports with their heightened claims to journalistic objectivity, betrays growing media sympathy for the Lawrences and their case. These reports, and the many hundreds of others that updated, told and retold the basic details of the Stephen Lawrence case across this period (see Table 4.3), served to construct the Lawrence case as a public narrative that had yet to reach its denouement. The public elaboration of the 'Stephen Lawrence story' in more politically inflected and morally evaluative terms, however, would be discharged principally by other forms of journalism.

STEPHEN LAWRENCE: FROM SIGN TO SYMBOL

The events leading up to and including the earlier CPS 'breach' had placed the name of Stephen Lawrence in the public eye, and, as such, it was available for further public circulation. News reports of other incidents of racial violence and murder, as well as institutional moves to bolster public confidence in the authorities' handling of these, increasingly made reference to the name of Stephen Lawrence. The *Times*, for example, did so in a long feature on the death of Joy Gardner, a black woman who had died whilst being forcibly restrained and deported by the Metropolitan Police, under the new Chief Commissioner Paul Condon:

A Question of Restraint

David Leppard

. . . Above all he is passionate about what he calls 'ethical policing', the touchstone of his new doctrine at the Yard. "We must have ethical policing" he kept repeating last week after Gardner's death. "This is the only policing we will tolerate."

Racial tension was already high in parts of London last weekend. The black community was unhappy about the dropping of charges against two white teenagers accused of the murder of Stephen Lawrence, a black teenager, with Jamaican-born parents, who was stabbed to death in a racial attack in Eltham, south London.

(*Times*, 8.8.93)

Unintentionally, but prophetically as it turned out, the name 'Stephen Lawrence' would later take up an even more central position in the public evaluation of the Metropolitan Police and commissioner Paul Condon, who had declared earlier that year that he would make racism the 'greatest challenge facing the force' (*Guardian*, 4.8.93, 2). For the moment though, Stephen Lawrence was one among many causes of concern that called into question the policing of black communities. His name, however, was beginning to feature in reports of other racist attacks and growing community anger at inadequate and/or hostile policing:

East End Bengalis Set to Fight Back in Face of Racist Attacks

Paul Lewis and Michael Durham

. . . As the older generation surveyed boarded-up shops, their children and grandchildren were determined to counter what they say is an unprecedented level of violence.

Quaddus Ali, 17, was last night in a critical condition at the Royal London hospital after he was left for dead by a gang of eight whites last Wednesday. A defence campaign was formed yesterday to represent 10 Asians arrested during the battles between police . . .

Tension is also fuelled by a current trial in which two men deny murdering an Asian taxi driver. The court heard that Fiaz Mirza was robbed and shut in his car last February, before being pushed into the Thames, where he drowned.

The case comes four months after black schoolboy Stephen Lawrence was stabbed to death in what police described as an 'outrageous and senseless racial attack'.

(*Guardian,* 12.9.93, 3)

Moreover, as Stephen Lawrence became an established point of reference in the latest reports of violent racist attacks, so press reports of the latest developments in the Lawrence case now also began to include references to other racist incidents and/or racism in different fields:

Family Demands Race Killers Be Brought to Justice

The family of the murdered black teenager Stephen Lawrence vowed last night to intensify its efforts to bring his killers to justice. . . . His mother Doreen handed a statement to journalists at the start of a torch-lit vigil and march in Eltham. . . . It said her family was "angry and frustrated that despite our co-operation with the police in providing them with an authentic list of suspects, no one has been arrested and convicted."

Nine Asian youths were remanded on bail at Thames magistrates court yesterday charged under the Public Order Act.

They were arrested during a demonstration on Friday outside the Royal London hospital where an Asian teenager is in a critical condition after being beaten by a white gang.

(*Guardian,* 14.9.93, 3)

The media name 'Stephen Lawrence', at first a 'sign' of the murder of a particular black teenager in southeast London, was now beginning to be aligned with other racist attacks and growing concerns about the criminal justice system and particularly the police. 'Stephen Lawrence' was gravitating from sign to symbol and beginning to act as a common focal point holding together diverse events and issues within the troubled field of 'race' and racism. As with all signs that carry political charge, however, this was open to multiaccentual inflection and political appropriation. What made the sign of Stephen Lawrence so potent, however, was its capacity to signify within and across the competing discourses of 'race', racism and identity within British society. None but the most rabidly racist could deny the inhumanity and injustice of his murder, nor its violation of the utopian civil society discourse.

But there were other features that also made 'Stephen Lawrence' such a universalising sign of racial injustice within white British society—as we have already heard. Young, black and gifted, Stephen Lawrence did not conform to the usual media stereotypes of black youths as criminal, disaffected or otherwise troublesome, and his parents seemingly matched the middle-England ideal profile of hard-working, god-fearing and self-improving first-generation immigrants content to make their own way in British society. The sign of Stephen Lawrence, then, spoke to the different discourses competing within the contested field of British race relations and registered with emotive force and political urgency something of the essential inhumanity and injustice of his murder—and, by extension, all those subject to racist violence.

Through this phase of mounting crisis, Stephen Lawrence would come to signify and symbolise even more than this, however, and this additional symbolic charge would be generated principally in and through two key moments of failed institutional redress: the private prosecution mounted by the Lawrences and their legal team, and the later public inquest into Stephen Lawrence's death. Each of these was characterised by moments of high tension and ritual drama, and each, as we shall see, irrevocably deepened the phase of mounting public crisis. The media progressively enacted these two key moments by increasingly arguing for and advocating specific changes on the basis of the case, and by flooding the Stephen Lawrence story with emotional affect and moral significance.

PRIVATE PROSECUTION AND PRESS ADVOCACY

The emotional tension of the Stephen Lawrence case palpably mounted following the failure of authorities to act, which the British press signalled. Only one newspaper, however, sought to performatively champion the Lawrences' cause.

A Performative *Voice* in the News Wilderness

The *Voice*, as we have seen, adopted a performative and politically combative stance from the outset, simultaneously inscribing and summoning into being a black solidarity on the basis of rising racist violence and perceived indifference on the part of the authorities. This performative enactment then continued with further double-page spreads, elaborate features, front-page items as well as campaigns to raise support funds, and even the offer of a reward for information leading to the conviction of Stephen Lawrence's killers. Headlines from this period illustrate something of this performative 'doing': WHEN THE KILLING HAS TO STOP (4.5.93); FIGHTING A COMMON FOE: Incidences of racial violence are on the increase and Britain's ethnic minorities must now realise that, despite their differences, they are all potential victims of racism and therefore need to fight it together (4.1.94, 8); DON'T PROCRASTINATE: LEGISLATE! (8.2.94, p. 10); RAISE CASH FOR JUSTICE

(2.5.95, 1); and £5,000 TO CATCH STEPHEN'S KILLERS (24.2.97, 1). The paper, performatively, also gave voice to critics of the police and those promoting political action, such as the Black Police Association under the headline BLACK POLICE JOIN LAWRENCE FAMILY IN CONDEMNING PCA CONCLUSIONS (22.12.97 & 29.12.97), and the Society of Black Lawyers (SBL):

Stop the Race Violence Now

The SBL calls for urgent and meaningful action to inspire the faith of Black people in the criminal justice system. We demand an independent enquiry . . . to investigate:

(i) The systematic pattern of racial violence in Britain,
(ii) The responses of the police and the crown prosecution service to racial violence; with power to make appropriate recommendations. The alternative is that more Black people will die. . . .

(Markbool Javaid, Chair, Society of Black Lawyers, Voice, 5.10.93, 6)

Sections of the mainstream media were not prepared at this time to adopt the performative and campaigning posture of the *Voice*, though some were now beginning to advocate institutional and/or legislative changes in respect to particular issues raised, and to engage also in strong criticism of institutional authorities. The *Mail on Sunday*, in a leader comment headlined, A DAMNING VERDICT, argued: 'In such a sensitive area as racial violence, there is an obvious imperative to move with care and discretion. In the case of Stephen Lawrence, the CPS showed all the subtlety of an elephant in clogs'. It went on to suggest that the boss of the CPS, Barbara Mills, 'would seem better suited to licking postage stamps in the outer office than being Director of Public Prosecutions' (*Mail on Sunday*, 1.8.93,20). Even the conservative *Times*, a paper not noted for its critical stance on public authorities, especially those enforcing law and order, felt uneasy about the CPS decisions in 1993, and again in 1994, not to prosecute, and stated so:

When Parents Prosecute

THE LAWRENCE CASE REVEALS DEEP FLAWS IN THE CPS

. . . A culture of excessive caution appears to have taken hold of the CPS, which has led to a tendency to pursue only those cases which are sure to yield either a guilty plea or a conviction. . . . It is difficult to avoid the conclusion that Mr and Mrs Lawrence would not have needed to bring a private prosecution had the CPS been doing its job properly. Two youths now stand accused of the murder of their son. The CPS stands accused too.

(Times, 13.9.95)

While the *Daily Mail* and the *Times* criticised the role that the CPS had played in the Lawrence case, both did so on grounds of bolstering the public credibility of the CPS rather than championing the cause of the Lawrences per se. The liberal/left-of-centre broadsheets, however, went further. The *Guardian*, for example, advocated legislative change in its criticisms of the incumbent conservative home secretary:

Bringing Race Bigots to Book

THE ONE AREA OF LAW WHERE MICHAEL HOWARD SHOULD GET TOUGH IS RACIAL VIOLENCE AND HARASSMENT. SO WHY IS HE REFUSING TO MAKE SUCH OUTRAGES SPECIFIC OFFENCES?

Geoffrey Bindman

. . . Against a background of escalating racially-motivated attacks, in which innocent teenagers like Stephen Lawrence, Rolan Adams and Ashiq Hussain have been murdered—and this very week a notably vicious and disgraceful assault on a black man has been reported, apparently provoked merely by the fact that he was with a white woman—the fear and frustration of the victims and their supporters approaches breaking-point.

Yet the Home Secretary, in a speech reported in the *Guardian* last Thursday, refused to endorse new offences of racial violence and harassment; nor did he propose any other measures to strengthen the law.

This is an abdication of responsibility. It is also bewilderingly inconsistent with his proposals for tougher measures against crime in general.

(Guardian, 20.10.93, 18)

The mainstream press, evidently, were now prepared to mount criticism and advocate changes, but they had yet to publicly commit themselves to the much deeper issues of race, racism and identity implicit to the case. The proceedings of the private prosecution and its later collapse in 1996, followed by the public inquest in 1997, provided the grounds on which the mainstream media, both press and television, would collectively begin to enact a more performative and politically engaged stance and one, importantly, that was principally mounted on the public elaboration of powerful emotions and appeals to moral solidarity and moral shame.

Originally Stephen Lawrence's murder had received limited reporting at best, which was confined to inside pages; three years later, with the opening of the private prosecution on 19 April 1996, it was being prominently replayed. The brutality of this act of racist violence was given extensive and dramatic headline attention across the British press: HACKED TO DEATH JUST FOR BEING BLACK (*Sun*); RACE-HATE LED TO BOY'S KNIFE KILLING (*Daily Mirror*); BLACK STUDENT KILLED 'OUT OF RACIST HATRED' (*Independent*); FRIEND TELLS COURT HOW A WHITE MOB KILLED STEPHEN LAWRENCE (*Guardian*); BOY 'KILLED BY RACISTS' (*Herald*). Under the headline BLACK TEENAGER 'MURDERED' BY RACE-HATE GANG, the *Times*, like other newspapers, reported the opening words of Michael Mansfield, Queen's Counsel for the prosecution, who unequivocally stated:

There can be no mistaking that this was an unprovoked, unwarranted attack by those who held not just racist views but racist views that involved the desecration of those who are black by injury and possibly death.

(*Times*, 19.4.96)

The *Times* report continued with descriptions of Stephen's last hours, eyewitness statements and graphic accounts of the attack and the knife that caused his fatal injuries. Press reporting, then, was giving full vent to the racist nature of the attack and its appalling violence. Through this relived violence, readerships were being invited to 'bear witness' and feel and see the hurt that this crime had caused.

When the case collapsed on 25 April 1996, after the judge ruled that both Duwayne Brooks's testimony and the video evidence were inadmissible, the media reported the evident disappointment and anger that attended this latest 'breach' of justice: ANGER AFTER RACE CASE COLLAPSES (*Guardian*); PARENTS FIGHT ON (*Times*); IT'S JUST NOT FAIR (*Sun*); SO WHO DID KILL STEPHEN? FATHER OF RACE MURDER VICTIM DEMANDS JUSTICE (*Daily Mirror*); DEVASTATED (*Voice*). Both the mainstream and minority press also followed up on the collapse of the prosecution and provided transcripts of the covert police video that, again, underlined the extreme racism of the prime suspects. Both the *Independent* as well as the *Times* (SPY FILM EXPOSED SUSPECTS' HATRED OF BLACKS, 26.4.96), for example, reproduced at length excerpts from the video. Given the extremism of the language and sentiments that these revealed, they could only serve to produce common feelings of revulsion from across the social-democratic spectrum.

Depth of Hatred Revealed in Covert Video

Neil Acourt brandished a knife, waved it around and thrust it into the wall or furniture uttering vile racist abuse.

"I reckon that every nigger should be chopped up mate and they should be left with nothing but fucking stumps."

His extremist views and his naked aggression were revealed in video tapes shot secretly by police and shown at the committal hearings. They provided a video of nasty racial hatred featuring Neil Acourt, Gary Dobson and Luke Knight, the three men whose trial for the murder of Stephen Lawrence collapsed for lack of evidence yesterday. . . . According to the stipendiary magistrate, David Cooper, who sent the three for trial, the video showed "a deeply held emphatic and sadistic loathing of all black people".

"This is not the sly and sniggering racism which is common in many sectors of society. It is not even the blatant racism used on the football terraces."

In another sequence David Norris said: "If I was going to kill myself do you know what I'd do? I'd go and kill every black c***, every Paki, every copper, every mug that I know. I would go down to Catford . . . with two sub-machine guns and . . . I'd set on one of them, skin him alive, torture him and set him alight. I'd blow their two legs and arms off and say 'go on, you can swim home now'."

(Independent, 26.4.96, 4)

The press also gave full exposure to the emotion and hurt that followed the collapse of the private prosecution. The *Daily Mirror,* for example, described how 'Heartbroken Neville Lawrence spoke out after three racist bigots walked free from the Old Bailey' before quoting him as saying, 'I believe in fairness and I don't think what has happened today is fair' (26.4.96, 15)—words that were reported widely. The next day, the *Guardian* in a lengthy feature, LOST DREAMS OF AN UNSPENT LIFE, gave prominence to the views and feelings of Doreen Lawrence, how she felt 'betrayed by British justice', and how it was 'as if Stephen had died again when the judge decided that the evidence of our main witness could not be presented before the jury' (27.4.96, 26). Touched by the understandable grief and sentiments of the Lawrences and repulsed by the grotesque display of verbal racism and acting out of racist violence—behaviour that fell outside of the spectrum of acceptable human behaviour as far as all mainstream media were concerned—the British press collectively became emboldened in its support for the Lawrences.

The *Daily Mirror,* a paper that hitherto had been relatively quiet about the Lawrence case, for example, opined:

Whining Brats Get a Lesson in Dignity; the Best and the Worst of Britain

Tony Parsons

Two British families were in the news this week because of their sons. One son was the repulsive little perpetrator of violence. The other its tragic victim.

Richard Wilding, 13, was expelled from his Nottingham school for persistent violence and bad behaviour. Stephen Lawrence, 18, was stabbed by racists at a bus stop in south London. . . . The very different stories of these two very different families pose an important question. What does it mean to be British today? Are there certain standards of behaviour we can reasonably expect from each other?

Many would say that being British means living your life with dignity, restraint and a respect for others. It means having a sense of fair play and an ability to show grace under pressure. It means, above all else, a quiet, fundamental decency.

The Lawrences are black. The Wildings are white. But which family would you say best embodies those British virtues?

I hope that Mr and Mrs Lawrence one day find the justice they seek and deserve.

(*Daily Mirror*, 29.4.96, 7)

Encoded within Tony Parsons's support for the Lawrences is the assumption that his readership presumes that black families may be less British than white families, a view that is seemingly challenged by his pedagogical use of the Lawrence case (at the same time that he instantiates it). But his performative homily also demonstrates how the Lawrence case has now become public knowledge and infused with common sentiments.

The *Observer* also sought to make use of a similar argumentative parallelism in its leading article STARK JUSTICE IN BLACK AND WHITE (28.4.96, 3). Its argumentative strategy was also clearly performative, as it compared the failure of the CPS and police investigation in the Stephen Lawrence case with 'Badrul Miah, a youth of Bangledeshi origin, who was convicted of taking part in the murder (though not of dealing the fatal blows) of the white 15-year old Richard Everitt'. According to the *Observer*, the police and Crown Prosecution Service handled these cases in markedly different ways. Unlike the Lawrence case, the police charged into the local Asian centre on the night of the murder of Richard Everitt and picked up any youths and forensic evidence they could find, and they interviewed no less than 300 Asians. The report concluded that 'the impression, already far too strong, that British justice is not colour blind, receives another dismal boost' (*Observer*, 28.4.96, 3).

The emotions, revelations and arguments that swirled around the private prosecution were elaborated, and often originated, within the forms of their journalistic expression, and they sustained the development of public sympathies. Even so, the name of Stephen Lawrence had still not become the powerful symbol that it later would; nor had the mainstream media fully committed to picking up the cudgels on behalf of the Lawrences' cause, though clearly they were now sympathetically propelling, as much as propelled by, the case.

CORONER'S INQUEST AND MORAL POLLUTION

The coroner's inquest in February 1997 attracted the full glare of media attention and once again placed the Stephen Lawrence case, as well as its unresolved tensions and threatened conflicts, on public display. At the outset, the emotional hurt and angry sentiments of Doreen Lawrence were granted universal exposure, whether through the liberal idiom of educated discourse under the headlines MOTHER ATTACKS 'RACIST' JUSTICE (*Guardian*, 11.2.97, 5) and THE JUSTICE SYSTEM IS RACIST (*Independent*, 11.2.97, 8), or through the populist vernacular of tabloid journalism:

Murder Mum Slams 'Racist' Legal System

The mum of murdered teenager Stephen Lawrence yesterday attacked the "racist" judicial system which she said meant his killers were "still walking the street".

His mother, Doreen, said: "The police saw Stephen as a criminal. He was stereotyped by the police, he was black, then he must be a criminal.

"Our crime was living in a country where the justice system supports racist murders against innocent people."

A-level pupil, Stephen, 18, was stabbed as he waited for a bus.

Mrs Lawrence wept as she gave evidence at a reopened inquest at Southwark Crown Court. . . . Mrs Lawrence said yesterday that she was not allowed to see Stephen as he lay dying in hospital.

And she claimed police ignored her when she gave them a list of suspects. "They were not taking my son's death as seriously as they should have.

"The value this white racist country puts on black lives is evident."

(*Daily Mirror*, 11.2.97, 14)

The public inquest was reported in detail. Police blunders were publicly revealed for the first time, and various police claims were challenged by the Lawrences' legal team. The refusal by the five accused to answer questions in the witness box produced universal press condemnation: FURY AS WITNESSES OBSTRUCT INQUEST ON BLACK STUDENT (*Times*, 12.2.97); WALL OF SILENCE FROM WHITE YOUTHS AT LAWRENCE INQUEST (*Independent*, 12.2.97, 7). In its mediatisation, the ritual drama and effect of the inquest was publicly elaborated and commented on by both the press and broadcasting institutions. By the time the inquest reached its final verdict, the story was guaranteed to receive extensive coverage and comment. The *Guardian* led with the story on its front page:

'Unlawfully Killed in an Unprovoked Racist Attack by Five White Youths'

Alison Daniels and Duncan Campbell

. . . The condemnatory words exemplified the strength of feeling the case has provoked during the Lawrence family's four-year campaign for justice. Juries are required only to return a verdict as to whether a death was unlawful, accidental or 'open'.

(14.2.97, 1)

All national papers reported the verdict: LAWRENCE FAMILY TO SUE MEN CLEARED OF RACIST MURDER (*Times*); WE'LL SUE POLICE WHO DIDN'T NAIL MY SON'S KILLERS (*Daily Mirror*). Many international newspapers covered the verdict as well, such was the story's national prominence: BRITAIN BRACES FOR ITS 'OJ CASE' (Australian, *Daily Telegraph*). The *Voice*, for its part, devoted its front page to the verdict and again enacted its own viewpoint: THE VOICE SAYS: A MOTHER'S GRIEF, BRITAIN'S SHAME (17.2.97, 1).

The next day the mainstream British press followed up on the verdict with detailed commentaries and analysis reflecting on the failure of the criminal justice system to deliver justice to the Lawrence family and, in the case of the *Guardian*, reflexively commented on the growing symbolism of the case:

Family's Fruitless Fight for Justice

Duncan Campbell

The murder of Stephen Lawrence has become symbolic of racial tension in London. . . .

It may only have been one of 170 or so murders in London every year but it has become symbolic of the simmering racial tension of the city, the distrust between some sections of the black community and the police, and the failures of the judicial system to bring to justice the strutting racists who carried out the attack. It has prompted supportive action for the victim's parents from the South African president, Nelson Mandela, and calls for changes in the law.

(*Guardian*, 14.2.97, 4)

The *Times*, however, unlike the rest of the mainstream press, had sought to distance itself from the mounting criticism of the police and the growing support for the Lawrences and their claims about injustice. On the same day that the coroner's verdict was reported, the *Times*, for example, granted the Metropolitan Police space to publicly defend their position against mounting public criticism:

Police Defend Inquiry

Lin Jenkins

The Metropolitan Police insisted yesterday that its officers had done everything they could from the beginning of the investigation.

Ian Johnston, Assistant Commissioner, said, "It is a matter of deep regret to me and to the officers involved in this terrible murder that we have not been able to see the murderers successfully prosecuted."

(14.2.97)

It was the *Daily Mail,* however, that truly set itself apart from the rest, with a dramatic, performative, intervention. On 14 February, under the headline MURDERERS blazoned across its front page (see Figure 6.1), it reproduced pictures of the five prime suspects subtitled 'The Mail accuses these men of killing. If we are wrong, let them sue us', and did so with the certain knowledge that none of the suspects would want to risk cross-examination and self-incrimination in a libel case. The *Daily Mail* defended its reasons for this unusual and bold act as follows:

. . . We are naming them because, despite a criminal case, a private prosecution and an inquest, there has still been no justice for Stephen. . . . This week the five refused to answer any questions at the inquest on Stephen, citing their legal right of privilege not to say anything which might incriminate them.

The Lawrence case threatens to damage race relations and the reputation of British justice.

(14.2.97, 1)

The paper's action, then, was not motivated by a coincidence of views with those of the Lawrences and their supporters, but appears to be based more on indignation at the way in which the process of criminal justice had been thwarted by, to use their terms, five 'moronic thugs,' which threatened to 'damage race relations and the reputation of British justice'. The *Mail*'s essentialist thinking on matters of 'race' and racial conflicts, discussed in the previous chapter, did not permit a more historically or contextually grounded understanding of racism and its institutional forms. Unsurprisingly, therefore, its editorial of the same day explicitly distanced itself from the views of the Lawrences:

Figure 6.1
Daily Mail, 14 February 1997, p. 1. © *Daily Mail*. Photos: *Photo News Service, Times/NI Syndication, ITN News.*

A Tragic Failure of British Justice

LEADING ARTICLE

IT IS no light matter when a national newspaper condemns as murderers five men who have never been convicted in court. But when the judicial system has failed so lamentably to deal with the killers of Stephen Lawrence, extraordinary measures are demanded. . . . A hard-working A-level student with his bright future all before him has been snuffed out by a pack of bigots who are still walking free and smirking at the thrill of getting away with it. Small wonder that Stephen's relatives feel betrayed. Or that they lash out in their grief at the police and the CPS for failing to bring the murderers of 'only a black boy' to justice.

But suggestions made by his grief-stricken mother that the police were less than assiduous because of Stephen's colour are surely misplaced. They committed huge resources in trying to catch the murderers. . . . The sorry truth is. . . . that our system has failed miserably. And while the murders walk free, it is a truth that diminishes us all.

(*Daily Mail,* 14.2.97,8)

Rhetorically the *Daily Mail* sought to attribute the arguments of Doreen Lawrence to an outpouring of grief that had caused her to lash out at the CPS and police. Emotion and feelings, it conservatively argued, were apt to cloud judgement and reason; and yet the *Daily Mail*'s editorial is no less emotion-filled, and, as we have seen, it was the emotional outpouring enacted by the press that had helped to drive the media story to this point. Unlike the statements of Doreen Lawrence, however, the *Mail* lacked a perspective that could account for the systematic failures and institutional nature of the British criminal justice system and its failure to deliver justice.

The *Daily Mail*'s intervention nonetheless prompted media reflexivity in the UK, and internationally: RACIAL KILLING BURSTS A BRITISH PRESS TABOO (*New York Times*, 18.2.97); PAPER JUSTICE (*Sydney Morning Herald,* 22.2.97). In the UK, Roy Greenslade, in a commentary for the *Guardian*, EVENING UP THE SCALES OF JUSTICE, argued, 'This was a free press at its best. The paper got it right. Editor Paul Dacre deserves the enthusiastic support of all who value a free press' (15.2.97, 3). The *Times*, as the self-appointed defender of the institutions of law and order, naturally preferred to admonish:

Two Wrongs

The vigilante is both an understandable and an unattractive creature. The English law may sometimes produce outcomes that barely resemble justice. That, by itself, does not excuse individuals or groups from putting themselves above the law and infringing the rights of others. . . . There have been many unsatisfactory aspects of this saga. . . . That does not, however, justify the *Daily Mail* in intervening in this way.

(*Times*, 15.2.97)

The *Voice* observed that 'The sense of shame has definitely hit middle England', and this was 'embodied by the *Daily Mail*'s sensible decision' (24.2.97, 11). Others, such as the *Daily Mirror*, pondered the apparent volte-face of the *Mail* from its early preoccupations with how "race militants hijacked a tragedy" (*Daily Mirror*, 15.2.97, 4). Media reflexivity, as well as increased reflection on the issues raised by the Stephen Lawrence case, were now picking up momentum. Television then began to play its part, too.

The Stephen Lawrence Story, a documentary about the Lawrences and their struggle, included film sequences with emotional and angry statements by Doreen and Neville Lawrence and heartrending scenes of Neville Lawrence breaking down at the grave of his son in Jamaica (see Figures 6.2 and 6.3). This aired on Channel Four on 15 February 1997, the day after the *Daily Mail* headline, to an audience of 958,000, and was repeated in April later that year. The program reflected on what it is to be black and British and gave voice to Stephen Lawrence's friends, both black and white. Doreen Lawrence interviewed on camera reflected:

The public have shown real disgust at how we've been treated and how the case has been handled. And for the press to have come out in the way in which they have, just in the fact that every paper has carried it, and it's front page news, is to show that we weren't wrong in what we were saying, that the police had messed up. . . . It doesn't restore my faith in justice because justice is still not done. . . . And what the press has done is highlight that even more so, and making it come home to people. The justice system has not done anything for me—they failed me and my family.

(*The Stephen Lawrence Story,* Channel
Four, 15.2.97, Director Kelvin Richards,
Producer Peter Lee-Wright)

Through the public mediatisation of the coroner's inquest, and the earlier private prosecution, the Lawrence story was now signalling issues of 'race' and racism as well as injustice at the heart of its public telling. Press advocacy, and the media's elaboration of the emotions and feelings generated by the case, had served to powerfully 'move' the story forward. This was not confined to the actions of the tabloids or the minority media; emotions and emotional appeals, which were enacted by the nation's media, broadsheets and tabloids, press and television, flooded the Stephen Lawrence

Figure 6.2
'Doreen Lawrence', *The Stephen Lawrence Story*, 1997. © Peter Lee-Wright/*Channel Four.*

Figure 6.3
'Neville Lawrence', *The Stephen Lawrence Story*, 1997. © Peter Lee-Wright/*Channel Four.*

story. On the basis of this mediatised groundswell of affect, the media also enacted wider cultural reflexivity in their public discussions and debates about issues of 'race', racism and cultural identity. They did this through the different journalistic forms and formats—features, accessed commentary, editorial, debate and polls—at its disposal and which now began to be used much more often. In 1997, for example, over 50 percent of all press output made use of these 'reflective' and 'media reflexive' formats (see Table 4.3). This cultural reflexivity was also performed through the presentation of differing views and voices, sometimes orchestrated into deliberative forms of engagement. The *Daily Mirror,* for example, ran the following debate, following it with an explicit editorial address:

The Monday Debate: Will We Ever be Able to Live in Racial Harmony?

Helen Weathers

. . . No one has been convicted of the killing, but last week a newspaper took the unprecedented step of naming five men as the murderers. The case has reopened the whole issue of racism in Britain. Here we examine whether it will ever be possible to live in racial harmony.

Yes, says Herman Ouseley Chairman of the Commission for Racial Equality . . . No, says Doreen Lawrence Mother of Stephen Lawrence, stabbed to death three years ago.

Divided We Fall

COMMENT ON STEPHEN LAWRENCE KILLING: VOICE OF THE MIRROR

The words of Doreen Lawrence on this page are chilling. Since the murder of her son Stephen, she has come to believe that we cannot live in racial harmony. If she is right, that is a terrible condemnation of this country. Efforts to drive out racism should be redoubled and redoubled again.

That would be the best legacy for the tragic and pointless death of Stephen Lawrence.

(*Daily Mirror,* 17.2.97, 6)

In turn, this was followed by a *Daily Mirror* poll that purported to 'represent' its readership views, though the terms in play were hardly likely to encourage anything other than the reported results:

You Back Race Peace

**MIRROR READERS SAY IT IS POSSIBLE TO LIVE IN
RACIAL HARMONY**

The mum of murdered black teenager Stephen Lawrence is wrong to think
we cannot live in racial harmony, say *Mirror* readers. You voted by a 3–1
majority in our poll that it is possible.

(Daily Mirror, 19.2.97, 16)

The *Times*, characteristically, responded to wider debates about British
identity and multicultural society in and through its own ideological prism
of business enterprise, achievement and success:

One Nation

The real Asian tigers are on our doorsteps. The spirit of enterprise that
has transformed the nations of the Pacific Rim is now taking over the
British high street. A list of Britain's 100 richest Asians in the journal
Eastern Eye reveals the extent to which ethnic diversity has underpinned
economic growth. The creation of a multicultural society has not, however,
been painless.

The difficulties were poignantly underlined yesterday by the presence
of the tragic yet dignified figure of Stephen Lawrence's mother at the London launch of the European Year Against Racism. The debate provoked
by the failure to bring his murderers to justice has forced an agonised examination of how society deals with racial tensions—but the creation of
One Nation depends just as much on celebrating achievement as acknowledging difficulties. The recognition of how much Britain now owes
to its new entrepreneurs can play a part in building tolerance and guaranteeing esteem for all minorities.

(Times, 19.2.97)

The *Guardian*, also characteristically, gave voice to black academics and
intellectuals who were now accessed, often at considerable length, to put
forward their views on the changing nature of multicultural society and
British identity. The U.S. academic, Henry Louis Gates, in a 3,250 word
feature article, BLACK FLASH, for example, reflected on 'how being black
was becoming a way of being British' (*Guardian*, 19.7.97); the British academic Stuart Hall was interviewed at length in THE TEBBIT TEST AND TRIBAL
GAMES AND RACES about his views on 'multiculturalism and Norman Tebbit's old hard-line views' (*Guardian*, 11.10.97, 5); and Martin Jacques, former coeditor with Stuart Hall of the new-left magazine *Marxism Today*

and coarchitect of the 'News Times' political agenda, reflected in THE MELT-ING POT THAT IS BORN-AGAIN BRITANNIA about how ethnic minorities would fare in Britain's cultural renaissance (*Observer*, 28.12.97, 14).

This general outpouring of cultural reflexivity directed at issues of multicultural British identity was unleashed by the Stephen Lawrence case and was enacted, as we have seen, across the mainstream press. Even so, the shared symbol of 'Stephen Lawrence', though encouraging a common revulsion at this and other racist murders, was not capable of completely warding off right-wing viewpoints that could only encourage racist sentiments and actions:

Tony Parson's Column

. . . It is, of course, a national tragedy that Stephen Lawrence died. But the fact that every decent person in Britain wants justice for Stephen, no matter what the colour of their skin, suggests that this is ultimately a successful multi-racial society.

But our multi-racial society is done no favours by allowing phoney asylum-seekers to settle here. And phoney asylum seekers are settling here in their droves. . . . This is a scandalous abuse of the welfare state. It is also an insult to British hospitality.

(*Daily Mirror*, 4.8.97, 9)

While right-wing commentators and newspapers sought to contain the political challenges supported by the new 'emotional mood' building on the basis of the deepening Stephen Lawrence crisis, the crisis gained increased urgency with every new report of a racist attack and inadequate police responses—and there were many:

Police Failed to Act as Race Hate Victim Died in Hospital

David Rose

FOR SIX days the family of a black musician who was set on fire in a street attack begged detectives to take a statement from him in hospital, but he fell into a coma and died before being interviewed.

The death of Michael Menson, 29, is now the subject of a murder inquiry. But, in an echo of the notorious Stephen Lawrence case, police sources admit that the prospects of bringing his attackers to justice may have been seriously weakened by their colleagues' slowness to act.

(*Observer*, 30.3.97, 3)

By this point, the symbolic status and signifying capacity of 'Stephen Lawrence' was firmly established through the media's extensive, and emotionally intense, exposure of the private prosecution and public inquest. A sense of moral solidarity informed the media's enactment of the case, even if the press then sought to particularise it and realign the groundswell of emotion and sentiments to run along preferred editorial tracks. Irrespective of their individual editorial outlooks and political ambitions, the mainstream press were now enacting the Stephen Lawrence case as a major *cause célèbre* and, in so doing, were appealing to a generalised moral collectivity. This solidarity invoked and presupposed in media discourse was evidently outraged and emotionally disturbed by continuing acts of racist violence, and had been forced to confront the possibility that the utopian discourse of civil society was not adhered to, or possibly even aspired to, in the daily practices of some of society's key institutions.

Stephen Lawrence had moved from sign to symbol, and the media had transformed the focus of the Lawrence case from an individual racist murder and the pursuit of justice for Stephen Lawrence and his family to concerns about wider racism and the (in)justice of the criminal justice system within British society. As such, this mediatised story had penetrated the profane order of institutionalised life and threatened to reveal the bankruptcy of society's deeper sense of itself as a moral collectivity, but it had also unleashed renewed attempts to construct a moral centre at the very moment that it was being called into question. The Stephen Lawrence story had entered into a moral realm in which symbolism and ritual would play an increasingly important part, which would determine how it discharged its political effects. Indications of this moral shift in public mood were clearly visible in the run-up to the staged public inquiry that took place in 1998.

Stephen Lawrence's memorial stone was defaced, for the first time, in an act of calculated, irreverent symbolism in March 1998. Such was the public prominence of the Stephen Lawrence case by this time that this act of vandalism required a public reaction from the prime minister, Tony Blair: 'He is appalled. His thoughts are with the family' (*Daily Mirror*, 9.3.98, 7). Sir William Macpherson, the appointed chair of the public inquiry, was also no less aware of the potent symbolism and moral sentiments surrounding the case when he visited Stephen Lawrence's memorial plaque, at the spot where he had been killed, stating, 'It seemed to me right to come here and remind people of the terrible events of five years ago' and 'to mark our disgust at the vandalism that was perpetrated. It was an unspeakable act' (*Guardian*, 14.3.98, 1).

The release of the preliminary report by the Police Complaints Authority in December 1997 before the public inquiry further contributed to the considerable sense of moral grievance, and anticipated findings that would surely result in criticism of the Metropolitan Police force at the inquiry and, possibly, vindicate the Lawrences' claims. Society's sense of itself as a moral collectivity was about to be publicly put to the test. Brian Cathcart, writing for the *Guardian*, summarised the PCA findings, and in so doing captured something of the moral compass now directing the Stephen Lawrence story, as well as its uncertain destination:

The Mental Ghetto that Hides Racist Killings

Brian Cathcart

FOUR years of arguments by the Metropolitan Police in defence of their conduct of the Stephen Lawrence case were brutally demolished this week, with Home Secretary Jack Straw's publication of the Police Complaints Authority's report.

There was no local 'wall of silence' impeding their inquiry into the murder of this black teenager; detectives did allow the forensic trail to go cold, as the Lawrence family always said; and the idea that black radicals obstructed the investigation by hijacking the case was shown up as nonsense. Above all, the PCA's interim report on Monday demolished the long-standing assertion of senior officers that even if there were flaws in the investigation, they could not have affected the outcome of the trial. This was a truly dreadful cock-up.

But it would be a mistake—even an injustice—to imagine that the police alone are responsible for the failure to bring Stephen's killers to justice; the Crown Prosecution Service and the political system must answer for their conduct, but most of all British society as a whole is entangled in the net.

(17.12.97, 17)

The molten lava of moral pollution was beginning to stir, on the basis of preceding and often emotionally intense feelings and sentiments circulated by the mass media. Institutional power holders recognised the threat and sought, where they could, to head off the flow. The Police Complaints Authority, for example, took the unusual step of announcing its recommendation that a senior serving officer involved in the Stephen Lawrence murder case face a disciplinary charge, and announced this just a few days before the beginning of the public inquiry (*Guardian*, 14.3.98, 1). Even the public inquiry chair, Sir William Macpherson, was not immune from the moral flows set in motion by sections of the press. The *Observer*'s investigation of Sir William Macpherson threatened to delay the start of the public inquiry when it reported that he had previously:

- Ruled a white parent could withdraw a child from a class with a large number of Asian children, even if the decision was motivated by racism.
- Argued that racial discrimination should not be tackled by law but by 'good sense'.
- Went to Royal Ascot when he was due to hear a case involving a race attack victim.
- As a High Court judge had one of the worst records for refusing leave for judicial review in immigration cases.
- Denied family and Commission for Racial Equality lawyers access to key parts of a Police Complaints Authority report on police handling of the Lawrence case.

(15.3.98, 5).

Clearly, some sections of the press were now performatively moving the Stephen Lawrence story forward and contributing to a growing sense of moral commitment and collectivity. Leading public figures and their reputations thereby became available for public criticism and censure.

SUMMARY

The private prosecution was reported widely as an unprecedented legal move, and one that implicitly criticised the CPS as well as the Metropolitan Police for failing to collect sufficient evidence or bring a prosecution against the prime suspects. When the private prosecution—potentially a moment of symbolic and legal redress—collapsed, the Stephen Lawrence case was once again tipped back into deepening crisis. The criminal justice system publicly appeared impotent in its ability to convict racist killers and unable or unwilling to fully commit to the necessary task of rebuilding damaged community trust in the conduct and efficacy of its key institutions. The public sense of grievance that was thereby opened up, and the sympathies and sentiments on which it drew its sustenance, was produced in large measure during the reporting of the private prosecution—a public event that was defined in emotional, revelatory and dramatic ways.

The coroner's inquest, and its unprecedented verdict, also generated palpable emotions and dramatic scenes, and these, too, served to underpin the growing sense of moral outrage and collectivity that was summoned by the media in its extensive exposition of the case, its reporting of the racist behaviour of the prime suspects and in its commentary on wider concerns of racism within British society. 'Stephen Lawrence', as sign and symbol, had now entered into public life and taken up a position on centre stage. The media had enacted this and were reflectively and reflexively discussing issues of 'race' inequality and identity as well as the multifaceted and deep-seated nature of racism, and they did so through the full panoply of different journalism forms and formats.

What the private prosecution and public coroner's inquest had not managed to do, notwithstanding their ritual potential to do so, was dissipate or head off mounting public unease and criticism being directed at key criminal justice system institutions and their evident failings. The Stephen Lawrence case had raised serious, potentially cataclysmic concerns that went to the heart of divisive concerns of 'race' and racism, identity and inequality, within British society and culture. But the various forms of institutional response or 'redress' by different agencies of the criminal justice system had so far only served to exacerbate the sense of deepening crisis, not ameliorate it. They had merely opened the wound symbolised by Stephen Lawrence, not cauterised it. This public wound demanded moral and institutional redress if community anger and public opprobrium was not to overspill and pollute core institutions of state and society, ruin public reputations or threaten serious civil unrest. At this juncture, clearly, the Stephen Lawrence story had entered into public life and was being played out on the media stage. Hopes for, and tensions surrounding, the public inquiry were high.

Seven

Redress

This brings us to the third phase, *redressive action*. In order to limit the spread of crisis, certain adjustive and redressive 'mechanisms' . . . are swiftly brought into operation by leading or structurally representative members of the disturbed social system. . . . It is in the redressive phase that both pragmatic techniques and symbolic action reach their fullest expression. For the society, group, community, association, or whatever may be the social unit, is here at its most 'self-conscious' and may attain the clarity of someone fighting in a corner for his life. Redress too has its liminal features, its being 'betwixt and between' and, as such, furnishes a distanced replication and critique of the events leading up to and composing the 'crisis'. This replication may be in the idiom of judicial process, or in the metaphorical and symbolic idiom of a ritual process, depending on the nature and severity of the crisis.

Victor Turner, *Dramas, Fields, Metaphors* (1974, 41)

The structurally inferior aspire to symbolic structural superiority in ritual; the structurally superior aspire to symbolic communitas and undergo penance to achieve it.

Victor Turner, *The Ritual Process* (1969, 203)

With each successive failure of the criminal justice system to deliver justice to Stephen Lawrence's family, and with each successive report of continuing racist attacks and murders in London and elsewhere in Britain, the Stephen Lawrence case accumulated symbolic power. This extended its signifying capacity and political charge to divisive concerns of racism in British society. An ordinary black family's pursuit of justice for their son murdered by known racists had metamorphosed in the glare of the media into a mounting public crisis. As symbol, Stephen Lawrence now embodied the particular and the general, expressed concrete and abstract forces of change, and also managed to condense surrounding discourses of 'race' and racism. The media breathed life into this symbol as it took a central position in a narrative that had yet to run its course. Here it served as an agent of change and prompted cultural reflexivity in respect to issues of 'race', racism and British identity.

As we have seen, the media based its enactment of mounting crisis in significant degree on the emotional resonance of the case, both extending and elaborating this throughout society. The role of emotions in ritual and moral solidarity, changing 'structures of feeling' and political events have all been commented on by other scholars (though not in respect to the part played by the media), and these ideas help to sensitise this discussion to the dynamics at work in the mediatised enactment of public redress. Randal Collins, for example, in his sociological theory of transient emotions, based on Durkheim's ideas, emphasises how rituals make use of emotional ingredients and produce feelings of moral solidarity (2003, 129–33). Rituals, he suggests, shape cognitions and leave a longer-term emotional energy. Emotions and feelings of social solidarity need not, therefore, be taken as secondary to cognition but are infused with, and often animating, them: 'we feel the emotions of social solidarity in the various ideas with which we think' and 'thinking those ideas allows those individuals to feel a renewed surge of socially-based enthusiasm' (132–33).

Raymond Williams, when struggling to find a language that captured the always formative, always 'experienced' processes of social being, coined the concept of 'structures of feeling' (1985, 128–35). Historically emergent 'structures of feeling' refer to 'affective elements of consciousness and relationships: not feeling against thought, but thought as felt and feeling as thought: practical consciousness of a present kind, in a living and interrelating continuity' (132). These ideas also help to remind us of the ways in which, in this case, the cultural forms and expression of mediatised ritual can be 'experienced' and 'felt', notwithstanding their freezing within retrospective analysis. Indeed, the concept of 'structure of feeling' in this context seems particularly apposite; it helps to map how past and emergent social sentiments about 'race' and racism in British society at a particular historical juncture 'moved' the contested field of British race relations. As William H. Sewell has argued, 'Tracking down the causes and character of structural transformations in political events may require us to be particularly sensitive to the emotional tone of action' (2003, 136).

This chapter now attends to how the media performed the emotional energy that had built across the preceding phases of Stephen Lawrence's murder and its aftermath and which had now become focused in the phase of judicial and symbolic redress. This began on 17 March 1998, the opening day of the public inquiry instigated by the government, included the release of the Macpherson report on 24 February 1999 and continued across the first wave of political responses and public discussion in March of that year. The chapter examines how the media performed the Stephen Lawrence case not simply in terms of the massive media exposure and outpouring that accompanied the reporting of the public inquiry (mapped in Chapter 4), but more qualitatively in respect to how the media helped to produce (as indicated in Chapter 6) a new 'emotional mood' that sustained a collective sense of 'moral solidarity' and directed flows of moral opprobrium and approbation. It was by these means that the media powerfully entered into the life of society, enacting the Stephen Lawrence case as a moment of potential catharsis or even transformation of British race relations.

MEDIA REPORTING MORAL DRAMA

Prior to the public inquiry, the molten lava of moral pollution, as we have seen, had publicly started to flow, on the basis of a general 'heating up' of the cultural terrain where public concerns about racist attacks, police treatment of blacks and British identity had surfaced, as well as growing media criticism directed at aspects of the criminal justice system. The five prime suspects in the murder of Stephen Lawrence had widely received public condemnation by the press, but so, too, had the CPS and its director, the conservative home secretary, Michael Howard, as well as the Metropolitan Police Service and its chief constable and, earlier in some sections of the press, antiracist organisations and their supporters. More recently still, the reputation and moral fitness of Sir William Macpherson, the inquiry chair, had been publicly questioned by the *Observer*—a challenge that he had only managed to fend off by the intervention of home secretary Jack Straw and personal assurances made to Doreen and Neville Lawrence. By the time the public inquiry was launched, public anticipation and media interest was high: the public reputations of prominent individuals and institutions were seemingly on the line, and public shaming was a distinct possibility.

The inquiry lived up to its preceding sense of anticipation. It opened with a minute's silence in memory of Stephen Lawrence, before rehearsing, to use Turner's appropriate terms, 'a distanced replication and critique of the events leading up to and composing the "crisis"' (1974, 41). This began with detailed scrutiny and criticism of the botched police investigations in the headlines: INQUIRY TOLD OF LAWRENCE CASE BLUNDERS (*Independent*, 25.3.98, 4); COPS WAITED TWO WEEKS TO QUIZ MURDER SUSPECTS (*Sun*, 25.3.98, 8); AMAZING TRAIL OF BLUNDERS BY POLICE: INQUIRY OPENS WITH CATALOGUE OF ERRORS (*Daily Mail*, 25.3.98, 1). Such criticisms were added to throughout the remainder of the inquiry as damning revelations came to light for the first time. The *Independent* reported, as did other papers, for example, on the BLOODY CLUES MISSED BY LAWRENCE POLICE and described how 'Peter Finch, a civilian photographer with the Metropolitan Police, watched two suspects carrying black plastic bags emerge from a house under observation on consecutive days but did nothing because he did not have a mobile phone' (*Independent*, 24.4.98, 6).

But it was the highly charged testimonies and emotional scenes of the inquiry itself as much as the disclosure of previously hidden details that helped sustain the collective effervescence now surrounding the case and infused in its public mediatisation. On the second day of the inquiry, Doreen Lawrence testified: MUM'S HELL AT MURDER OF STEPHEN (*Sun*, 26.3.98, 8); THE ANGER AND ANGUISH OF MRS LAWRENCE (*Guardian*, 26.3.98, 2); A MOTHER'S TORMENT: 'I GAVE A POLICE OFFICER THE FIVE SUSPECTS' NAMES. HE FOLDED THE PAPER INTO A SMALL BALL. I WAS SO ANGRY.' (*Daily Mail*, 26.3.98, 19). The following day this emotional intensity was deepened even further with the heartrending testimony, publicly aired for the first time, of a couple who had cared for Stephen Lawrence as he lay dying: YOU ARE LOVED, WOMAN PASSER-BY WHISPERED AS STEPHEN SLIPPED AWAY (*Daily Mail*, 27.3.98, 27). The *Independent* ran the following account:

Poignant Last Seconds of Stephen Lawrence 'Died in My Arms'

Kathy Marks

A POIGNANT account of the last few minutes of the life of Stephen Lawrence was given yesterday by a couple who looked after him as he lay dying in a pool of blood on the pavement.

Conor Taaffe told the public inquiry into the black teenager's death that he and his wife, Louise, knelt down beside him after he was stabbed. Mrs Taaffe held Stephen's head in her hands and spoke into his ear, telling him: "You are loved, you are loved."

Neville Lawrence, Stephen's father, left the room during Mr Taaffe's evidence and several people in the public gallery wept.

(27.3.98, 4)

Duwayne Brooks's testimony, a little later in the inquiry, also proved to be emotionally charged and was reported at length by the media:

'They Killed Steve and Ruined My Whole Life'

Kathy Marks

A powerful and moving account of Stephen Lawrence's final moments was given yesterday by his close friend, Duwayne Brooks, who also delivered a stinging attack on the conduct of police who investigated the murder.

"Steve and I were young black men. Racist thugs killed Steve and shattered my life," Mr Brooks told the public inquiry into Stephen's death. "I think of Steve every day. I'm sad, confused and pissed about this system where racists attack and go free, but innocent victims like Steve and I are treated like criminals."

(*Independent*, 16.5.98, 2)

The intensity of the emotional discharge at the inquiry was not reliant on spoken testimonies, however, but inhered in the drama, theatricality and pathos of the event itself. A particularly charged moment came when the prime suspects gave their 'evidence' to the inquiry, witnessed by the Lawrences. The press sought to capture this dramatic moment and deployed their rhetorical powers to do so. The *Independent*, for example, portrayed this encounter on its front page where normally a more restrained prose style of news reporting may have been expected:

Passing Before Their Eyes, One By One, Were the Racist Thugs They Believed Killed Their Son

Kathy Marks

IF HE felt the slightest twinge of self-consciousness, he did not show it. Jamie Acourt swaggered into the room, glanced at the massed ranks of hostile faces and settled down in the witness box, adjusting the lapels of his freshly pressed suit.

Twenty feet away, Neville and Doreen Lawrence gazed steadily at this young man, with his slicked back dark hair and insolent demeanour. Acourt slouched back in his chair, unfazed by the attention.

(30.6.98, 1)

The press unanimously condemned the unconvincing and evasive testimony of the five prime suspects, who refused to answer questions put to them: LAPSES OF MEMORY AND STILL BRAZENLY DEFIANT (*Daily Mail*, 1.7.98, 5). Headlines ran transcripts of their responses: INQUIRY HEARS FROM LAWRENCE PRIME SUSPECTS (*Times*, 30.6.98); 'BLACK PEOPLE CALL EACH OTHER NIGGERS, SO WHY DOES IT MATTER IF WHITE PEOPLE SAY IT?' (*Independent*, 30.6.98, 4). As they left the inquiry under police escort, the suspects were subjected to a hail of abuse from the awaiting crowd and responded violently in a dramatic moment captured by television cameras and photojournalists, discussed later in this chapter.

Expectation of public drama also informed the participation of the Metropolitan Police at the inquiry, building to a climax as public apologies were belatedly offered by senior representatives of the Met and, declined by the

Lawrences, and as calls for Sir Paul Condon's resignation began to be heard. This was now essentially a moral drama being played out on the media stage and in which public accountability, humility and shame were seemingly demanded and, periodically, offered up as a means of demonstrating public contrition—and of slowing the flow of public opprobrium being directed at the police as an institution. The former deputy assistant commissioner, who was in charge of the area of southeast London where Stephen Lawrence was murdered, was the first to publicly apologise: AT LAST, AN APOLOGY BY LAWRENCE POLICE (*Daily Mail*, 10.6.98, 28). This was followed a week later by a further police apology, but again not from the commissioner himself. The *Daily Mail* reflected on this in its editorial, whilst reminding its readers where their scorn should principally be directed:

When Justice Weeps

LEADER

POLITICIANS would regard it as damage limitation. To lawyers it must look like throwing yourself on the mercy of the court. For priests it would be akin to confession.

Yesterday one of London's most senior police officers offered his 'deepest apologies' to the parents of murdered black teenager Stephen Lawrence. . . .

The contrast could hardly be more humiliating. While the police confess their faults, the murderers of Stephen Lawrence stay tight-lipped and strut free. It is enough to make justice weep.

(*Daily Mail*, 18.6.98, 10)

The broadsheets also reported the belated public apologies from the Metropolitan police.

Finally, Police Apologise to the Lawrence Family

Kathy Marks

The apology was made through the assistant commissioner, Ian Johnston, the third highest-ranking officer. . . . "We have let you down. We could have and should have done better.

"On behalf of myself and the commissioner, who specifically asked me to associate himself with these words, and the whole of the Metropolitan Police, I offer my sincere and deep apologies to you", he said.

(*Independent*, 18.6.98, 1)

The *Independent*, in contrast to the *Daily Mail*, however, was less magnanimous in its reading of such public apologies, interpreting this event for its readership as a public relations move on behalf of the commissioner:

Sorry, Sir Paul, an Apology is Not Enough

Peter Victor

SO, THE Metropolitan Police are sorry. Sorry that Stephen Lawrence was murdered; sorry that his murder was not investigated properly; sorry that the killers are not behind bars; sorry they have "lost the confidence" of black people. So what?

The only person likely to gain from this apology is Sir Paul Condon, the Metropolitan Police Commissioner: he might avoid further humiliation. He does not relish the prospect of being dragged through cross examination . . . so this week he sent his emissary, assistant commissioner Ian Johnston to atone in his place.

(19.6.98, 4)

By the time Sir Paul Condon was required to take the stand, public expectancy was palpable. How would he respond to the criticisms of the Met, and would he accept the charge of 'institutional racism' now being levied against it? The *Guardian* described the event as follows: 'For a little over two hours he ignored the shouted calls for his resignation as he was forced to acknowledge and apologise for a damning series of shortcomings in his force. . . . Sitting at a desk a few feet from Stephen's parents, both impassive throughout, Sir Paul said he felt it was right that as commissioner he should experience "the anger and frustration" felt by many in the community about the tragic death' (2.10.98, 10). The *Guardian* displayed this dramatic event on its front page, performatively enacting it as a significant moment, whilst pointing to the entrenched interests at stake behind the public rhetoric:

Lawrence Family Spurns Met Chief's Personal Apology Over Racist Murder: When Sorry is Not Enough

David Pallister

There were just two words that Sir Paul Condon could not bring himself to accept yesterday. They were words that, in truth, probably would have condemned him as a traitor in the eyes of the 27,000 officers in the Metropolitan police. No matter how hard he was pressed by Sir William Macpherson and his colleagues . . . Sir Paul resolutely and repeatedly refused to accept that the Met was infected with "institutional racism" . . . Sir Paul's performance cut little ice with Stephen's parents. "That is a PR job," Mrs Lawrence said.

(2.10.98, 1)

The *Times* also reported Sir Paul Condon's apology and the Met's sense of shame, but it chose to emphasise his denial of institutional racism:

Met Chief Denies Police Racism
in Lawrence Case

Stewart Tendler

The Commissioner of the Metropolitan Police publicly apologised to Stephen Lawrence's parents yesterday for the failure to catch his killers. However, Sir Paul Condon denied that it was attributable to corruption or racism.

Sir Paul, giving evidence at the inquiry into the events surrounding Mr Lawrence's death, said: "I deeply regret we have not brought Stephen's racist murderers to justice. I have set out my personal sorrow and regret at having failed Stephen, his parents and Londoners. There is a sense of shame in the Met about many aspects of this tragic case."

(2.10.98)

The *Times* then followed up on this, publicly defining its own political position in respect to the mounting criticisms of the Met and suggesting how the chief constable should pragmatically respond to the growing public criticisms of his force:

Black and Blue

The Commissioner of the Metropolitan Police may not believe that his force is 'institutionally' racist. But after the casual, callous incompetence displayed by the officers investigating the murder of the black teenager Stephen Lawrence, Stephen's grieving parents can be forgiven for thinking otherwise.

Sir Paul Condon took the opportunity yesterday to apologise directly to Neville and Doreen Lawrence for his force's failings. The sincerity of Sir Paul's regret is not in doubt, nor is his commitment to the sensitive policing of a multicultural society. . . . The Commissioner may consider that it would be counterproductive to accept that his force is 'institutionally' racist, and it is certainly invidious to tarnish the Met's many fine officers with so sweeping a condemnation. . . . Sir Paul will not wish to pre-empt the inquiry's conclusions, but he will be better placed to endure any criticism if he can point to substantive measures already in place to tackle painful failures he has already, honestly, acknowledged.

(2.10.98)

By the end of this stage of the inquiry, prior to the release of the report, the *Independent* had no doubts about the threat that the case now posed to Sir Paul Condon's personal standing: SIR PAUL'S SPIN CANNOT ALTER THE

UNCOMFORTABLE TRUTH; OF ALL THE PLAYERS IN THE LAWRENCE CASE, IT IS THE MET'S COMMISSIONER WHO HAS THE MOST REASON TO SWEAT (*Independent*, 8.2.99, 4).

The inquiry also produced its own violence when the Nation of Islam stormed the inquiry prompting the *Daily Mail* to report on the UNWELCOME PRESENCE OF MEN IN THE RED BOW-TIES (30.6.98, 4), though this provided an opportunity for the *Independent* to reflect on how the media's pursuit of images of violent black men validated white British fears (1.7.98, 4). Clearly, the Lawrence case was now attracting universal media interest, but so, too, was it being interpreted and appropriated through the differentiated politics of 'race' encoded by different media. As the inquiry pressed harder into issues of police incompetence, institutionalised racism and wider racism in society, so political fault lines opened up. Over preceding months and years, the press had played its part in stirring the tectonic plates of racial identity; now, as the inquiry began to publicly bite into difficult issues and entrenched institutional interests, so some newspapers became uneasy with the momentum that they had helped to unleash. The *Times*, for example, began to distance itself from the inquiry, even before its conclusion and publication of recommendations.

The Police Prepare to Work in Handcuffs

Melanie Phillips

The Stephen Lawrence affair has developed an alarming momentum of its own. . . . As they dig themselves ever deeper into a hole, the police can only gaze with impotent horror at the destruction of their own moral authority. But there's an uneasy feeling that both the Lawrences and the police are being used to promote a less than constructive agenda.

(*Sunday Times*, 31.1.99)

Evidently, the Stephen Lawrence case was exerting itself as a force within society, and this was a force that some institutional interests found unwelcome.

Press Performance as Cultural Reflection and Media Reflexivity

Alongside and contributing to the daily mediatised enactment of the public inquiry, the press now also produced an upsurge in background pieces, news features, opinion pieces and editorials both contributing to and expressing wider processes of cultural reflection (see Figure 4.1). They also reflexively monitored and commented on this media outpouring (see Table 4.3 and Figure 4.5). Across 1998–1999, no less than 545 features, 352 comment/opinion pieces, 194 letters to the editor, 146 editorials and 88 profiles informed this voluminous press output in our sample of British newspapers. This profusion of press outpouring augmented the earlier 'indicative' journalism of information and dissemination with a 'subjunctive' journalism of discussion and deliberation now focusing on wider problems and perspectives for change.

Ten percent of all Stephen Lawrence-related press items in 1999, for example, focused on discrimination and ethnic minority representation in different sectors of society, including the probation service, social services, housing and education, and a further 10 percent of all items focused specifically on police racism and minority ethnic recruitment in both 1998 and 1999 (see Table 4.2). This produced such headlines as: SHAME ON THE RACISTS IN OUR POLICE RANKS (*Times*, 9.8.98); FORGOTTEN VICTIMS OF RACE HATE: THE MURDER OF STEPHEN LAWRENCE WAS NOT AN ISOLATED INCIDENT. NOR WAS THE BUNGLED POLICE RESPONSE TO HIS DEATH (*Observer*, 7.2.99, 11); STRAW DEMANDS MORE BLACK COPS (*Sun*, 10.2.99, 2); WHY RACISTS FLOURISH IN AN ANTI-RACIST FORCE (*Independent*, 24.2.99, 4).

The press reflexively focused on itself and other media in an upsurge of 292 such pieces, or nearly 10 percent of all press output in 1999 (see Table 4.3 and Figure 4.5). For example: RACE IN THE MEDIA: IN PLAIN BLACK AND WHITE . . . AND BARELY A BLACK FACE IN SIGHT (*Independent*, 1.12.98, 15); GUILTY AS CHARGED, OFFICER—THE NATION MUST SEE THE COLOUR OF JUSTICE, THE HARROWING PLAY BASED ON THE LAWRENCE INQUIRY (*Guardian*, 14.1.99, 9); DESPITE ITS COVERAGE OF THE LAWRENCE CASE, THE DAILY MAIL HAS REVERTED TO TYPE ON RACE (*Independent*, 9.2.99, 13); HOW MURDER BECAME A MEDIA EVENT (*Guardian*, 25.2.99, 22).

Liberal broadsheets also reflected on the symbolic status acquired by Stephen Lawrence in the media and situated this historically alongside other watershed cases, thereby extending and deepening both its historical and political reach and significance: LAWRENCE BECOMES BLACK ICON (*Independent*, 20.12.98, 8); ICON FOR A SCEPTICAL AGE (*Observer*, 10.1.99, 12); TRAGEDIES THAT SHAPED PERCEPTIONS (*Guardian*, 26.2.99, 6).

This media reflexivity grew across the mounting crisis and redress phases, but assumed its most prominent aspect following the release of the Macpherson inquiry report on 24 February 1999. Before the report was officially published, however, a further crisis attended its publication when it was leaked to the *Sunday Telegraph* four days in advance. The press reported some of its key findings and reflected in particular on whether Sir Paul Condon would resign following Sir William Macpherson's criticisms and the commissioner's refusal to accept the report's definition and charge of the Metropolitan police as 'institutionally racist: REPORT LAYS BARE RACISM AT MET (*Guardian*, 22.2.99, 3). The home secretary then sought to place an injunction on further reporting until its official release on 24 February 1999.

SYMBOLIC REDRESS: THE POLITICAL CENTRE UNITES

On the day of the Macpherson report's release, public anticipation was high, and media interest intense. This potentially cathartic (or socially cataclysmic) moment of symbolic redress, six years in the making, was now at hand and the political centre of society came together to publicly demonstrate their support for the Lawrences, acknowledge their collective sense of shame and lend support to symbolic processes of redress. This all-party support was embodied in the statements by leading politicians in the House of Commons on 24 February 1999, which were broadcast live and in full by television as well as in abridged form later that same day, and then reported in the press the following day. These public pronouncements symbolised a united commitment from the political centre of society to processes of change and, in Turner's term, 'redress'. Collectively they expressed a position of 'civic universalism', a shared moral and political commitment to how civil society should and could be. This aspect of the 'social imaginary' was elaborated through the declarations of prominent political leaders reasserting their commitment to the moral collectivity of civil society, a place that the Stephen Lawrence case had threatened to expose as a sham. There were no better figures to publicly display this renewed national commitment to the social imaginary of an inclusive civil society than the most senior politicians in the land, and there was no better place than from the televised seat of governance, the British parliament's House of Commons:

Prime Minister, Tony Blair: Madam Speaker, I think it right today to praise Doreen and Neville Lawrence for their courage and dignity. We should confront honestly as a nation the racism that still exists within our society. We should find within ourselves as a nation the will to overcome it. The publication of today's report on the killing of Stephen Lawrence is a very important moment in the life of our country; it is a moment to reflect, learn and to change. It will certainly lead to new laws, but more than that it will lead to new attitudes, a new era in race relations and a new more tolerant and inclusive Britain.

(*Westminster*, BBC2, 24.2.99)

William Hague, the leader of the opposition, also pledged his party's support and reiterated his commitment, and that of 'decent' people everywhere, to the civic universalism of justice and respect for others. This was then followed by a further statement from the prime minister pledging to back up words with policy deeds:

William Hague, Leader of the Opposition: Madam Speaker, would the Prime Minister agree that every decent person in this country, regardless of politics, will wish to show sympathy and support to the family of Stephen Lawrence and will feel shame and disgust that his murderers have not been brought to justice? Will he agree that if some good is to come out of this appalling crime all of us need to learn the lessons of what went wrong and commit ourselves to build a nation in which every citizen regardless of colour or creed is treated with justice and respect?

Tony Blair: Our recommendations, that will deliver the most comprehensive agenda in improving race relations this country has seen for many decades, and the test and the sincerity as law-makers in this House, is not how well we can express sympathy with the Lawrence family but how well we implement the recommendations that will insure that this type of thing never happens in our country again.

(*Westminster*, BBC2, 24.2.99)

The home secretary, Jack Straw, then followed with a lengthy and detailed exposition of the Labour government's endorsement of the Macpherson report, its analysis, findings and recommendations. Importantly, it spelled out Macpherson's definition of 'institutional racism' as well as the report's intended cathartic impact in terms of unleashing positive initiatives for change. Informing the home secretary's carefully worded speech was the powerful symbolic aura of Stephen Lawrence, whose killing was described once again at the outset and then explicitly referenced once more towards the close of his address. These words, sentiments and images represent perhaps the cathartic pinnacle of the Stephen Lawrence story, which had now penetrated to the very seat of government and challenged the political centre of society to redress the hurt and injustice that had become symbolised and condensed within his name. The home secretary's words lay bare the express need to revitalise the utopian discourse of civil society and deepen society's commitment to social inclusion, multiculturalism and justice. These words are worthy of extended quotation:

Jack Straw, Home Secretary: . . . The House will share my sense of shame that the criminal justice system and the Metropolitan Police in particular failed the Lawrence family so badly. The Commissioner has asked me to share with the House that he feels that sense of shame too. . . . On the critical issue of institutional racism the inquiry's definition is as follows: 'Institutional racism consists of the collective failure of an organisation to provide an appropriate and professional service to people because of their colour, culture or ethnic origin. It can be seen or detected in processes, attitudes and behaviour which amount to discrimination through unwitting prejudice, ignorance, thoughtlessness and racist stereotyping which disadvantage minority ethnic people'. And the inquiry found on this definition, and again I quote, 'Institutional racism exists within both the Metropolitan police service and in other police services, and in other institutions country wide'. . . . The report then expresses the hope that the catharsis of this inquiry will lead to constructive action and not to further divisive views or outcomes. Madam Speaker, this is a new definition of institutional racism that I accept and so does the Commissioner. . . .

This report challenges us all, and not just the police service, and I want to use the opportunity the report gives us to tackle discrimination wherever it is found. So today I can announce to the House that we shall be extending the Race Relations Act to cover not just the police, as the report recommends, but all the public services. . . . The police do have a special responsibility in our society because day by day they are the immediate guardians of fairness and justice but we would all be deluding ourselves if we believed the issues thrown up by this inquiry affect only the police. . . . [T]he very process of the inquiry has opened all our eyes to what it is like to be Black or Asian in Britain today, and has revealed some fundamental truths about the nature of our society and some of these truths are uncomfortable but we have to confront them. I want this report to serve as a watershed in our attitudes to racism. I want it to act as a catalyst for permanent and irrevocable change not just across our public services but across our whole society. . . .

The vision I believe is clear; to create a society where every individual regardless of colour, creed or race has the same opportunities and respect from his or her neighbour. On race equality let us make Britain a beacon of the world. . . . This report must mark the beginning of this process and not the end.

Madam Speaker, in her evidence to the Lawrence inquiry Mrs Lawrence said this, 'I would like Stephen to be remembered as a young man who had a future. He was well loved and had he been given the chance to survive maybe he would have been the one to bridge the gap between black and white'. On this report we must build a lasting testament to Stephen.

(hear, hear. . . .)

(*Westminster*, BBC2, 24.2.99)

Clearly, the Stephen Lawrence case had now galvanised action and symbolic response from the centre of political society, but the media's enactment of this cathartic moment had only just begun.

'SOCIETY IN ACTION': MEDIATISED
COLLECTIVE EFFERVESCENCE

Following the official release of the Macpherson report on 24 February 1999, the media performed a spectacular 'collective effervescence' of media outpouring comprising voluminous reportage, commentary and criticism, which dominated the media sphere on this day and for many days and weeks thereafter. This outpouring was enacted across the mainstream and minority media, press, broadcasting and internet and through an 'ensemble of expressive cultural genres' (Turner 1981, 158). Together these instantiated the emotion, anticipation and political mood that had built throughout the preceding weeks and months and which now crystallised in this pinnacle moment of symbolic and judicial redress (see Figure 4.1). The press, for its part, certainly did not undersell the occasion; it made full use of all the resources at its disposal and enacted this as a liminal moment grounded by an evident sense of communitas. This was performed on front pages, in double-page spreads, supplementary pages and special reports, all making full use of page layout, visual impact and championing headlines (see Figures 7.1–7.4).

The liberal broadsheets publicly enacted this national moment of symbolic redress in terms of collective acknowledgement and shame: STEPHEN LAWRENCE'S LEGACY: CONFRONTING RACIST BRITAIN (*Guardian*); A FAMILY TRAGEDY, A POLICE FORCE DISGRACED AND A NATION SHAMED (*Independent*). This moment of liminal reflexivity was carried through on inside pages. The *Independent*, for example, produced a special twelve-page report that included the following headlines: STRAW AND CONDON SPEAK OF THEIR SENSE OF SHAME; 'INSTITUTIONAL RACISM'—THE OFFICIAL MEANING; an account by Doreen Lawrence that made explicit reference to the dark history of British slavery, THE POLICE OFFICERS BEHAVED TOWARDS US LIKE WHITE MASTERS DURING SLAVERY, positioned, symbolically, above an article about Sir Paul Condon, WE FEEL SHAME AT HAVING LET DOWN STEPHEN'S PARENTS. Various background pieces were also featured, including: A BOY FULL OF LIFE, NOT JUST AN ICON; THE CLOSE FRIEND; HOW A CRAVING FOR TRUTH TURNED INTO A CRUSADE: THE PARENTS; DID THEY KILL HIM? WE MAY NEVER FIND OUT: THE SUSPECTS; STREETS WHERE RACE HATRED IS THE NORM; JUDGE WHOSE SYMPATHY SURPRISED ALL; THE INQUIRY TEAM; POLICE FACE RADICAL RACE LAW CHANGES; and CALL FOR CONDON TO RETIRE EARLY.

The *Daily Mail*, as expected given its earlier MURDERERS front-page and clarion call for justice, also underlined the momentous nature of the Macpherson report on its front page: JUDGE'S DAMNING REPORT ON RACE MURDER WILL CHANGE BRITAIN and THE LEGACY OF STEPHEN. In contrast to the *Independent*, however, its inside pages focused more on the report's criticisms of the police investigation, THE BLUNDERING OF THE FIRST VITAL HOURS, and Sir Paul Condon's response, MY SHAME AT POLICE BUNGLES, BY CONDON; the suspects, I WANT KILLERS TO FEEL HUNTED SAYS SIR PAUL, and STILL HE SMIRKS: BOUNCY AND SWAGGERING THUG FLAUNTS HIS DEFIANCE; as well as THE PARENTS WHOSE LIVES THEY RUINED, and FOR THE LAWRENCES, ONE STARK REALITY REMAINED: JUSTICE WAS NOT DONE. It also printed the full list of Macpherson's seventy recommendations under the headline RADICAL MEASURES and provided Macpherson's definition of institutional racism.

The *Sun* headlined its front page with STRAW WAR ON RACISM, and the *Times* reported how LEGACY WILL BE SOCIAL CHANGE and stated, RACIST MURDER AN AFFRONT TO SOCIETY. The *Daily Mirror*, belatedly and with no likely chance of legal success, now sought to take up the cause: THE LAWRENCE INQUIRY REPORT: NAIL THEM; MIRROR OFFERS £50,000 TO CATCH LAWRENCE KILLERS and editorialised on the DAMNING VERDICT THAT SHAMES THE NATION. The *Sun* and the *Times*, like the *Daily Mail*, also began to question some of Macpherson's recommendations, but gen-

Figure 7.1
Guardian, 25 February 1999, p.1. © *Guardian and Observer.*

Figure 7.2
Independent, 25 February 1999, p.1. © *Independent.* Photo: David Rose.

Figure 7.3
Daily Mail, 25 February 1999, p. 1. © *Daily Mail.* Photo: *Reuters.*

Figure 7.4
Voice, 22 February 1999, p. 1. © *Voice.*

erally, as we have seen, all the press felt obliged to enact this moment as one of shared public communitas.

The *Voice* had adopted a championing and performative stance from its very first report of Stephen Lawrence's murder. Unsurprisingly, therefore, it took the opportunity of the leaked Macpherson report to trailblaze media calls for action in its earlier Monday edition. The theme of its front page (see Figure 7.4), Now CHANGE MUST COME, continued in its special inquiry report which included: TIME FOR CHANGE; THE LESSONS THAT MUST BE LEARNED and WE HAVE DONE OUR PART, LED BY THE COURA- GEOUS LAWRENCE FAMILY. NOW IT'S UP TO THE GOVERNMENT TO TAKE REAL ACTION.

Britain's mainstream media, then, collectively reported the response from the political centre of society as a moment of historical import. This 'cultural flooding' also signalled it as a liminal moment outside of routine political time and party politics and thereby helped to promote a sense of national renewal and moral solidarity. While different newspapers sought to emphasise certain aspects of the case and not others, for a while at least they evidently felt obligated by a shared recognition of national shame and the need for a moral commitment to change.

Press Performance as Iconography: 'How to Do Things with Pictures'

Throughout the period of the public inquiry, the press had collectively performed the Lawrence case, making full use of dramatic developments, narrative progression, emotional testimonies and startling revelations. This was also powerfully discharged through the use of symbolic images. Susan Sontag, in her essay *Regarding the Pain of Others* (2003), reminds us that 'The photographer's intentions do not determine the meaning of a photograph, which will have its own career, blown by the whims and loyalties of the diverse communities that have use for it' (39). This is true of course, both semiotically and in terms of the ways in which the photographs are used by newspaper editors (Cottle 1998). But whereas photojournalists usually exercise little control over the subsequent use made of their pictures by audiences, newspaper editors have a greater capacity to ensure that the intended meanings, from their editorial point of view, are in fact read. Editorially, pictures are subject to careful processes of selection and cropping and are positioned, juxtaposed, headlined and thereby framed and inflected in ways that conform to the informing editorial view and idiom of the paper and are designed to be read by particular readerships. In this sense, the democratic currency of news images is often more constrained than may be the case for pictures displayed in other contexts. The press powerfully visualised the Stephen Lawrence story, providing highly symbolic images that both expressed and literally embodied the emotions and feelings that the story had given rise to, and did so for good reason: 'Photographs lay down routes of reference, and serve as totems of causes; sentiment is more likely to crystallize around a photograph than around a verbal slogan' (Sontag 2003, 85).

The press images of Doreen Lawrence undoubtedly served to place her in the public mind as dignified, determined and aggrieved—attributes that helped mobilise public sentiments. A series of strikingly aesthetic portraits, all carefully lit against a black background, were used time and again and seemingly exhibited Doreen Lawrence's inner calm and sublime qualities. Such 'saintlike' portraits helped, semiotically, to canonize Doreen Lawrence and undoubtedly helped to position her and her cause on moral high ground (see Figure 7.5). This is not to criticise the evident aesthetisation at work in such press images. As Sontag has observed, 'the dual powers of photography—to produce documents and to create works of visual art—have produced some remarkable exaggerations about what photographers ought or ought not to do' (2003, 76). But it is to say that the press performatively deployed these images for effect. These 'sacred' images, in both Christian and Durkheimian terms, implicitly challenged the more mundane images of officialdom and politicians associated with the case, as well as the 'profane' if not animalistic world of unthinking aggression, violence and defiance that was symbolised in the repeated use of a limited range of dramatic pictures of the five suspects (see Figures 7.6 and 7.7).

The image of the five suspects reacting violently to the awaiting crowd when exiting the public inquiry on 30 June 1998, captured by Paul Hackett of Reuters, was subsequently used repeatedly, such was its symbolic capacity to seemingly reveal their 'true' nature as well as the public's odium towards them. According to Sontag, 'Uglifying, showing something at its worst . . . invites an active response. For photographs to accuse, and possibly alter conduct, they must shock' (2003, 81). When circulated by the media in the context of the known Stephen Lawrence story, this image of the aggressive and violent suspects could only elicit condemnatory reaction from all but the most callous. The picture also invited media reflexivity when it was given 'Best Picture of The Year' at the 1998 Picture Editors' Awards: 'Young, white male aggression killed Stephen Lawrence and its ugliness was defined in this moment captured by Paul Hackett of Reuters' (*Independent*, 28.12.98, 12).

Paul Hackett's picture assumed iconic, albeit 'profane' status also, through its repeated press rehearsal. Its use in the *Guardian* report, as we can see, visually undermines the suspects' mothers' claim, carried in the report, that their sons are innocent. When juxtaposed against the angelic image of Stephen Lawrence, the suspects' photographed violence seemingly betrays their mothers' statement.

This small image of Stephen Lawrence—unassuming, ordinary, mundane, but now inevitably read with mortal gravitas—became *the* public

Figure 7.5
Observer, 14 February 1999, p.7. © *Guardian and Observer,* Mark Honigsbaum.

Doreen Lawrence on the inquiry
'I'm angry that even now we're still being kept in the dark and have to read the newspapers to find out what is going on.'

...on the suspects
'I will never forget their smiling arrogance at the inquest. They came off as if they were untouchable.'

...on the police
'I naively assumed that they would do everything they could to catch Stephen's killers, but the reality was they weren't doing anything.'

...on racism
'My son's crime was that he was walking along the road. Our crime was living in a country that supports racist murderers against innocent people.'

Doreen Lawrence: 'I gave birth to Stephen, I nurtured him, I was there when he cried. Nobody has the right to take his life.'　Photograph by Richard Saker

Figure 7.6
Guardian, 20 February 1999, p.2. © *Guardian and Observer.*

'They can't keep persecuting our sons. Their lives are ruined'

Mothers break six-year silence to defend suspects in Lawrence case

Edited transcript of Radio 4 interview yesterday:

Q: What effect have the past few years had on your sons?

A: They cannot get a job now, they have absolutely ruined their life. Our sons were 16 and 17 years old when it started and they've got no chance of getting a job because their names are known all over ... and everywhere they go people recognise them.

Q: The bulk of the criticism, loathing ... has been directed at your sons. How much of it has come in your direction?

A: We had death threats, all of us. We had to leave a number of times. I've got a daughter who's an anorexic because of this and another daughter suffers from nerves. What's happened to us I wouldn't...

...their names and pictures, and it was in every home office... There was nobody there that could help us. Every week I... tied this country. The police know I would stake my life on it, so all our sons were that I... was under pressure to arrest where... well, so will get you sued help with libel actions.

Luke Knight (left), Neil Acourt (partially obscured), David Norris (centre), Jamie Acourt (throwing punch) and Gary Dobson (back right) are pelted with eggs while leaving the inquiry last June into the police handling of the murder of Stephen Lawrence (top left)　PHOTOGRAPH PAUL HACKETT

Figure 7.7
Observer, 28 February 1999, p. 9. © *Guardian and Observer,* Trevor Phillips.

STEPHEN LAWRENCE

The aftermath A special report

'We're not racist but...'

The Stephen Lawrence report has prompted an agonising scrutiny of race relations in Britain. But already there are signs that complacency could overwhelm our response to the tragedy. Here, leading commentator and broadcaster **Trevor Phillips** opens a special Observer report with a challenge to those who in the past week have failed to acknowledge some of the country's deeply held racist attitudes

Neil Acourt, one of those originally accused of Stephen Lawrence's murder, leaves the Macpherson inquiry in defiant mood.   Photograph by Alex Sturrock

image of the murdered youth. Above all others, it was repeatedly used by the press, television and online web pages and news sites. As the story became a major public crisis, the press even used it as a kind of visual logo, either accompanying or inserted directly into the relevant page layout (see Figure 7.1). This need not, however, be seen as morally depleting or exhausting the meaning of the image. To again quote Susan Sontag, 'there are cases where repeated exposure to what shocks, saddens, appals does not use up a full-hearted response. Habituation is not automatic, for images (portable, insertable) obey different rules to real life. Representations of the Crucifixion do not become banal to believers. . . . Pathos, in the form of a narrative, does not wear out' (2003: 82–83).

The performative iconography of the press was not only populated symbolically by the 'sacred' Lawrences and 'profane' criminal suspects; it also encompassed a wider cast of public characters, many of them occupying more ambivalent or precarious moral positions. Sir Paul Condon, for example, had to publicly fight for his professional reputation as well as that of the Metropolitan Police, both of which had received unrelenting rebuke in the media. Symbolically, Sir Paul Condon was confronted by the sacred aura and elevated status now attached to the Lawrences and their cause, which drained the commissioner's own capacity to deploy strategic communicative power as well as the Met's formidable public relations capability (see Figure 7.8). Through its public mediatisation of the Lawrence case, the commissioner was symbolically positioned on the same terrain as the Lawrences and publicly obliged to address their agenda.

Not that all police officers were tarnished by the Metropolitan's increasing public disrepute. John Grieve, formerly head of the celebrated antiterrorist force of New Scotland Yard, had been appointed to root out racism in the Metropolitan Police Service. Significantly, and one suspects symbolically, his appointment had been made prior to the publication of the Macpherson inquiry, which was widely predicted to be highly critical of the Metropolitan Police. Through prominent press exposure, John Grieve arguably came to personify and symbolise the 'great white hope' for salvaging the damaged reputation of the Metropolitan Police Service (see Figure 7.9).

But it was the Lawrences, their supporters and legal team, and Doreen Lawrence above all, who had secured public recognition and respect, and who used this symbolic power to gain the ear of the powerful—and it was the powerful who were publicly obliged to be seen to be listening (see Figures 7.10 and 7.11).

Visual symbolisation played a key part in media performativity and in the public expression of generalised hopes and aspirations that had now become infused in the Stephen Lawrence story and sustained its enactment as a form of mediatised collective effervescence. The sense of communitas sustained by this media outpouring following the release of the Macpherson report rendered reports the next day of the vandalism of Stephen Lawrence's memorial stone all the more shocking (though it had been attacked on previous occasions). In this context, such an act could only be felt by most people as an act of desecration directed at Stephen Lawrence's name and the sense of moral solidarity to which his name had given rise. The *Guardian* registered the sense of depravity of this deliberate act against the new public mood on its front page (see Figure 7.12), and thereby contributed to a sense of Manichean struggle that would become even more palpable over the coming weeks and months.

Television Enactments: Constituting 'Civic Common Ground'

The failure of the private prosecution followed by the coroner's verdict had earlier granted the Stephen Lawrence case national prominence and led to the production of *The Stephen Lawrence Story*, a powerful documentary that aired twice on Channel Four in 1997. But it was not until the

Figure 7.8
Independent, 28 February 1999, p. 13. © *Independent*. Photo: Peter Macdiarmid.

FOCUS

Mission impossible

Sir Paul Condon has held onto his job by the skin of his teeth. But many, both inside and outside the police, believe that his position has been made untenable by the Stephen Lawrence inquiry. If he's failed to make the Met work in six years as Commissioner, how can he do it in the 11 months left before he retires?

BY KIM SENGUPTA

OVERLEAF
Stephen's legacy for multi-ethnic Britain, page 14; Copper who changed sides, page 15

The man who traps racist colleagues

BY JASON BENNETTO

Figure 7.9
Observer, 31 January 1999, p. 15. © *Guardian and Observer*, Mark Honigsbaum.

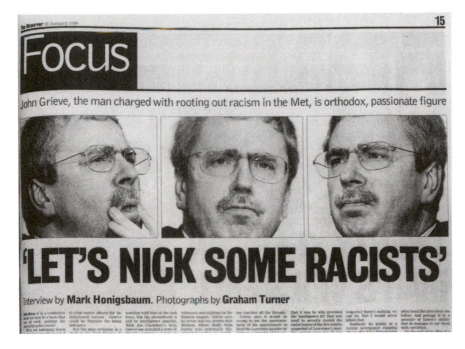

Figure 7.10
Observer, 28 February 1999, p. 11. © *Guardian and Observer*.

Figure 7.11
Guardian, 25 February 1999, p. 4. © *Guardian and Observer.*

government's instigation of the judicial inquiry that television took its belated cue to produce a stream of current affairs and documentary programmes, many of them scheduled to coincide with the release of the public inquiry report. Up until this point, the medium had followed the lead of the national press with news bulletins occasionally reporting key institutional developments, but otherwise declining to put its energies (and different programme forms) behind the growing public interest in the case.

As a national and non-party political medium, television addressed the Stephen Lawrence case through an imagined national middle ground and, unlike the press, held back from performatively enacting more politically engaged views or invoking particularised publics. Television's imagined audience was typically assumed by programme makers to occupy a 'civic common ground'. This was an imagined terrain of presumed national sentiments, common feelings and collective morality, united in its sense of outrage towards racist violence and the injustices at the heart of the Lawrence case. For the most part, television's presumed audience positioned in this civic common ground was white, irrespective of the particu-

Figure 7.12
Guardian, 26 February 1999, p. 1. © *Guardian and Observer.*

The trouble with Tim —
the man who knows
Sport99

Spike Lee tells a story
of racist murder
Friday Review

NEWSPAPER OF THE YEAR

The Guardian

45p
Friday
February 26 1999
Published in London
and Manchester
www.guardianunlimited.co.uk

White
paint
splattered
over the
memorial
to Stephen
Lawrence.
The racist
answer to
a new
beginning
for Britain

White paint splattered across Stephen Lawrence's memorial in Eltham yesterday. The racist vandals might have been caught on camera - but police had moved it elsewhere

Blunder follows blunder

Lawrence report list withdrawn after suspects sent informants' names

Jack Straw and Doreen Lawrence in Eltham yesterday

Racists deface memorial which was guarded by dummy camera

Stuart Millar

Reports, pages 4-6;
Decca Aitkenhead and
Duncan Campbell, page 22;
Leader comment and letters,
page 23

lar programmes and genres that addressed the case. These can be briefly described before we examine something of their distinctive, and characteristic, forms of expression.

Panorama, the BBC's flagship current affairs series, produced 'In Stephen's Name', (BBC1, 11.1.99, Producer Jay Hunt), which focussed on the struggle of Neville Lawrence and asked whether the police had learnt anything from the mistakes that had informed their investigation into his son's death. *Granada*'s 'The Murder of Stephen Lawrence' dramatised some of the key events in the Stephen Lawrence case with the help of actors and aired on ITV (18.2.99, Director Paul Greengrass). *The Colour of Justice,* Richard Norton-Taylor's acclaimed play reenacting key moments from the public inquiry transcripts, was also staged specially for BBC television and broadcast on the day before the Macpherson report was published (BBC2, 23.2.99).

National television news also increasingly reported on the various developments in the Macpherson inquiry, often with the help of filmed reconstructions and repeated use of television footage of the five suspects throwing punches and spitting with grimaced faces at the angry crowd when leaving the public inquiry. Television, like the press, repeatedly used these violent images, though not quite as often as they made use of the symbolic portrait of Stephen Lawrence that routinely featured as a background image in news presentations and studio discussions (see Figures 7.13 and 7.14). BBC2's *Newsnight* extended its normal running time and devoted two full sixty-minute programmes to the inquiry and Macpherson report (BBC2, 19.2.99 and 24.2.99) and included, as did ITN news, filmed reconstructions of Stephen Lawrence's murder and subsequent police investigations. News studio panels and audiences also featured in these more elaborate *Newsnight* programmes, which provided public fora for the deliberative engagement of different perspectives, arguments and points of view (see Figure 7.14).

On the day of the report's release, *Westminster* (BBC2, 24.2.99), the BBC's afternoon parliamentary coverage programme covered live, in full, and with breathless anticipation, both Prime Minister Tony Blair's and Home Secretary Jack Straw's statements in the House of Commons before moving to analyse with the help of a live studio discussion some of the key points of the report. Later that night, *Despatch Box* (BBC2, 24.2.99), the BBC's late-night parliamentary analysis programme, also focused on the release of the Macpherson report and, with the assistance of a *Daily Mail* editor, reviewed national newspaper front pages and their various stances towards the inquiry and its recommendations. *Question Time,* the BBC's popular audience/panel discussion programme hosted by Sir David Dimbleby, displaced the advertised programme following the release of the Macpherson report (BBC1, 25.2.99) and devoted its entire prime-time slot to 'The Lawrence Inquiry' (see Figure 7.15).

Figure 7.13
Newsnight, BBC2, 24 February 1999.

Figure 7.14
Newsnight, BBC2, 19 February 1999.

Figure 7.15
Question Time, BBC1, 25 February 1999.

Less prominent amongst the schedules was BBC2's *Black Britain* series
and its programme 'Why Stephen?' (20.2.99, Director Charles Wheeler),
which aired in the same week. Perhaps because of its target black audience,
this broadcast felt able to take a hard look at why, amongst countless other
racist attacks and murders, the case of Stephen Lawrence had attracted the
media spotlight and how it had produced such impetus for change. In the
course of the program, presenter Charles Wheeler deliberately referenced
racist killings in Britain as 'lynchings', and interviewed Marc Wadsworth
of the Anti-Racist Alliance (ARA). Wadsworth argued that the ARA had
consciously pitched the Stephen Lawrence case to the mainstream press, including the tabloids, as a way of summoning the support of middle England, whilst strenuously avoiding the media tag of black extremism—a
phenomenon that had diminished public support for the campaign following the murder of the black schoolboy Rolan Adams. Wheeler's program,
exceptionally, challenged some of the media myths that had grown around
the Lawrences and their fight for justice, and it critically examined the in-
herent racism of the media's own performance.

Six weeks after the release of the Macpherson report, Channel Four also
produced a media reflexive programme, *The Siege of Scotland Yard* (6.4.99,
Director Roger Graef). This documentary provided a rare fly-on-the-wall

view of the Metropolitan Police and the public relations battle that both the commissioner and his expanded team of public relations advisers had conducted whilst trying to ward off growing mediated criticism of the Met and the commissioner's own reputation.

This prolific, if long overdue, televisual presentation of the Stephen Lawrence story, then, took the case into people's homes and placed it into everyday media routines and familial and domestic contexts, and it did so in ways that perhaps only the medium of television can. 'Stephen Lawrence' had arrived 'home' and, for a time at least, was part of the everyday world of media consumption and televisual culture. Viewers were invited to witness the hurt and see the pain of the Lawrences and relate this to wider issues of injustice and the vexed questions of 'institutional racism'. By these same programme means, television also invited audiences to imagine themselves as part of a wider, multicultural society moving towards a more inclusive and less discriminatory future. Contending, sometimes challenging discourses about 'race', racism and British identity were presented from the televisual stage, and these pulsated through different programme forms and formats, some inviting wider deliberation of the issues addressed. Different journalism forms served to discharge this upsurge of public interest, emotional energy and debate. And some televisual forms, as we have already seen, also demonstrated critical reflexivity towards the media's own performance in this mediatised discharge of effervescence.

These programme forms enacted television's 'civic common ground' in characteristic ways. ITN, Britain's main provider of national and international television news for the commercial ITV network, at the height of the Macpherson inquiry chose, for example, to focus on the experiential and private torment of the Lawrences and how this had affected their marriage and led to their separation. This stance and focus was very different, for example, from BBC2's *Newsnight*, which characteristically led with a more interrogative and 'incredulous' line of questioning directed at the Metropolitan Police:

ITN News

Newscaster: Shiulie Ghosh has a special report on the tragedy that goes way beyond the killing of a black teenager.

Ghosh, reporter: Neville Lawrence is an intensely private man, but events have forced him into the public eye. Here in London he runs a trust in his son's name to help students of architecture, the profession Stephen had eventually wanted to join. . . . Everyday brings a bag load of mail from people all over the country who have been moved by their campaign for justice.

Neville Lawrence: My family was a private family and wasn't used to any kind of publicity; and it was very hard for me at first to understand what was happening for quite a long time because it was the death of one of my child. . . .

Doreen Lawrence: It still hasn't brought Stephen's killers to justice and they are still walking the streets.

Ghosh: It's been a long frustrating search for the truth for Neville and his wife Doreen but again and again the adjective used to describe them is dignified. Neville shrugs that off.

Neville Lawrence: For me, I feel that it is just a father trying to get to the truth and to learn exactly what happened regarding the loss of a child and I feel any other mother or father or family would do the same.

Ghosh: But the strain of the last few years has told on their marriage, though they both appear in public together, Neville and Doreen have now separated. Their friend and councillor, Ross Howell, says they have dealt with their grief in different ways . . .

Ros Howell: As a family, the bonding hasn't happened. The grief has not bonded them, yet. . . .

Reporter: The murder of Stephen Lawrence has captured the attention of the nation in a way that rarely happened before. Stephen has become a symbol for those who stand against injustice, violence and racism. There have been countless documentaries and in London a play about the public inquiry. With the inquiry report now published, the Lawrences can look to the future. Neville says he is trying to repair their relationship.

(*ITN News*, ITV, 24.2.99)

BBC2 *Newsnight*

Presenter Jeremy Paxman: Good evening. There's been no more disturbing public inquiry in recent years than that into how a gang of white racists stabbed to death an innocent black teenager waiting at a bus stop in South London in 1993. The scenes at that inquiry, the swaggers of the young suspects, the defiance of black Muslims, the unprecedented apology from the police have thrown light on a side of British life that we'd all prefer to forget. Tonight we're going to explore what this inquiry has told us about ourselves with the Assistant Commissioner who says he can't think of a murder inquiry that has been as badly handled as this one, with Stephen Lawrence's father and with black and white policemen talking about whether the police are intrinsically racist and with others who have experienced racism at first hand. . . . Assistant Commissioner, can you think of a murder investigation that the Met has handled worse than they have handled the Stephen Lawrence investigation?

Assistant Commissioner Ian Johnston: Um, no I can't but then neither can I think of a murder investigation that has been subject to such rigorous, and proper, examination . . .

Presenter: Now, your apology to the Lawrence family, was that an apology for incompetence or for racism?

Assistant Commissioner: Um, it was an apology in essence for not giving them the type of service that they expect from the Metropolitan police . . .

Presenter: How many people have been disciplined for incompetence shown during that investigation?

Assistant Commissioner: Well, right, as you know the majority of the senior investigating officers, in fact all the investigating officers have retired because this was a case in 1993–1995, some five years ago.

(*Newsnight*, BBC2, 19.2.99)

BBC1's *Question Time* (25.2.99) enacted the same civic common ground but did so through its populist variant of a public arena. This elicited, rather than led with, forthright views from a selected panel of speakers, which included the black editor of the *Voice*, Annie Stewart, all in front of a selected studio audience. The programme began as follows:

Question Time

David Dimbleby: Good evening, welcome to this special edition of *Question Time,* and whether you are watching on television or watching this worldwide on the Internet. The Macpherson report into the murder of Stephen Lawrence wants us all to change, white or black, in or out of the criminal justice system. Tonight we have a specially invited panel and audience here to discuss the issues raised by it.

(*Question Time*, BBC1, 25.2.99)

Question Time provided a forum for the public display and discussion of some of the issues raised in the report, as well as for criticisms of some of the views of the programme's invited speakers. The first public release of the Macpherson report had failed to conceal the identities of witnesses promised anonymity at the inquiry, who were still listed in the report's appendices. Glen Smyth, chair of the Police Federation and one of the *Question Time* panelists, sought to argue that this was very similar to the 'innocent mistakes' made by the investigating officers working on the Stephen Lawrence case, a point of view publicly rebutted by a member of the studio audience:

Glen Smyth: It just shows you how an innocent mistake can have massive repercussions. . . . [I]ts very similar to . . . the Stephen Lawrence inquiry.

Studio audience member: I think it's a bit rich coming from the Police Federation to now try and twist this issue and say that this somehow explains their behaviour during the Lawrence inquiry. . . . This is what the Police Federation and the Metropolitan Police have been attempting to do for the last two days (applause).

A little later on, the editor of the *Voice* questioned the informing assumption at the heart of the Macpherson report as well as the *Question Time* agenda, namely, that the presumed white readership was shocked by the report's 'revelations', which were hardly new to the black community:

David Dimbleby: Annie Stewart, can we come back to the point about predominantly black and Asian areas and the policing of them. . . .

Annie Stewart: I don't think it will be harder for the police. The majority of black people are decent honest citizens and we don't want criminals lying about on the streets of London. We want to live in a society whereby it's fair and just . . . The report is telling us what we live! We live this every day. What I think has happened is that it has opened the eyes of the wider white society to what is going on, and I do really think that we need to move this debate forward.

On Channel Four, *The Siege of Scotland Yard* publicly revealed the public relations battle that had been carefully waged from inside the Met at the height of the Macpherson inquiry. As it did so, it revealed the tactical moves discussed by Sir Paul Condon and his media advisors attempting to manage the growing public criticism now being directed at the chief constable and the metropolitan police. This form of documentary provided, then, rare insights into the inner sanctum of the metropolitan police and its public relations strategy, which was composed in a moment of mounting pressure.

Narrator: The core issue is simple, the commissioner accepted that there were racists in the Met, but he resisted the term 'institutional racism', he believed it labelled all 26,000 officers. Now he must accept the report which is expected to include a new definition of institutional racism. But can he avoid the humiliation of retracting his earlier words? His credibility is at stake.

Sir Paul Condon: I, and we, have challenged some of the definitions of institutional racism. . . .

Superintendent Sarah Thornton, Lawrence Inquiry Response Team: I'm not sure how we can maintain the current line given the report's finding on institutional racism, but I also think to try and deflect it on to the rest of society will unravel. And that would be my fear with the line that you are suggesting, and it will sound either grudging or in denial, and that's the difficulty with it. And that then becomes the focus, you know 'Met guilty of racism' and there's an argument about it, rather than 'Met guilty of racism' and we've got to try and move on.

(*The Siege of Scotland Yard*, Channel Four, 6.4.99)

These different television programmes, then, publicly enacted the Stephen Lawrence story at the height of the institutional and judicial redress phase, doing so in and through the available forms of television journalism. These gave characteristic televisual expression—by way of display, discourse and deliberation—to this moment of extensive and intensive public introspection on the nature of British society and questions of 'race', racism and identity. They also constituted this moment, as in-

dicated, on the basis of an imagined 'civic common ground'. This imagined public space was typically both oriented from, and spoke to, a white
perspective on the problems raised by the Macpherson report. It was
white England that was principally addressed in and through the medium
of television, and it was television that sought to give expression to widespread concerns about how the British criminal justice system, and the
police particularly, could have been so publicly and devastatingly found
wanting.

The Stephen Lawrence Story Goes International

As the Stephen Lawrence case became a mediatised public crisis in the mainstream British media, it became mediated through the full panoply of journalistic forms. This also included the internet. Mainstream news providers,
including the BBC and the *Guardian*, for example, produced their own web
pages with sections devoted to the Stephen Lawrence case and with easy access to summaries of earlier news reports. Minority and alternative sites also
disseminated information and commentary on the Stephen Lawrence case,
avoiding mainstream editorial positions and control. Blink, the Black Information Link, for example, carried all the transcripts of the Macpherson inquiry and received 60,000 hits on the day of its publication. Far-right political
organisations such as the National Front and the British National Party sought
to counter the 'media hysteria' and 'media circus' to which the Stephen
Lawrence case had given rise. By such means, the Stephen Lawrence case and
its public articulation was both extended by mainstream media providers and
simultaneously circumvented by alternative, minority and extremist perspectives. 'Stephen Lawrence', evidently, no longer belonged to a particular perspective or political project, or any one medium of communication.

The Stephen Lawrence story also radiated geopolitically outwards. International newspapers, especially those based in countries and regions
with strong British connections, picked up on the case. As they did so, the
story inevitably became inflected or appropriated by different cultural identities, social interests and political agendas. Scotland's press, for example,
reported the main developments in the case, occasionally prompting reflection on Scotland's own situation: SHADOW OF RACISM HANGS OVER
SCOTS POLICE FORCES (*Scotsman*, 4.3.99). It also mentioned the case in respect to similar racist murders: 'Three people were arrested with the murder of Surjit Singh Chhokar . . . yet nobody has been convicted of the
killing . . . racial sensitivities had been heightened by the inquiry report into
the murder of black teenager Stephen Lawrence' (*Scotsman*, 20.3.99).
Northern Ireland's *Belfast Telegraph* also sought out possible parallels as
well as personnel with an Irish connection—RAP FOR ULSTER EX-MET OF-
FICER (*Belfast Telegraph*, 25.2.99)—but went further in its use of the
Lawrence case to interpret its own political violence:

The Voice of Westminster

Des McCartan

The murder of Stephen Lawrence in London and the gruesome brutal paramilitary attack on an Armagh woman may not, at first sight, have a lot in common. But both, in their respective spheres of violence, are motivated by the reality that an endemic hatred exists within their communities.

(*Belfast Telegraph*, 25.2.99)

The Australian press (*Sydney Morning Herald, Courier-Mail, Age, Advertiser, Australian, Daily Telegraph*), given its strong readership connection to Britain, reported the Lawrence story in culturally consonant ways, deferring mainly to the known public details of the case. The Canadian press, in contrast, was less deferential and took the opportunity to voice a more independent view:

Race Murder Rocks U.K.

Matthew Fisher

. . . The British take on race relations has always been a little absurd. Britain is the nation which perfected maritime imperialism and the slave trade and which has latterly become infamous for religious mayhem in the province of Northern Ireland and for its black- and Arab-hating soccer hooligans.

But there it is. Countries which are hyper-critical of other countries often have trouble acknowledging how deeply screwed up they may be about some things themselves.

(*Toronto Sun*, 10.7.98, 5)

The U.S. press exhibited closer links to the UK but evidently felt the need to translate the Stephen Lawrence case into terms that would immediately be recognised by their readership:

Black Anger at British Police Abuse Boils Over

Sarah Lyall

. . . For years, black and Asian Britons have complained about what they see as overt and tacit police racism, and except at times of particular upheaval—like during race riots in Brixton in 1981—no one in authority in Britain has paid much attention.

But in the last few months, the issue has been at the forefront of the country's consciousness. . . . The impetus for all this is the six-year-old case of Stephen Lawrence . . . 'Rodney King without the video'.

(*New York Times*, 22.2.99, 3)

Newspapers in China and India, for their part, exhibiting historical and diasporic connections, tended to reflect on how their own communities fared in Britain and in respect to the culture of racism publicly revealed through the Lawrence inquiry:

Chinese Enter Racism Debate

Simon Macklin

At a belated Lunar New Year reception in north London last weekend, most of the attention was centred on who had won the lucky draw but the streets outside bore evidence to an uglier issue which has been preoccupying Britain. . . . Most of the attention has focused on the relationship between the police and the country's black community but the ethnic Chinese community is increasingly being drawn into the debate.

(*South China Morning Post*, 2.3.99, 17)

Intolerance Universal

. . . India is not the only country where intolerance is practised. Discrimination, hatred, violence and murders are openly perpetrated on the minorities in the U.K. However, the minority situation there is not based on religion or caste, but on colour. . . . While it is comforting that in debating the religious intolerance, particularly the murders of Christians, in India, Britain has not taken a holier-than-thou attitude, India should take steps to draw attention in the Lok Sabha to the harassment, intimidation and murder in the U.K. of citizens of Indian origin.

(*The Hindu*, 3.3.99)

In such ways as these, then, the Stephen Lawrence case circumnavigated the globe and, as symbol, collected further cultural layers of meaning and was put to work in other peoples' causes and concerns. At the heart of all these different semiotic and political layers of meaning grafted onto the symbol of Stephen Lawrence, however, resided a common core, which centred on issues of 'racism', cultural identity and struggles for social inclusion. Such was the signifying power of the Stephen Lawrence symbol and story now registered in disparate outlets of the world's global media.

SUMMARY

The Macpherson inquiry, without doubt, was a high-level, state-sanctioned institutional and judicial response that accurately mirrored Turner's ideas about the 'redress' stage within a social drama. This government-authorised and officially controlled inquiry proved to be momentous, both in terms of its initial impact on public debate and discussion and also on subsequent policy formation. It is doubtful whether it would have been authorised at all if the media had not earlier animated wider public sentiments and unease about the case, which had built through the earlier mediatised phase of mounting crisis. The institutional phase of redress was then publicised and visualised in the media spotlight, and its emotional charge was thereby extended across society and even radiated outwards to countries around the world. But clearly the media did much more than this. They enacted the drama, discharged the intense emotions, steered the flows of moral pollution, displayed the symbols and deliberated the difficult issues raised by the inquiry. And, importantly, they summoned and directed both the emotional and moral force of the case outwards, and downwards, into society. They served, in other words, to energise and give shape and substance to the collective effervescence and communitas unleashed by this public moment of ritualised redress. A new 'emotional mood', a new 'structure of feeling', a new 'cultural habitus' had been created, which structured the form, and possibilities, of enacted politics.

Status elevation and status reversal, to use Turner's terms, were also clearly evident in the public performances and symbolism that helped constitute this liminal moment 'outside' of the normal strictures and structures of institutional, hierarchical power. High-energy symbols took up position on sacred moral high ground, and signs of moral depravity possessed the 'profane' moral low ground, but all entered with affective force and cultural resonance into the public drama that threatened, symbolically at least, the moral centre of society—and which thereby challenged the strategic deployments of communicative action by powerful vested interests.

Social solidarity became rearticulated and reworked with respect to (white) society's shameful secrets concerning racist murders and violent assaults in British society, as well as the racism embedded in some of its core institutions. Mediatised, the Macpherson inquiry unleashed an avalanche of cultural reflection and reflexivity that uncovered the stain of British racism and prompted, experientially as well as deliberatively, a moral solidarity based on declared commitments to change. Media performativity collectively enacted this latest stage in the unfolding story of Stephen Lawrence, and it also invested it subjunctively with hope and generalised ambitions for the future. But where could, and where would, these cultural flows of energy and moral collectivity go next?

Eight

Reintegration/Schism

The final phase I distinguish either as reintegration of the disturbed social group or of the social recognition and legitimization of irreparable schism between the contending parties.
Victor Turner, *Dramas, Fields, Metaphors* (1974, 41)

The release of the Macpherson report, as we have seen, was accompanied by an outpouring of mediatised cultural effervescence, which remained palpable for a considerable time and helped to sustain the momentum for redressive action. It also contributed to the production of a lasting legacy in Stephen Lawrence's name. But did it lead to 'reintegration' or lasting 'schism'? In one sense, it would be unrealistic to presume that the Stephen Lawrence case, or any other event, could single-handedly overturn the fractured realities, identities and inequalities of 'race' and racism in British society. Even so, it is beyond doubt that the Lawrence case unleashed widespread changes at the level of public policy, organizational behaviour and institutional practices, which can clearly be documented (see Appendix 4). These responses are both real and extensive, and they cannot be dismissed as of little consequence or as mere palliatives for ingrained realities of 'race' and racism. In its mediatisation and performative enactment, the Lawrence case contributed in meaningful ways to cultural shifts in multicultural sensibility and improved social understanding of continuing racial inequalities and racism in British society. In these important respects, the British field of race relations was certainly reconfigured by the Stephen Lawrence case. Our focus here is principally on the media and its continuing contribution to these dynamics of institutional and cultural change in the post-redress phase.

This chapter explores how the media followed up on their earlier performance and continued to breathe life into the story as Macpherson's seventy recommended reforms made their way into policy and processes of legislative enactment. As we shall see, this momentum was not only sustained through institutional reportage now referencing political as well as criminal justice arenas but was enacted also on the basis of the cultural effervescence that appeared to spark off similar issues in the media sphere. 'Stephen Lawrence' was now, so to speak, in the 'cultural air', oxygenating news events and fuelling them with added significance and meaning. This helped to sustain public expectations that the momentum of redressive action would keep moving forward and did so as the media often sought to revitalise public solidarities performed earlier.

Turner's discerned stages of social drama have thus far helped to chart, in broad terms, the institutional developments and cultural dynamics characterising the progression of the Stephen Lawrence story as it moved through time and space. But the various twists and turns of the case, as we would expect from the complication of social forces at work and cultural identities at play, have also demonstrated more complexity than Turner's schema. Each phase not only built on the momentum of the preceding ones, but also condensed 'mini-phases' within themselves. The phase of judicial and institutional redress, for example, built on the earlier momentum of mounting crisis, but so, too, did it produce its own breaches of public trust that led to further potential crises that threatened to delay or otherwise discredit the political centre's moment of symbolic redress. These included the public challenge posed to Sir William Macpherson as inquiry chair; the premature leaking of the report followed by the home secretary's attempts to rectify this through a court injunction; and the incompetent inclusion of 'protected' witnesses' names in the first publication of the report. The redress stage also condensed within itself the beginnings of Turner's reintegration/schism phase in that it simultaneously served to symbolise processes of healing directed at the public wound that had opened up around the name and symbol of Stephen Lawrence. No less than the prime minister of the day and leaders of all major political parties had publicly acknowledged the shame and the hurt of the Stephen Lawrence case and collectively pledged their support to bring about meaningful change. This same phase had also, of course, promised more practical forms of reintegration based on Macpherson's extensive list of recommendations (see Appendix 4).

Following the announcement by the prime minister and home secretary in the House of Commons on 24 February 1999, the Labour government embarked on turning Macpherson's seventy recommendations, and some of its own, into policy over subsequent weeks and months. Meanwhile, on the basis of established public interest, the media continued to performatively enact the Stephen Lawrence story, often seeking out new angles and engineering new developments. The collective effervescence generated pre-

viously, both within and without the media, was too socially and emotionally charged to be ignored, and it was on this basis that the media continued to represent the Stephen Lawrence story as a watershed in British
race relations. This did not, however, preclude some sections of the media
challenging the pace of reform or the validity of the concept of 'institutional racism', or even refuting claims of widespread police racism. But the
mainstream media nevertheless evidently felt obligated to a deeper collective sense of 'society,' one now in need of repair after its bruising from the
Stephen Lawrence case. Following the political centre's acknowledgement
of the Lawrences' cause and the legitimacy of their expressed grievances,
this was a necessary collective project if British civil society was once again
to take for granted an image of itself, though mythical, as a place of even-
handed justice and social inclusion protected, rather than undermined, by
the forces of law and order.

MEDIA, MORALITY, MOMENTUM

In order for the Stephen Lawrence story to continue to discharge moral
effects (and affect) after the cultural flooding that followed the Macpherson report, the story needed to find renewed momentum. It needed, as far
as the media were concerned, somewhere else to go. As it turned out, the
moral energy and momentum of the Stephen Lawrence story was boosted
from unexpected quarters in the weeks and months following the release
of the Macpherson report.

Sacred Society's 'Other' Profane Racism

The public odium directed at the five suspects offered one possible route
for further media exploration—or exploitation. In their public pillorying,
the suspects represented an index of the continuing sense of collective moral
grievance within society. Unsurprisingly, given their previous behaviour
and display of racist attitudes caught on video, considerable controversy
erupted when ITV launched its new populist current affairs series, *Tonight*,
hosted by Trevor Macdonald, and announced that the first programme
would be devoted to exclusive interviews with the five prime suspects—
their first television interviews. This produced vociferous media comment
both prior to and following the broadcast and prompted the programme's
producer to respond to the gauged public mood by stating that the interviews by Martin Bashir would be 'tough, searching and unremittingly hostile' (*Guardian*, 3.4.99, 7). The programme also carefully made use once
again of previously circulated film images of the suspects, clearly signalling
its intention not to assist in their bid for public rehabilitation. It opened as
follows:

Tonight exclusive interviews with murder suspects in the Stephen Lawrence case. For the first time their conflicting evidence on the night, (Suspect: "It doesn't look too good on the face of it; no it doesn't"); for the first time their fascination with knives and violence (Suspect: "I never used the kosh, I had it in my hand"); and for the first time their extreme racism (Martin Bashir: "Am I what you would call a Paki?" Suspect: "Well some people would call you a Paki, Martin, yes"). In agreeing to speak to us, clearly they had their own reasons: perhaps they were hoping to change public perceptions and counter these images of a swaggering gang, arrogant and defiant. (Images of suspects entering and leaving the public inquiry) . . . We wanted to submit them to the interrogation they've never had and shed more light on what really happened on the night Stephen was killed. . . . [U]nlike the public inquiry no questions were off limits.

(*Tonight*, ITV, 8.4.99)

In the *Daily Mail*, the article A DISGRACE TO BRITISH TELEVISION (9.4.99, 10) condemned the programme as a 'tawdry, demeaning stunt' and an 'affront both to viewers and justice', a point of view shared by the *Voice* in TRUTH OR TRASH? (12.4.99, 9), which argued, 'The Stephen Lawrence case may have been the worst piece of incompetence in the history of the Metropolitan Police but it has also exposed investigative journalism to be, at best, a makeover for celebrity'. Similar views were widely expressed by much of the press: LAWRENCE 'STUNT' LEAVES NASTY TASTE (*Independent*, 9.4.99, 7); HOW THE TRASH LET THEIR TRUE COLOURS SHOW (*Daily Mirror*, 11.4.99, 25); SELF-SERVING SUSPECTS AND FRANTIC WANNABE TV. WHAT A SPECTACLE (*Guardian*, 9.4.99, 20); JUSTICE—NOT JERRY SPRINGER (*Observer*, 11.4.99, 30).

Through this reflexivity, then, the media continued to performatively enact the moral mood of society and threw into sharp relief the widespread opprobrium that now publicly surfaced towards sacred society's 'Other': profane racism. The mythical centre of enlightened society—invoked and given political substance when leaders of all major political parties acknowledged the hurt and injustice of the Stephen Lawrence case—summoned into being a common cause against morally indefensible acts of violent racism and racists. This sacred centre was mythical not in the sense that it was a deliberate distortion, entirely without foundation or untrue, but rather that it constituted an imaginary discursive place underpinning assumptions about the nature of democratic society, its freedoms and equalities. This mythic centre, hitherto for the most part implicit to much public discourse, had now been forced through the thick crust of institutional denial and media complacency towards racism, and was being subjected to public criticism and moral evaluation—in the full glare of the nation's media.

The collective sentiments publicly stirred by the extensive mediatisation of the Macpherson inquiry also provided a powerful cultural ambience that could envelop new developments. This cultural energy was principally sustained by widespread anticipation of thoroughgoing reforms and disbelief that the political centre could in fact deliver on its pledges. But the Stephen Lawrence story also found an additional infusion of moral energy from an unexpected source, which manifested itself when sinister forces of violent racism appeared to attack the sacred idea of society in a backlash deliberately targeting the new subjunctive mood. Up until this point the locus of public odium against violent racism had been focused for the most part through the 'profane' images of the five prime suspects, recycled time and again. It was these images, discussed previously, which had helped to personify and literally 'embody' racism within the media's collective representations. Importantly, the more diffuse processes, practices and outcomes of institutional racism had proved much more difficult for the media to represent or symbolise—though Sir Paul Condon's public appearances had, on occasion, risked being represented as the face of the Met's institutional resistance to change, if not institutional racism. The desecration of Stephen Lawrence's memorial stone earlier, filmed at the height of the cultural flooding of the nation's media, had also seemed a deeply sacrilegious act at the time and lacerated the new public mood. But even this didn't compare with the dramatic shock that befell the new subjunctive mood when a nail bomb exploded in a bustling Brixton market, a centre of black culture in London, injuring thirty-nine people on 18 April 1999.

The media immediately suspected a racist backlash: 'The Brixton bomb was probably the work of racist thugs' (*Sun*, 19.4.99, 4). This view was seemingly placed on firmer ground when claims of responsibility were reported to have been made by far-right extremist groups: MIRACLE ESCAPE AS COMBAT 18 CLAIM BOMB (*Daily Mirror*, 20.4.99, 1). When further bomb explosions followed in the East End of London nine days later, the perception and fear of a racist backlash was now firmly embedded: RACE TERRORISM FEAR AS BOMB BLASTS EAST END (*Independent*, 25.4.99, 1); BOMBER PICKS TARGETS TO SPREAD RACE TERROR (*Times*, 25.4.99). Confronted by such assaults on society and its sacred revitalization, the press united in moral condemnation and closed ranks once again against the racists. 'Communitas', according to Turner, 'tends to be inclusive. . . . This drive to inclusivity makes for proselytization' (1982, 51). So it did in the British media:

Voice of the Mirror: Together We Can Defeat Racist Thugs

Extremist bigots want to unleash a race war on the streets of Britain. They must not be allowed to succeed with their sick plan. The bomb blasts in the East End of London on Saturday and in Brixton nine days ago have shocked the nation. . . . The overwhelming majority of British people are justly proud of the multi-cultural society in which we live. Racism can be beaten. The racists can be made outcasts from society. Working together we can build a better Britain.

(Daily Mirror, 26.4.99, 6)

What the Bombers Want

Two bomb explosions in London's multi-ethnic communities in consecutive weekends are clearly calculated to spread fear, arouse suspicion and incite racial tension. The injuries of passers-by are a means to that end. If we are to defeat the bombers, it follows that we must do all we can to deny them their real ambition, which is to destabilize good race relations. Their aim is to turn Londoners against themselves and replace neighbourliness by neighbourhood wars. However long it takes to catch them, they must not succeed.

(Sunday Times, 25.4.99)

These immediate press responses to the bombings demonstrate how the news media were in fact caught up in the liminal sense of expectation generated with the release of the Macpherson report, and how this informed their interpretation of new events—cognitively, emotionally and morally. The generalised climate of fear of racist violence also found more personalised expression in the tabloids when it was reported that Martin Bashir, the interviewer of the five suspects for *Tonight*, had received racist death threats aimed at both himself and his family: MARTIN FEARS FOR HIS LIFE . . . AND HIS FAMILY, HE IS GOING THROUGH A TERRIBLE TIME (*Daily Mirror*, 11.5.99, 7). At the time, such developments served to produce a renewed sense of communitas and a united press front against violent racism in defense of society. The sacred idea of society unleashed in public responses to the Macpherson report was now seemingly producing its antithesis when the forces of white racism, normally invisible to white society, crawled out from under their stone. This tightened even further the sense of moral collectivity enacted by the media who positioned violent racists as sacred society's 'Other'. When a third bomb killed three people in the Admiral Duncan pub in Soho, a place frequented by members of the gay community, the presumption that a racist conspiracy was responsible or that this was a backlash aimed specifically at the new Macpherson public mood was weakened. Over a year later in July 2000, David Copeland, who declared that he was a 'righteous messenger from God', was sentenced to six life sentences for the bombings. While he stated that he had aimed to 'start a race and homophobic war', he had in fact acted alone and did not claim to have been responding to the Stephen Lawrence case (*Guardian*, 1.7.2000).

Caught up within, and actively performing, the liminal sense of expectation unleashed by the Macpherson report, the press had responded to these bombings in ways that seemingly endorsed the sacred idea of society at the very moment that it was presumed to be under assault. This 'Other' of violent racism was pathologised and depicted as irrational and amoral. In such dramatic ways, this media depiction of racism could only remind white society of the (in)human face of racist violence and its horrific consequences, but it thereby distanced ideas of institutional racism as a seemingly more diffuse, opaque and, in these respects at least, 'less real' phenomenon.

The Agency of Moral Sentiments

The moral force of the Stephen Lawrence story enacted by the media that generated a public sense of moral concern and communitas was available for further media mobilization. Previously expressed moral sentiments could thereby easily be put to work. Continuing racist violence and accounts of police racism in this cultural climate could only generate widespread media condemnation:

Voice of the Mirror: Race Hatred That Shames Our Nation

SOME crimes are so appalling that they defy comprehension. The murder of former paratrooper Ben Kamenalagi is one such crime. . . . [His attackers] shouted racist abuse as Ben lay defenceless and dying. . . . [B]lack police advisors at the scene of the Paddington rail crash . . . claim to have suffered extreme and continuous racial abuse from officers. . . . [T]hey raise the deeply worrying possibility that some of the police in London have yet to learn the lessons of the Stephen Lawrence debacle.

(*Daily Mirror*, 16.10.99, 6)

The Met's Shame

. . . The Met is supposedly committed to ridding itself of the 'institutional racism' uncovered by the enquiry into the case of Stephen Lawrence. But the force's own race relations advisors say they were abused by officers at the Paddington rail disaster. . . . Post-Lawrence, the Met is supposed to be a new, open, inclusive force. Right now it looks mired in racism, and firmly stuck in the past.

(*Guardian*, 17.10.99, 28)

The moral force of the Stephen Lawrence case, then, became a player in the contests and conflicts played out in his name, and this extended to the political party arena. When William Hague, leader of the Conservative opposition, argued later that year that the Macpherson inquiry had in fact damaged police morale and led to less vigorous policing in black areas and a consequent rise in black crime, he badly underestimated both the longevity and potency of the public sentiments surrounding the Stephen Lawrence case. His intervention immediately brought forth widespread media condemnation, and eddies of moral pollution once again began to swirl: Mr Hague Has Shredded His Credibility with This Cynical and Disgraceful Speech (*Independent*, 15.12.2000, 3); Voice of the Mirror: Shame of a Tory Leader at new low (*Daily Mirror*, 15.12.2000, 6); How Hague mugged Macpherson (*Guardian*, 15.12.2000, 3). Even the right-wing Sunday tabloid *News of the World* felt compelled to come out against Hague's transgression of the public mood:

Have You No Shame, Hague?

Sion Simon

Hague's initial reaction to the inquiry into police mishandling of Stephen Lawrence's murder was that all decent people would feel 'shame and disgust' . . . and that we must 'build a nation in which every citizen, regardless of colour and creed, is treated with justice and respect'. . . . By last week all he cared about was getting maximum numbers of the death-or-glory Tory blue-rinse brigade to pull on their surgical stockings and do it for him one more time.

The reason it's called 'playing the racist card' is that Hague's outburst was nothing to do with whether the police are racist. . . . By alleging that the Macpherson report has 'contributed directly to a collapse of police morale and recruitment and has led to a crisis on our streets', Hague was sending a coded signal to all those retired colonels and old maids who might, just, save his bacon next year.

He was appealing to their basest instincts.

(7.12.2000, 11)

The *Daily Mail* had in fact adopted the same line as William Hague some time earlier under the headline Muggings Soar as Lawrence Case Criticisms 'Paralyze' Police (15.5.99, 18), but even the *Daily Mail* had reported, in the wake of Macpherson, sympathetically on the continuing horrors of violent racist assaults and murders: Why We Have To Go On Fighting for Justice For Our Murdered Son: In A Moving Account, The Father of Asian Waiter Surjit Chhokar, Explains his Family's Torment (16.6.99, 12).

Police actions were also more likely to incur media wrath in reports of further police incompetence and racism in their dealings with blacks, and all the more so when the police were so crass as to assault the sacred aura that continued to publicly envelop Neville Lawrence: Neville Lawrence—

I Thought the Police Had Got Better . . . Until I Was Stopped Because I'm Black; Grieving Neville Lawrence on His New Agony
(*Daily Mirror*, 5.2.2000, 8). The aura that surrounded Doreen Lawrence
was also reanimated through her continuing association with Nelson Mandela, who pledged support in their 'battle for compensation from Scotland
Yard' (see Figure 8.1).

Sections of the press, then, continued to performatively enact the new
subjunctive mood and championed new cases thought to demonstrate parallels with the Stephen Lawrence case. The *Guardian* reported on the case
of Ricky Reel: The police said he had fallen into the river and
drowned but Ricky Reel's mother is determined to prove he was
the victim of a racial killing (*Guardian*, 12.7.99, 4). The case even-

Figure 8.1
Guardian, 30 June 2000, p.7. © *Guardian and Observer.*

tuated in further criticism of the Met: Jury's rejection of Met claims
that Asian student's death was an accident applauded by family
(*Guardian*, 9.11.99, 1). The *Independent* performatively went further. It
picked up and championed a story over many months about two black men
in the small town of Telford who had apparently committed suicide (or
been lynched), and showed how, as in the Stephen Lawrence case, police
responses were less than determined and seemed not to consider the possibility that racism could be at the heart of the case. When the
Independent's suspicions concerning the case were subsequently found to
be unproven, however, the newspaper found it necessary to publicly explain its actions to both its readers and media critics the *Sun* and *Daily
Mail*:

It Is Our Job to Ask Questions

The purpose of *The Independent*'s reporting of these cases was never to
assert definitely that the men were murdered, or that they were the victims of a racially motivated lynch-mob. But there was enough doubt about
the speedy presumptions of suicide to require a fuller police investigation.

There was also the possibility that, despite the recent lessons of the
Stephen Lawrence case, the police in Telford had been insufficiently sensitive to the concerns of the family of the men simply because they were
black.

(*Independent*, 3.4.2000, 3)

The case is illustrative of the determination of some sections of the press
to performatively carry through the new subjunctive mood, with its implicit public mandate to expose continuing institutional racism and acts of
racist violence. Even the *Daily Mail* was not immune from this new found
sense of commitment, notwithstanding its criticisms of the *Independent*:
Lynched? . . . Could This Young Black Student Have Been the Victim of A Mob Execution In A Surrey Park? (6.9.99, 16). The *Times*,
though also caught up in the increased sensitivity to reporting racist attacks
and murders, nonetheless sought to use such occasions to congratulate
rather than condemn the role of the police while also challenging the validity of the concept of 'institutional racism':

Manhunt After New 'Lawrence Stabbing'

Tim Reid

The family of a black student were traveling from France to be at his hospital bedside in London yesterday as police investigated how he was
stabbed in an attack that bears striking similarities to the murder of

Stephen Lawrence. . . . In a vivid demonstration of the profound effect of Lord Macpherson of Cluny's damning report on the Lawrence investigation, more than 40 officers were on the scene within ten minutes of being alerted early on Saturday. The next day hundreds of officers took part in door-to-door inquiries and a traffic check.

(*Times*, 28.9.99)

Lawrence Casts a Dark Shadow Over Peckham

Magnus Linklater

Ethnic murders now invariably lead to accusations of police racism.

So deeply embedded is the Stephen Lawrence case in our national conscience that any attack on a black youth instantly raises the spectre of racism. The way police handle the murder of Damilola Taylor, the 10-year-old Nigerian boy stabbed to death in London on Tuesday evening, will inevitably be judged in the light of the Lawrence report, though here, at first glance, it is institutional neglect rather than institutional racism that is to blame. . . . [I]t [institutional racism] is a phrase . . . that has proved to be, in many ways, counter productive—a barrier to race relations rather than an aid. It is a blunderbuss description. It brands a whole police force with a collective taint of guilt.

(*Times*, 30.11.2000)

Clearly, acts of racist violence summoned a shared sense of moral collectivity and outrage, both in respect to the actual victims of assault and also in the perceived attack upon the sacred idea of society. While the press as a collectivity was both responding to and enacting the new public mood, each paper also sought to differentiate itself in the competitive media and wider political fields. As they did so, they summoned particularised publics differently aligned towards Macpherson's and the New Labour government's agenda of reforms. This then began to undermine the press and public solidarity manufactured at the height of the cultural flooding unleashed by Macpherson in the redress phase.

Press Performance as Calendrical Ritual

Victor Turner in his discussion of ritual observed how liminality can often inhere within seasonal and calendrical events, but also how communitas can seldom be sustained for long, given its tendency to generate new social norms and structures (1982). The performative commitment of the press to enact, and thereby sustain, the liminal quality (and potentiality) of the new subjunctive mood was demonstrated one year after the release of the Macpherson report. The Lawrence family's supporters had recognised the symbolic and political value of anniversaries from the outset of their campaign, publicly marking Stephen Lawrence's birthday and the day of his murder, and holding torch-lit vigils and remembrance ceremonies. This had variously helped to win media publicity for their cause. During this period, sections of the media themselves inaugurated their own calendrical ritual, which was used as a further means of performatively maintaining the momentum for change.

Exactly a year after the publication of the Macpherson report, sections of the press enacted this as a ritual public occasion—a 'time-out' to comment on what had changed in the twelve months since the release of this 'historic' report and to evaluate the pace and depth of the reform process. This, too, was performed by the press in characteristic ways. The *Guardian*, for example, performatively made full use of its front page, juxtaposing a saintly portrait of Doreen Lawrence and her expressed feelings, as well as the hard-hitting headline POLICE RACE FAILURES EXPOSED based on the paper's own recruitment survey of ethnic minority police officers, timed to coincide with the anniversary. It also used biting satire in the form of a cartoon to underline claims about continuing police racism (see Figure 8.2). The cartoonist, Austin, depicts a police officer holding a copy of police recruitment statistics saying, 'We had one Black applicant but he fell down stairs'.

Press performativity also encompassed reflexivity towards questions of identity in multicultural Britain at the end of the millennium. Like most anniversaries, this was as much a result of the felt need to reassert solidarities and identities of the present as to remember those of the past. But the news media, especially those positioned by market ecology and professional commitments to responsible news journalism and objectivity, need something to hang their hat and coat on, and anniversaries are one artificial means for finding a legitimising story peg. In the case of the Macpherson inquiry, this peg was bigger and more resonant than most, with emotions and sentiments still running high. The *Guardian* produced its SPECIAL REPORT ONE YEAR AFTER MACPHERSON, which opened with a rhetorically powerful commentary from its black journalist Gary Younge. This simultaneously sought to identify and instantiate the meaning of the Stephen Lawrence case and the Macpherson inquiry one year on. It began:

A Year of Reckoning

Now that the dust has settled and the rubble has been cleared, it is time to check the foundations. The Macpherson report fell like a bombshell on the political and cultural landscape. Into what appeared to be a fairly simple narrative between good (the Lawrence family) and evil (the five young men suspected of murdering their son), William Macpherson introduced a new and far more complex character: institutional racism.

Figure 8.2

Guardian, 24 February 2000, p. 1. © *Guardian and Observer*.

Suddenly a term that most of England had never heard before was all over the nation's breakfast tables. . . . This was no longer a debate about how to contain the problems that black people cause by their very presence. This was white people talking to other white people about the problems engendered by their racism.

All black people did was, literally and metaphorically, die for it. Stephen Lawrence died for it. Rohit Duggal, Rolan Adams, Michael Menson and many others died for it. . . . At last, here was proof of what black people had been saying for years. That they have been falling foul not just of the law of the land, but of the law of probabilities; evidence that there is a persistent and consistent propensity to shove ethnic minorities to the bottom of every available pile and not only leave them there but blame them for being there as well.

(21.2.2000, 2)

The *Guardian*'s special report also gave voice to, amongst others, the views of Ambalavaner Sivanandan, 'Britain's foremost black intellectual' (21.2.2000, 4) and editor of *Race and Class*; Boris Johnstone, editor of the rightwing *Spectator*; Hanif Kureishi, writer and novelist. A 'distinguished panel,' including the academic Lola Young, Faisal Bodi, the news editor of *UK Muslim*, and John Grieve, deputy assistant commissioner of the Metropolitan Police, also discussed issues of identity, employment and inequality post-Macpherson (21.2.2000, 12).

This reflexivity to the post-Macpherson period and questions of identity and inequality, then, was not only enacted by the accessing of a wide spectrum of different views and perspectives, but also in and through different formats that facilitated deliberative forms of engagement as well as the display of difference. This performative use of press formats included a succession of inserts, titled IDENTITY PARADE, in which ordinary Britons, black and white, answered the same questions: 'How would you describe yourself?'; 'What is the worst racial prejudice you have encountered?'; 'Do you think Britain has become more or less racist, and in what ways?'; and 'What lessons can we learn from the Stephen Lawrence incident?' This cultural reflexivity around issues of race and identity was also explored further through personal reflections and commentaries under such headings as WHOSE IDENTITY IS IT ANYWAY?, where it was argued that it was vital to keep talking about race. And the *Guardian* performatively ensured that its writers, and indirectly its readers, did just that.

The *Voice*, for its part, was less interested in exploring questions of identity and more concerned with examining the progress of the reforms since Macpherson. It declared in the report, A YEAR OF BROKEN PROMISES: 'This week marks the first anniversary of the Macpherson Report. Many remain convinced that little of substance has been enforced' (*Voice*, 21.2.2000, 10). Later that year, however, it reported, approvingly in RACE

RELATIONS VICTORY of the introduction of the Race Relations (Amendment) Bill outlawing racial discrimination, both direct and indirect, as well as victimisation in public authorities previously not covered under the Race Relations Act of 1976. Noticeably, the *Voice*'s performative enactment of the Stephen Lawrence story was seeming to wane by this time. Whereas the mainstream liberal press was reflecting on questions of identity and British culture, this popular minority newspaper evidently felt no necessity to examine questions of identity through the prism of the Stephen Lawrence story. Confident in its own black readership, which it addressed through a distinctive populism of black celebrity, consumer features and hard-hitting reports on continuing racism, the *Voice* eschewed the wider public debate then being played out in the mainstream press concerning questions of British identity and multicultural society.

The conservative press, like the liberal mainstream press, also engaged performatively with questions of identity at this stage but, crucially, only did so in reactionary mode and in opposition to the increased social and cultural reflexivity. The *Times*, for example, in line with its discomfort engendered by the recommendations of the Macpherson report and the new wave of reforms pursued by the Labour government, performed a reactionary response one year after the report's release. The views of rightwing commentator Melanie Phillips were given full vent as she referenced the 'witch-hunt atmosphere generated in the wake of the murder of Stephen Lawrence' in articles such as NOW WE KNOW THE TRUTH: THE POLICE ARE NOT RACIST (*Times*, 24.9.2000). The release of the report 'The Future of Multi-Ethnic Britain' by the Runnymede Trust (Parekh 2000), a race equality charity, also occasioned ferocious criticism in such reports as THEY'RE DOING THEIR LEVEL BEST TO DESTROY BRITAIN'S IDENTITY, which argued, 'Isn't the real racism to deny minorities access to a common, equalizing culture?' (*Sunday Times*, 15.10.2000). Questions of identity and difference here typically found short shrift as traditional nostrums of British homogeneity, traditionalism and supposed tolerance towards others were reasserted against the perceived climate of revisionist thinking in British history, culture and identity:

They're Doing Their Level Best to Destroy Britain's Identity

Melanie Phillips

. . . But my forebears came to Britain because it was tolerant and fair. Those immigrants and their children prospered only because the schools taught them the culture, values and history of the nation to which they belonged and so enabled them to take their place in it as equals. We were all British, a neutral handle that allowed us to share a civic identity while retaining a separate ethnic identity.

Yet according to last week's report by the Runnymede Trust, British identity is 'racially coded'. . . . This report provides yet another defining marker on the agenda of British self-hatred. . . . The report also repeats and expands on the big lie peddled by the Macpherson report on the Stephen Lawrence murder that every British institution is racist. What it fails to acknowledge is that the racist attacks from which many black people suffer are fuelled not by too much British identity but too little: a destabilizing cultural rootlessness, resulting from the remorseless campaign of national denigration of which this document is such a choice specimen.

(*Sunday Times*, 15.10.2000)

Thus we find that mainstream newspapers, though all caught up in and actively contributing to the new cultural mood or 'structure of feeling' produced by the Stephen Lawrence case, nonetheless staked out their positions quite differently on the post-Macpherson political and cultural terrains. Each nonetheless evidently felt obligated to take a stand on these shifting sands, constructing particularised identities and summoning moral collectivities with which to either hold back the winds of change or give them a helping blow.

SUMMARY

In this chapter we have seen how the media variously contributed to symbolic and, indirectly, to practical processes of 'reintegrating' and 'reconciling' society following the public trauma of the Stephen Lawrence case. In its mediatisation, the story was performed in ways that continued to publicly enact a sense of communitas and collective effervescence. At the heart of these collective representations were symbolic appeals to moral solidarities and the dramatisation of sacred and profane forces in society, as well as more deliberative uses of reasoned commentary, analysis and debate within 'reflective' press formats. It was by these representational means that the sacred idea of society once again became symbolised and enacted by the press. This was elaborated in response to the perceived backlash of violent racism, which reanimated a sense of collective opposition and produced a united media front.

At this time, the media also continued to champion the new public mood by actively seeking out racial injustices and holding the forces of law and order to public and moral account—William Hague, for example, discovered to his detriment that the moral sentiments unleashed earlier continued to exert moral authority within society and could even derail base political ambitions within the realm of party politics. Here the media played their part in circulating and sustaining this sense of collective moral vitality. Sections of the press also performatively enacted their own calendrical

ritual under the legitimising mantle of the Macpherson report's first anniversary. This, too, sustained further reflexivity on issues of identity in
multicultural Britain, as well as critical commentary and analysis on the
progress of the Macpherson and Labour government reforms.

As time moved on, however, so the press began to reassert their editorial independence from the surrounding 'communitas' or inclusive public
mood—a mood that they themselves had helped earlier to produce. Political fractures once again began to open as the sacred sense of society unleashed by the media and the Macpherson inquiry was subjected to
intensified criticism and challenges. Some newspapers then sought to slow,
if not derail, the momentum of reform and criticism being directed at the
forces of law and order, and the police particularly; others stoked the en-
gine of change and encouraged the New Labour government to release the
brakes. All nonetheless were caught up in, and contributed to, the story's
continuing momentum. On the basis of this continuing press performativity, the schism of 'race' and racism in British society, which had too often
been covered over in the past, found continuing media exposure, doing so
at a time when practical as well as symbolic processes aimed at reintegration were moving forward and encountering inevitable political dissent and
opposition. By now, the name of Stephen Lawrence had become embedded
within the institutional and cultural fields of British society and was historicised as an obligatory referent in the discussion of changing race relations. The name also, however, continued to contribute powerful
sentiments and even exert benchmark authority in future-oriented projects
for change—the subject of our final empirical discussion.

Nine

Ebbing/Revivification

I am well aware that the social drama is an agonistic model drawn after a recurrent agonistic situation, and I make no claim that there are no other types of processual unit. . . . Nevertheless, I would persist in arguing that the social drama is a well nigh universal processual form. . . . [T]here is an interdependent, perhaps dialectic, relationship between social dramas and genres of cultural performance in perhaps all societies.
Victor Turner, *From Ritual to Theatre* (1982, 71–72)

In its mediatised generalisation throughout society as well as in its more particularised canalisations, the Stephen Lawrence case acted as a litmus test of where society had been, where it was now and where it wanted to be. This social, cultural and institutional reflexivity, spurred on by the release of the Macpherson report, did not come to an end, however, with the recommendations and then instigation of a raft of policy reforms. The high-water mark of the Macpherson inquiry would not be matched again, but such was the cultural and emotional flooding produced and circulated by the media in this period that a deep cultural reservoir of sentiments and meanings was created. This was now available to periodically replenish the ongoing dynamics and struggles centering on inequalities and identities of 'race'.

By January 2001, nearly two years after the momentous release of the Macpherson report, 'Stephen Lawrence' had become established as a major historical reference point and now increasingly became deployed as a benchmark for measuring and evaluating processes of reform and cultural change. This often brought forth vociferous criticism and challenge. The Stephen Lawrence story, then, did not come to a neat resolution following

the stage of symbolic and political redress, or the succeeding phase of rein-
tegration/schism—and nor could it. Such are the cultural complexities of
identity and the embedded structures of racial inequality that the Stephen
Lawrence case was always destined to be at most an agent or catalyst of
change within the wider parameters and dynamics of British society—albeit one, as it turned out, that accrued tremendous symbolic power and ex-
erted momentous impetus for change. The case continues to this day to
exert agency and to reverberate in the contested field of race and identity
in British society, and looks set to do so into the future.

Here, too, the media have played a performative part in these longer-
term processes of change. A final fifth 'stage' can here be added to Turner's
schema. Though remaining dependent on the preceding stages, this last
phase draws away from them through time and, in its mediatisation, dis-
seminates the cultural resonance and fallout of the Stephen Lawrence story
into the future. This process of ebbing and revivification was, and continues to be, publicly enacted by the media and it is here that 'Stephen
Lawrence' has principally been constituted as historical reference, political
benchmark and cultural residue. This last empirical chapter, therefore, examines how the media continues to perform the Stephen Lawrence story in
the post-Macpherson period, starting in January 2001, nearly two years
after the release of the Macpherson report, and moving through 2003, ten
years after Stephen Lawrence was murdered. During this time, the media
periodically revivified the collective sentiments to which they had earlier
given such powerful expression but that now, through the ebbing of time,
had begun to settle as a deposit within the multicultural sensibility of British
society and culture. As we shall see, the aura, political charge and agency
of 'Stephen Lawrence' nonetheless remained available for reenactment, and
it continues to exert agency in the struggles and contests of the present and,
possibly, those in the future (see Postscript).

PRESS PERFORMATIVITY: SOCIAL REFORMS AND CONTINUING RACISM

By January 2001, nearly two years after Macpherson's report, many
wide-ranging social reforms had been implemented, while others were still
under public discussion (see Appendix 4). How the press positioned themselves, and their readerships, in relation to these reforms served to publicly
signal the continuing reverberations of the Stephen Lawrence case within
society and culture—as well as the political nature of press performativity.

The *Guardian* continued to enact its liberal social-democratic agenda and
did so by reporting on, investigating and pushing for the need for reform
across diverse social and cultural fronts: SETTING THE PACE ON RACE: ETH-
NIC EQUALITY INQUIRY TO SHAPE SOCIAL HOUSING AGENDA (*Guardian*,
10.1.2001, 4); FALLING BEHIND IN THE RACE: AS FORCES STRUGGLE TO AT-
TRACT ETHNIC MINORITY OFFICERS CLARE DYER REPORTS ON THE SIKH PO-

LICEWOMAN WHO CLAIMS SHE WAS HOUNDED OUT OF HER JOB BY COL-
LEAGUES (*Guardian*, 30.1.2001, 16).

SPECIAL INVESTIGATION: The hidden truth behind race crimes in
Britain: Jay Rayner has spent two months creating a race map of Britain
that reflects the true rates of recorded abuse and assault. Two years after
the Lawrence inquiry, he finds that it is rural areas, not inner cities, that
are the flashpoints.

(*Observer*, 18.2.2001, 8)

The *Independent* also performed its support for ongoing processes of reform, often displaying its commitments in more emphatic tones:

The Unpleasant Stench of Racism

'THESE CASES SUGGEST THE PROBLEMS OF INSTITUTIONAL RACISM UNCOVERED BY THE MACPHERSON REPORT HAVE NOT BEEN DEALT WITH AT ALL'

Deborah Orr

An internal investigation launched at Feltham Young Offenders' Institution,
in west London, after the murder of Zahid Mubarek, has produced 'very,
very troubling findings'. This is not the least surprising. In a prison where
a 19-year-old Asian, sentenced for very minor offences, is placed in a cell
with a violent self-styled Nazi and is beaten to death hours before his release, any findings are bound to be troubling.

(23.1.2001, 5)

When the *Guardian* took stock two years after the Macpherson report
and produced a balance sheet of reform, it usefully summarised something
of the scale and enormity of the social reforms that had been placed on the
statute books, which were then in various stages of implementation. But
more than this, it also demonstrated its own positive evaluation of these
events and its continuing political commitments to reform processes. It is
worth citing at length:

Racism One Step Forward: Straw's Record on Fighting Racism is Impressive, Even If Its Extension to Public Services Was Belated.

Malcolm Dean

Will the Macpherson report into the racist killing of Stephen Lawrence go
the same way as the Scarman report? Twenty years ago, Scarman's re-

port into the Brixton riots received an ecstatic welcome and an ocean of warm words, but it achieved little long-term change. . . . [O]n its [Machpherson report's] second anniversary last week the momentum for reform was still being maintained.

Of course, there have been reverses. The backlash began in week one, when the Mail and the Telegraph sought to distort the report by suggesting its 'institutional racist' findings against the Met, meant every officer was a racist. It meant no such thing. What it spelled out was that unintentional as well as intentional racism can cause serious harm. . . .

Last Saturday's Guardian survey showed that new officers from ethnic minorities dropped this year (155) compared to a year earlier (261). This makes home secretary Jack Straw's ambitious target of 6,000 extra ethnic officers by 2009 look even more distant. Currently, there are only 2,900 in a force of 125,000.

Yet progress on other fronts continues. The 100% increase in reports of racist incidents is good news. It shows ethnic minorities are more ready to come forward—and police more ready to prosecute, with 1,500 convictions for racial violence or harassment.

In April, the Race Relations (Amendment) Act comes into force, outlawing discrimination in all public services and placing a statutory duty on public bodies to promote race equality. Institutional racism is not confined to the police. It infects all services: heath, education, armed services, civil service and judiciary. . . .

Stop and search continues—as Macpherson wanted—but pilot programmes show stops can be reduced, while the proportion of arrests increases. The ninefold increase in stops between 1986 and 1996 was absurd. It led to gross discrimination, with black people five times more likely to be stopped.

Straw can take a bow. His record on fighting racism is impressive.

(28.2.2001, 7)

In these evidently performative ways, then, the broadsheet liberal press continued to commit their support to the Labour government's portfolio of reforms whilst seeking to ensure that their readerships and wider public support for change did not dim through time. The conservative and right-wing press, of course, performed a very different public stance. As time moved on so they deliberately sought to distance themselves, and their readerships, from the subjunctive public mood, the 'structure of feeling', that had been produced through the Macpherson inquiry and which had seemingly tamed their reactionary disposition on questions of 'race', racism and identity. With the passing of time and in response to the new Labour government agenda of reform, these sections of the press now began to mount a more vigorous backlash against the perceived shift in public sensibility.

This backlash targeted concerns of policing but extended to all social and cultural fields: RACE-ROW OFFICER GETS SEVEN TIMES MORE COMPENSATION THAN MACHETE VICTIM LISA (*Daily Mail*, 14.2.2001, 11); EVERY DAY 2,363 PEOPLE ACROSS THE COUNTRY ARE BURGLED AND 250 MUGGED. SO WHY ARE THE POLICE STAKING OUT CURRY HOUSES LOOKING FOR RACISTS? (*Times*, 1.4.2001).

Why Sir William Was Wrong About Race

Martin Mears

. . . In the wake of the Macpherson report, the liberal establishment underwent a kind of nervous collapse. It is not too late, however, for others to subject it to the critical analysis it should have received when it first appeared.

(*Times*, 1.5.2001)

The 255-Page Code for New Race Rules; 40,000 Public Bodies Ordered to Produce Equality Policies

Steve Doughty

The public services were saddled yesterday with extensive race target rules similar to American 'quota' systems.

(*Daily Mail*, 4.12.2001, 14)

The right-wing tabloids as much as the conservative broadsheets enacted this backlash and did so in characteristically sensationalist ways that could only reinforce ingrained racist stereotypes:

Get Tough on Crime . . . Wherever it Happens

Jane Moore

The wave of political correctness that swept through the police force after the murder of Stephen Lawrence has led to the problem being allowed to mushroom out of control. Last week, Lambeth police chief, Brian Paddick, announced he was to ban sniffer dogs from Brixton because he claims they upset the Afro-Caribbeans living there.

What he means is they upset the Afro-Caribbeans who are selling drugs or carrying guns.

(*Sun*, 6.3.2002, 11)

'Great and Good' Have Blood on their Hands

Sun Says

We're in an abyss of murder and mayhem . . .
HOW THE HELL HAS BRITAIN GOT ITSELF IN THIS SHAMEFUL STATE?
The blame lies four square with the soft liberal left. . . .
MEDDLERS like Sir William Macpherson whose report into the murder of Stephen Lawrence branded the police 'institutionally racist' and triggered a collapse in police morale and a surge in street violence as the use of stop and search tactics fell by half.

(*Sun*, 9.3.2002, 8)

This political backlash also appropriated new stories in its political efforts to split public opinion from the perceived new cultural sensibility. When the Damilola Taylor murder case resulted in no convictions, the right-wing press seized on this high-profile and disturbing case and claimed that its failures were a direct result of changed policing practices following the Macpherson report. Paradoxically, but seemingly unnoticed, the right-wing press now sought to discursively uncouple Macpherson from his public reputation as the judge who had been appointed to respond to British injustice, and actively sought to reposition him as the architect of injustice now being perpetrated in the post-Lawrence period:

The Shaming of British Justice

Branded both inaccurately and counterproductively as 'institutionally racist' in the Macpherson report into the Stephen Lawrence tragedy, police were overzealous to secure a conviction this time.

(*Daily Mail*, 26.4.2002, 18)

Discursive realignment also apparently characterised a *Voice* editor's calls for renewed 'stop-and-search' policing to curb violent crimes in black areas. This, too, was widely reported by the mainstream press, and with evident approval by the right-wing papers not known to take any interest in minority media views: VOICE EDITOR CALLS FOR STOP 'N' SEARCH (*Sun*, 5.3.2002, 14); BLACK EDITOR'S CALL TO BRING BACK 'STOP AND SEARCH' IN WAR ON GUN CRIME (*Daily Mail*, 5.3.2002, 10). Clearly, this was performatively enacted by these papers in support of their own political agenda—one, in fact, very different from that of the *Voice*, which continued to try to deepen, not derail, the momentum for change. On the second anniversary of the Macpherson report, the *Voice* displayed its evident commitments and continuing concerns about the pace and extent of the reform process (see Figure 9.1).

Moral Vengeance and Rewards

The right-wing press was on more comfortable ground, both politically and morally, when reporting on the remaining criminal justice developments in the Stephen Lawrence case. When David Norris and Neil Acourt were tried and sentenced in 2002 for racial assault on an off-duty black police officer (on the same road where Stephen Lawrence had been murdered), the tabloids enacted their glee, inviting their readerships to do the same: JUSTICE AT LAST (*Sun*, 25.7.2002, 1); JUSTICE; BEHIND BARS AT LAST, THE RACIST THUGS WHO HAVE NEVER ANSWERED OUR CHARGE OF MURDER (*Daily Mail*, 7.9.2002, 6). The *Sun*'s editorial, ABOUT TIME TOO, was explicit: 'The streets of Britain will smell a little sweeter this morning. Two nasty racist thugs are behind bars at last' (7.9.2002, 8). The right-wing press, including the *Sun*, then went even further than this and gave vent to feelings of vengeance also: LAWRENCE THUGS FACE HELL IN JAIL (*Sun*, 7.9.2002, 6); YOU WILL DIE; EXCLUSIVE: PRISONERS THREATEN LAWRENCE SUSPECTS (*Daily Mirror*, 26.7.2002, 7). In its article ROT IN HELL, the *Voice* expressed the same sentiment: 'The Voice supports calls for evil racist thugs to do time' (30.7.2002, 1). When both Acourt and Norris were released early under a government initiative to ease prison overcrowding this, understandably, was reported in similar emotional terms: ANGER AS RACE HATE PAIR FREED (*Sun*, 25.1.2003, 21). The *Guardian* offered a rare dissenting note amongst the moral certitude and vengeful feelings voiced by much of the British press: INNOCENT UNTIL PROVEN RACIST (31.7.2002, 7).

The moral approbation that had publicly enveloped the Lawrences earlier, and which gained additional charge from the moral opprobrium performed by the media and directed at prime suspects, now resulted in a number of public 'rewards' and awards ceremonies. These were reported by the media and further helped to recycle the name of Stephen Lawrence and symbolised society's continuing recognition of the justness of the cause conducted in his name. 'THIS HONOUR IS FOR STEPHEN'; LAWRENCES DEDICATE THEIR OBEs TO THE SON MURDERED BY RACISTS. The *Daily Mail* article continued: 'The parents of murdered black teenager Stephen Lawrence are honoured today for their unswerving courage and dignity through a decade of despair' (31.12.2002, 4). The key moral personae in the Stephen Lawrence story, then, continued to generate periodic press interest because of their earlier projection to national prominence, or infamy. But the moral vitality that had animated the Stephen Lawrence story earlier, inevitably, was beginning to ebb as the years passed by and notwithstanding the im-

Figure 9.1
Voice, 19 February 2001, p. 1. © *Voice.*

portance of the social reform process still rolling out across society. These institutional processes, by definition, were difficult to personalise, moralise and dramatise, and it was these forms of cultural expression, traditionally the terrain of tabloid journalism but not confined to these by any means, that had been performed earlier with such moral effect. And it was by these means, also, that the press had earlier summoned their particularised publics and enacted their differentiated political appeals.

POST-LAWRENCE, POST-MACPHERSON

The Stephen Lawrence story had become stitched into the cultural and institutional fabric of society, and its effects and affects had been distributed far beyond the particularities of Stephen Lawrence's murder. The public name of Stephen Lawrence, at first referent and signifier of racist murder, later became, as we have seen, a potent symbol and catalyst for change. It also underwent one further, perhaps final, transmutation. This immortalised the name of Stephen Lawrence, historicising it as an obligatory point of reference—some would say turning point—embedded in the institutional and cultural history of Britain, and as a catalyst for increased reflexivity towards issues of identity, 'race' and racism. This final transmutation was enacted principally by the media.

This referential history, given the social, political and cultural identities at play and the interests at stake in the present, remains, of course, highly contested. From the beginning of the Macpherson inquiry in 1998 to its publication in 1999, the term 'post-Lawrence' had been used as a shorthand descriptor of the new frame of reference that had been put in place by this very public case. (In our press sample, the term was used explicitly on thirty-eight occasions, though the frame of reference signaled by it informed many, many more.) Condensed in this term, as we have seen, was a wider recognition of the injustice perpetrated against Stephen Lawrence, both by the prime suspects and by the criminal justice system itself, and this received widespread public exposure and condemnation. The designation 'post-Lawrence', then, helped to signal this growing public awareness and sensibility that all was not right in Britain's multicultural society or its criminal justice system. 'Post-Lawrence' signalled that these important issues had now been placed on the public agenda, some of them for the first time, and that all of society was thereby challenged to rethink its views about society, 'race' and racism: 'Post-Lawrence, the Met is supposed to be a new, open, inclusive force. Right now it looks mired in racism, and firmly stuck in the past' (*Observer*, 17.10.99, 28).

Following the Macpherson inquiry, the term 'post-Lawrence' became superceded by 'post-Macpherson' (used in our sample on sixty-eight occasions). This proved to be a more contested signifier. In the terms of Volosinov (1973) it was a 'multi-accentual' sign, a sign that had strategic significance and, as such, was publicly fought over and given new direction and meaning by contending interests. 'Post-Macpherson' denoted a state of change (and change of state) in the political will to carry through wide-ranging reforms aimed at addressing inequalities of 'race' and outlawing forms of institutional racism. These reforms and the public discussion surrounding them were often couched in terms of a new commitment to social inclusion and positive recognition of cultural diversity in multiethnic Britain. Issues of identity as well as inequality were thereby placed on the wider public agenda, and these were bound to call forth political opposition to the new public mood and the impetus for reform now underway.

While the liberal press deployed the signifier 'post-Macpherson' to reference the desired shift in prevailing cultural sentiments and the raft of institutional reforms unleashed in the wake of Macpherson's inquiry, when viewed through a conservative lens these same forces of change could only be seen as politically misguided and as a threat to British society, its traditions and way of life. These differing takes on 'post-Macpherson' were played out across the press in largely predictable, often highly performative ways. The *Mail on Sunday*, for example, enacted its consternation by seeking to displace moral concerns about 'race' inequality raised in the post-Macpherson period with concerns about the immorality of different policing strategies purportedly used to police different communities. Questions of shame, so central to the media's representation of the Macpherson inquiry and its public drama, were now dearticulated from their former public discourse and rearticulated into a discourse about the felt need to return to 'law-and-order':

The Black and White Divide that Shames Britain's Lawless Cities

Lauren Booth

Since the Macpherson report turned the media gaze on to attitudes in the police, there has been a disastrous, hands-off policy towards groups of young black criminals. These aren't kids who just need a telling off or a good father figure to put them right, they are part of a violent subculture who prey first and foremost on their own communities.

But post-Macpherson the message went out that it was better to let them roam the estates at will than cause a race riot trying to stop them.

(*Mail on Sunday*, 19.1.2003, 27)

Questions of British identity had also been raised by the Macpherson inquiry, its public mediatisation and the raft of resulting social reforms. The term 'post-Macpherson' was, therefore, also likely to incur the full wrath of right-wing sentiments concerning British identity, especially insofar as these touched deep nerves in concepts of 'nation', 'heritage' and 'tradition'—a reaction that we have already witnessed in respect of the right-wing press's hysterical response to the measured tones and arguments of the Parekh Report. Notions of identity are also constituted through discourses of gender and sexuality as much as nation and cultural ethnicity, and these, too, proved to be no less challenging for right-wing beliefs and values. In the social imaginary of populist tabloid discourse, it was perhaps not surprising that Macpherson would also be a target for public pillorying alongside other identified (identity) 'threats' to the moral well-being of society. The *Sun*, for example, ideologically condensed rabid homophobia with a public denouncement of 'post-Macpherson' as leading to an emasculating cultural climate:

We Want Robocop, Not Village People

Richard Littlejohn

Commander Brian Paddick brings a whole new meaning to the expression 'bent copper'. He wears his homosexuality on his sleeve like a Boy Scout badge and is clearly very pleased with himself. Like a lovestruck adolescent he logs on to a website and bares his soul to the world. He finds anarchy attractive and condones the use of drugs such as cocaine and ecstasy. Commander Paddick is a member of one of London's most popular gay nightclubs, frequented by celebs such as Elton John and Dale Winton. If he were a bus driver or a chartered accountant, none of this would matter. What he does in his spare time, what he thinks about the price of fish, wouldn't be anyone's business but his. However, Brian Paddick is one of London's most senior policemen. He commands a district riddled with rampant street crime and drug-taking. Yet he adopts a 'softly softly' approach to drugs. . . . Scotland Yard is terrified of being called 'homophobic' and consequently has allowed Mr. Paddick plenty of slack. . . . Post-Macpherson there is an absolute obsession with diversity, gender and sexuality.

(22.2.2002, 11)

Inadvertently, but no less tellingly, the *Sun*'s despicable tirade identifies a cultural truth about the Stephen Lawrence case, that is, that it had reached into the heart of British society and culture and exposed some of its darkest secrets about institutional racism and racist violence, and had galvanised a groundswell of public opinion and sentiment, by which many felt the shame and injustice of this state of affairs and genuinely hoped for change. No wonder the *Sun* felt compelled to performatively enact a public opposition to this perceived momentum of change. Gary Younge, writing for the *Guardian* on the anniversary of Stephen Lawrence's death in 2001, expressed this new public reflexivity towards issues of race and British identity in a discussion of the 'legacy of Macpherson':

What Was All That About?: Race Row: The Prolonged Debate is a Problem for Whites. Black People Aren't Really Bothering to Listen

Gary Younge

It is through the prism of race that we are beginning to ask questions to which all of Britain has long sought answers. What does it mean to be British? Are you confident about what Britain might be or do you mourn the passing of what it was? Do you think that everyone should be treated equally, or do you believe that some should have privileges and other disadvantages inherited from birth? In that sense race is becoming the road map by which we navigate our way through a whole host of national issues, such as class and equality of opportunity.

(26.4.2001, 19)

Such potentially transformative sentiments had surfaced through the public enactment of the Stephen Lawrence story earlier and were now being pitted against the right-wing and conservative backlash that developed as time moved forward and the currency of 'Stephen Lawrence' began to lose value. With the ten-year anniversary of Stephen Lawrence's murder, the subjunctive mood for change was performed by the press and revivified one more time.

Media Performing Stephen's Legacy Ten Years On: Not Forgetting

Ten years after the murder of Stephen Lawrence, the media publicly enacted this commemoration and momentarily revitalised something of the subjunctive mood, the 'structure of feeling', that had earlier invested the story with such transformative energy. Right-wing tabloids again bowed to the sacred aura that surrounded the name of Stephen Lawrence and publicly acknowledged the far-reaching energies that his name had previously stirred, even if politically they weren't committed to them. The *Sun*, for example, reported the words of the prime minister and, in typical *Sun* style, sensationalised them in terms of war, (BLAIR: STEPHEN'S LEGACY IS OUR WAR ON RACISM, Lawrence Murder: 10 Years on) but now refrained from criticising the post-Macpherson reforms or shift in wider sensibilities towards issues of race, racism and identity (*Sun*, 23.4.2003, 26).

The *Daily Mail* produced a series of lengthy articles to mark the ten-year anniversary, opening with:

Why I Forgive My Son's Killers;

HERE, STARTING A MAJOR MAIL SERIES ON THE LEGACY OF THE MURDER THAT SHOOK BRITAIN, HIS FATHER REVEALS HOW THE TRAGEDY TORE HIS MARRIAGE APART . . . AND WHY, ASTONISHINGLY, HE FEELS NO BITTERNESS FOR THE KILLERS. STEPHEN LAWRENCE: TEN YEARS ON.

David Jones

(*Daily Mail*, 5.4.2003, 28–30)

This experiential and personalised view was followed up with an interview with Doreen Lawrence, I CAN'T FORGIVE MY SON'S KILLERS (7 April 20–21), a feature on the suspects, TODAY WE REVEAL WHAT HAS BECOME OF THEIR SORDID LIVES—AND WHY, SHAMEFULLY, THE LAST REAL CHANCE OF A CONVICTION IS GONE (8 April, 34), and then a report on the family's memorial service for Stephen Lawrence, TEN YEARS ON, THEY CAME TO REMEMBER THE BOY WHOSE DEATH SHOCKED THE NATION (23 April, 8). On the same day, a *Mail* commentary, WHAT HAVE WE LEARNED FROM STEPHEN'S DEATH?, used the occasion to reiterate its criticism of the concept of institutional racism and demonstrate its pre-Macpherson commitment to ideas of colour-blind policing, and to criticise the acknowledgement of institutional racism made by Commander Cressida Dick, 'head of the curiously named Metropolitan Police Diversity Directorate' (23 April, 10). The *Daily Mail*'s enactment of the ten-year anniversary was, then, for the most part channelled into the personal and experiential dimensions of the key protagonists with relatively little commentary on the changes unleashed by the Stephen Lawrence case. This contrasted with the relative silence of the *Times*, which chose not to enact the anniversary as a major opportunity to reflect on the last ten years, though it did lament, once again, the supposed threat posed by Sir William Macpherson's definition of institutional racism:

Murders Are Not Solved by Anti-Racist Nonsense

Peter Briffa

. . . Today is the tenth anniversary of the death of Stephen Lawrence.

I feel for the parents of Stephen Lawrence. I hope that whoever murdered him is brought to justice.

The best way of remembering Stephen Lawrence is hoping that justice will be done.

Which is why it is such a tragedy that the Macpherson inquiry, which tried to learn the lesson of his death and the botched investigation that followed, produced nothing but nonsense. Vacuous nonsense at best, dangerous nonsense at worst.

(*Times,* 22.4.2003)

The liberal broadsheets, by contrast, sought to performatively enact the ten-year anniversary as a major event and thereby maximize the opportunity to raise issues and reflect on questions of race, racism and British identity. The *Guardian* (and its Sunday *Observer*) and the *Independent*—newspapers that had belatedly championed the story of Stephen Lawrence but then vigorously enacted it as a major catalyst of change and steered it towards issues of social reform and questions of cultural identity—now performatively demonstrated their continuing commitment. The black broadcaster, writer, and chair of the Commission for Racial Equality, Trevor Phillips, reflected in the *Observer*, for example, on what the Stephen Lawrence case had meant to Britain and British identity (see Figure 9.2). He also sought to invoke the legacy of Stephen Lawrence and apply it to the new wave of asylum seekers and migrants experiencing racism—both institutional and personal—in Britain as he wrote.

Stephen Lawrence, 10 Years On: A Special Issue: How Tragedy, Trial and Error Brought Us All Together

A DECADE AGO A YOUNG STUDENT WAS LEFT TO DIE ON A SOUTH LONDON STREET. IT LED TO A WAVE OF REVULSION AND A SOUL-SEARCHING DEBATE ABOUT BRITAIN AND RACISM. TODAY WE ARE A NATION THAT THRIVES ON DIVERSITY—BUT WHAT ARE THE DANGERS FOR THE NEXT GENERATION?

Trevor Phillips

. . . When Jack Straw commissioned Sir William Macpherson's report, I doubt he realised what he was letting himself in for—unprecedented heartsearching in government followed the creation of the new law. About 43,000 public bodies, including almost all branches of government, now have to do their jobs without racial bias—and, more important, have to show that they are practicing what they preach, by drawing up a race equality scheme and regularly publishing figures. And if they don't, the Commission for Racial Equality now has sanctions to make them comply. It's a very new and different world. . . .

The Lawrence affair marked a watershed in Britain's attempts to deal with the aftermath of one of the waves of migration that have made the country what it is. Contrary to much of the sentimental claptrap about some mystical essence of Englishness that has been peddled in recent times . . . most of our identity has been consciously constructed in the past few centuries. . . .

One thing that we could learn from Stephen Lawrence's death is that we must not wait 50 years to create a legal framework that protects the new migrants.

(Observer Review, 6.4.2003, 1)

Figure 9.2
Observer Review, 6 April 2003, p. 1. © *Guardian and Observer.*

A full ten years after the murder of Stephen Lawrence, then, Britain's liberal broadsheets continued to performatively invoke the subjunctive mood galvanised by the Stephen Lawrence case and sought to periodically revitalise and extend its catalytic force. The sign, symbol, and historical referent of 'Stephen Lawrence' refuses to die and continues to exert agency within the fields of 'race', racism and identity. Perhaps it never will, so long as a collective sensibility exists that is shamed by his murder and the social injustices of racism within British society.

SUMMARY

The Stephen Lawrence story has inevitably ebbed through time, but such was its earlier impact and so deeply was it etched into the historical memory of society that it remains to this day available for periodic revitalisation. It continues to hold charge, partly because the issues and identities that surfaced through its cognitive and affective mapping of society remain contested terrains, but also because it accrued to itself symbolic power that burnt brightly and accusingly in the glare of the media. Let there be no mistake, however: this is contested terrain; and how could it not be given the material inequalities and identity politics at issue? The press, always the main media protagonists in the Stephen Lawrence case once the story had been propelled to national attention by the Lawrence family and their supporters, continued to perform the story ten years after the death of Stephen Lawrence and even many years after the 'high-water mark' of the Macpherson inquiry and the wave of reforms that it generated.

Over time the press has variously positioned and repositioned itself in relation to the longer-term trajectories of social, political and cultural change that it helped to shape through the Stephen Lawrence story. Both tabloids and broadsheets have, for the most part, however, continued to perform the Stephen Lawrence story 'post-Macpherson', committing editorial energies and political viewpoints into propelling it forward or seeking to stop it dead in its tracks. For the reasons already stated, the name of Stephen Lawrence is likely to remain part of media discourse and wider public sensibility for the foreseeable future (see Postscript).

Ten

Conclusion

Mediatized public crises . . . tend to increase the distance between the
indicative and the subjunctive, thereby giving to civil society its greatest power for social change. In these situations, the media create public narratives that emphasize not only the tragic distance between is
and ought but the possibility of historically overcoming it. Such narratives prescribe struggles to make 'real' institutional relationships
more consistent with the normative standards of the utopian civil society discourse.

  Jeffrey Alexander and Ronald Jacobs, 'Mass Communication, Ritual
                                  and Civil Society' (1998, 28)

The study of mediatised public crises provides unique insights into the complexities of media performance and public transformation and reminds us
of the powerful ways in which media today can intervene in the life of society, its schisms and struggles for change. Ritual, dynamics, symbolism
and performativity are constitutive of mediatised public crises, and it is in
and through these potent forms of cultural expression that some of society's most deep-seated conflicts and self-definitions are periodically played
out, and sometimes reconfigured. Overly rationalist conceptions of media
approached as a 'public sphere' of information transmission and deliberation, and post-modern views of media representations as socially ground-
less or inconsequential in their effects, are both found wanting on the basis
of this study and its examination of a major mediatised public crisis. The
mediatised story of Stephen Lawrence was given narrative and expressive
form by the media and was progressively enacted into a major public crisis that opened up deep-seated and troubled issues of 'race', racism and
British identity. It was this troubled field that granted the story its signifi-

cance, meaning and charge; but it was the media that progressively enacted the case within wider society and helped to release its transformative energies.

The Stephen Lawrence story was played out within, and opened up to public view, the chasm between normative views of civil society defined in terms of social inclusiveness, equal opportunities, tolerance and legal justice, and the continuing realities of racial inequality, murderous racist violence and anachronistic views of British identity, reinforced in the injustices of the criminal justice system. This contradiction surfaced through the media's representation of the Stephen Lawrence case and was progressively signalled as a moral indictment of British society and its inability to live up to the utopian discourse of civil society. At the height of this process, cultural and emotional flooding enveloped the nation at the very moment that 'the nation' became the subject of mediatised reflection and reflexivity, and as questions of 'race', racism and identity were publicly discussed. The media helped to bring into being a new subjunctive mood and this, in turn, helped to prepare the possibility of change.

This study has demonstrated how the British media, exceptionally, performed the Stephen Lawrence case and enacted it into a transformative moment in British race relations. Ten years after the brutal murder of Stephen Lawrence, the fallout continues to reverberate throughout British society and a raft of extensive social reforms has been legislated, many of them consequential (see Appendix 4). Today the name of Stephen Lawrence is institutionalised in these widespread reforms and is also sedimented in society's memory, where the symbolic charge, borne of this challenge to British racism, continues to act as a critical benchmark in ongoing antiracist struggles. So far, the moral and cultural charge of 'Stephen Lawrence' refuses to become historicised and de-moralised as a dead sign of the past. This concluding chapter now underlines some of the principal findings of this study and their relevance for wider considerations of media theory and research.

At the outset of this study I defined mediatised rituals as follows:

Mediatised rituals are those exceptional and performative media phenomena that serve to sustain and/or mobilise collective sentiments and solidarities on the basis of symbolisation and a subjunctive orientation to what should or ought to be.

This definition recognizes different forms of mediatised ritual and indeed accommodates diverse theoretical frameworks including approaches to moral panics, media events, mediated political scandals and mediatised public crises. The progression of the Stephen Lawrence story through time and climaxing (but not culminating) in a moment of staged ritual redress that demanded public response from the political centre of society clearly positions this media phenomenon as an instance of mediatised public crisis. The dynamics of the case, as we have seen, also follow to a remarkable degree Victor Turner's scenario of breach, crisis, redress and reintegration/schism. Importantly, however, these stages were in large measure either constituted within and/or principally played out through the mass media; such is the central role performed by the media in many of today's social conflicts. Expanding further on Turner's original insights, however, we have also observed how each stage in this mediatised public crisis also displayed its own internal dynamics. And we have also observed a further developmental stage, a fifth phase termed here as ebbing/revivification. This last phase, as discussed, temporally stretched the Lawrence case, post-Lawrence and post-Macpherson, into the future, where it took up position as historical referent, cultural residue and political benchmark—important 'post-crisis' attributes that can also be observed in other mediatised crises, from 'post-Watergate' to 'post-9/11'.

The media, principally the press but later broadcasting as well, progressively enacted the Stephen Lawrence case across these developmental phases, thematically extending and, importantly, emotionally deepening it throughout society. They did so in part on the basis of the institutional processes enacted elsewhere; generalising the successive failures of the criminal justice system and thereby helping to publicly fuel the growing sense of grievance about the case; but also canalising these same sentiments in respect to particularised publics embodied in differing political and rhetorical appeals. It is in these culturally expressive, dynamic and developmental ways that the media performed the Stephen Lawrence story over a long period of time, and which eventually served to release pent-up social pressures for change. This complexity of media performance, of media enactment or media 'doing' over the long term, demands to be taken seriously by media researchers today. The mediatised story of Stephen Lawrence drew its critical charge, as we have seen, from the surrounding and contested terrain of 'race' and racism in British society, and it also depended in part on institutional dynamics unfolding elsewhere.

The criminal justice system could have served to redress and thereby cauterise the public wound that was opening up around 'Stephen Lawrence', which threatened to symbolically discharge throughout society. If determined and effective police investigations had been conducted, if the CPS had recommended prosecution, if criminal trials had taken place, if the private prosecution had not been brought to a peremptory close, and if convictions had been secured, then the media interest in the case would surely have waned and its social sting of the case could have been dissipated—at least as far as the mainstream media were concerned. This, manifestly, did not happen.

The dynamics of the story did not develop only on the basis of the institutional logic of events played out in the criminal justice system. The Stephen Lawrence story also gathered its charge from the wider contention

within the field of 'race'. In the context of rising racist attacks and growing anger in black communities at the lack of response by the authorities,
the Stephen Lawrence case became a potent trigger in this field long primed,
post-Scarman, by community distrust of the police and their ability to rid
themselves of racism and racist officers. Fifty years after the arrival of the
SS *Windrush,* the ideas and sentiments of multicultural, multiethnic Britain
had also put down firmer roots in the British 'social imaginary'. Abhorrence of racist violence in Britain, though clearly not universal, was and is
today widespread. This, too, informed the cultural outlook of mainstream
British society and fed into the media's enactment of the case, as well as
its emotional and moral resonance.

The study has made a point of attending to the developmental dynamics of the Stephen Lawrence story as it unfolded over a period of ten years.
These long-term dynamics would have remained hidden if the study had
only focussed, for example, on the pinnacle moment of mediatised redress.
A criticism made early on in our discussion of studies of media events was
that these often decontextualise such moments from preceding and surrounding social dynamics, and they thereby fail to properly theorise their
determinants. A longer-term frame of reference can help to better ground
media phenomena within society and can also sharpen our understanding
of the complex cultural dynamics and determinations involved.

Ten years ago, I published a study on how British television routinely reported on the problems of the inner city and outbreaks of rioting in some
of Britain's major cities. *Television News, Urban Conflict and the Inner
City* (1993) examined the changing production environments and professional practices of television journalists and how these structured the cultural forms of television that routinely informed the public representations
of 'race', riots and urban inequality at this time. Ten years on, this latest
study examines an exceptional moment in the moving field of 'race', and
has explored how the media performatively enacted this. Both studies, in
their different ways, are concerned with questions of cultural mediation
and how the forms of journalism publicly represent the contending views
and values of 'race' and identity. While the earlier study principally examined these processes of mediation in the context of routine media production, professional practices and the changing parameters of corporate
organization, and deregulation and political economy, this study has deliberately focussed on questions of cultural mediation at the moment of its
performative enactment as expressed in and through the different forms
and narratives of contemporary journalism.

The media story of Stephen Lawrence story was, of course, informed by
political economy processes, organisational logics and the professional
practices of journalists working within a differentiated ecology of news,
just as the earlier reporting of the problems and issues of the inner city had
been. And it was also informed by strategic and tactical media interven-

tions by different, often powerful, vested interests, as well as the supporters of the Lawrence campaign. This study does not underestimate the importance of these interventions, and we have made reference to how some of these key players variously managed their public performances throughout this study. However, this mediatised public crisis, by definition and media performance, was in many ways exceptional. And here we needed to attend to how the cultural forms of journalism not only mediated the story in characteristic and routine ways, but also how they performatively enacted it. As we have seen, through time the media—principally the press—generalised, canalised and actively propelled the story forward, by increasingly making full use of all the communicative architecture and expressive means at their disposal. It was the media that progressively enveloped the case with emotional and moral intensity, and it was this that augmented its political charge. Importantly, this performative 'doing' was conducted in ways that would 'touch'—emotionally, affectively and, therefore, experientially—readers and audiences, as well as their sentiments about 'race' and racism in British society. Dissemination and deliberation, cognitions and affect, and information and moral solidarities were all deeply intertwined in this 'media doing', and this was enacted in and across the spectrum of different journalism media, forms and outlets—both popular and tabloid, serious and broadsheet.

Though the Stephen Lawrence story progressed through various criminal justice arenas, then, its narrativisation, emotional elaboration and growing social and political charge was principally and forcefully delivered culturally by the media. At the outset, the Lawrence family and their supporters had campaigned to attract media support, but this at best had gained only partial impact on a differentiated, largely complacent and, as we saw, sometimes hostile media. Nonetheless, a number of factors, including the 'respectability' of Doreen and Neville Lawrence, the 'innocence' of Stephen Lawrence, the 'aura' of Nelson Mandela and then the bombshell decision by the CPS not to prosecute, had helped to publicly signal a breach, which attracted some media interest early on. Thereafter, however, some sections of the media took it upon themselves to develop the story. Over time the press slowly began to enact the story and ratcheted up its emotional and political intensity.

By these means, they helped to generate a new emotional mood and gave cultural expression to the wider sensibility that now began to surround the case, and, by extension, issues of 'race', and racism. The media performatively summoned a subjunctive view of how society should be, which mandated the flows of moral opprobrium and approbation that penetrated both culture and polity with affect. In these culturally expressive and morally impregnated ways, right-wing and social-democratic tabloids, liberal and conservative broadsheets, minority newspapers and, eventually, mainstream television and internet sites all propelled the Stephen Lawrence story

into people's homes, as well as into the seat of government, where it demanded a response.

The moral flows set in motion by the media resulted in public shaming
and conditioned the public performances of political elites and various institutional authorities. A sacred sense of 'society' was brought into being,
which, for a time at least, conditioned the media's own performance. Even
the right-wing and conservative press seemingly found it difficult at times
to ignore or go against the new public mood, the sense of communitas, that
had become infused in media dissemination and discussion. Importantly,
this public mood was sustained not only on the basis of middle England's
recognition of Stephen Lawrence as an innocent student and Doreen and
Neville Lawrence's respectability as hard-working parents, but also on the
basis of the Lawrences' emotional anguish and private trauma that became
exposed to public view.

Here at last was a racist murder that was granted a public face by the
media and which thereby entered into people's homes and feelings. How
many people today can recall the faces or the cases of Lakhvinder 'Ricky'
Reel, Michael Menson, Farhan Mire, Uppadathil Divakaran or Zahid
Mubarek and the many, many others who have been wounded and killed
from racist attacks in Britain over recent years (IRR 2002a, 2003; see Appendix 1)? But many in Britain will still be able to recall the face of Stephen
Lawrence. Through repeated media use, the image of Stephen Lawrence
gained iconic status and became publicly known, familiar and ordinary and,
thereby, rendered human. From very early on, the media (and not just the
tabloids) had referred to Stephen Lawrence by his first name, and this, too,
had helped to personalise him as someone who belonged to friends, family and perhaps to the audience of readers.

The Stephen Lawrence case became suffused with intense emotions and
sentiments, and it also produced feelings of shame and anger. Through dramatic reenactments, graphic descriptions of violence and emotionally
charged testimonies, the media contributed to what could be termed a 'politics of pity' (Boltanski 1999). But this should not be dismissed as superfi-
cial sentiment. Sentiments—collective cognitions plus affect—were
undoubtedly flowing through the mediatised story of Stephen Lawrence and
were necessary if it was to captivate imaginations and contribute to a collective sense of moral solidarity. But these feelings were not based on a
'spectacle of suffering'. The contested field of 'race', racism and cultural
identity charged the Stephen Lawrence case from day one, and insofar as
a 'politics of pity' was flowing through the story's mediatisation, this
merged with feelings about 'race' as well as widespread liberal sentiments
about the murder of innocents. Together these elements proved capable of
producing a more socially engaged politics—a 'politics of shame'. The
Stephen Lawrence case, uniquely perhaps, managed to humanise, moralise
and, on this basis, shift to some degree the 'structure of feeling' of society

in respect to prevailing ideas, issues and identities of 'race', and as it did so, it forced the political centre to acknowledge the deep-seated and continuing nature of racism(s) within Britain's multiethnic, multicultural society. These racisms could now be publicly acknowledged and, in the case of 'institutional racism', named for the first time within public legislative discourse.

The mediatised story of the Stephen Lawrence case, then, demonstrates that ideas of moral solidarity, far from being rendered theoretically redundant in these new times of social fragmentation and fluid identities, remain crucial for understanding contemporary processes of social integration and change. Moral solidarities based on shared normative outlooks about how society is, or should be, remain foundational within civil society discourse, and these, as we have seen, were actively summoned in the media's performative enactment of the story. These generalised appeals to a moral solidarity, united in its abhorrence of violent racism and shamed by the failures of the criminal justice system to deliver justice to the Lawrences, were enacted on the basis of collective sentiments and a widely held 'utopian discourse of civil society'. The media also intertwined within this utopian discourse appeals to particularised publics that were canalised in respect of the wider cultural-political field of 'race'.

This canalisation was performed most obviously by the British press. The *Voice* not only championed the cause of the Lawrences from early on, immediately inserting the case into a preceding context of rising racist attacks, but simultaneously inscribed and invoked a sense of black solidarity united in its defence against these attacks. Performatively it summoned a particularised black solidarity in and through its deployment of expressive journalism forms and in its explicit editorial appeals. Right-wing and social-democratic tabloids (the *Sun, Daily Mail, Daily Mirror*) variously, sometimes inconsistently, staked out their position in relation to the case and the wider issues that it helped throw into public relief, doing so through the characteristic and populist idioms that inform their respective readership appeals and editorial positions. Sometimes this reportage became muted as the Stephen Lawrence case looked set to advance multicultural agendas and sensibilities that went 'too far'; sometimes these papers produced full-scale campaigns that reacted against the momentum of change; and sometimes these same papers became caught up in the sympathetic public mood enveloping the case. The *Times*, for its part, pontificated on the legal questions raised by the case and continued in its self-appointed role as guardian of the nation's institutions of law and order and traditional identity; but even the *Times* found it hard to completely ignore the shifts in public mood, and on occasion it advanced criticisms of the way the criminal justice system had mishandled the case. Liberal broadsheets, the *Independent* and the *Guardian,* invested huge amounts of energy in summoning liberal sensibilities and also sought to communicate something of the lived, experiential realities of the case, as well as of being black or Asian in a predominantly white British society. Together they produced a considerable outpouring of analysis, commentary and often eloquent rhetoric to 'move' their readerships and collectively position them in support of the social reform process and wider tides of change underway.

In these different and sometimes explicitly contending ways, then, the British press summoned moral solidarities and particularised publics by performatively making full use of all the expressive and rhetorical means at their disposal. Together these canalisations also contributed to the wider generalisation of the case and produced a collective sense of 'society' as deeply troubled and in need of moral repair. National television positioned itself, albeit belatedly, on 'civic common ground' and gave expression to the play of difference and sense of shame produced at the height of the Lawrence story. Here the different genres of television journalism were finally put to work and helped to constitute and disseminate the cultural effervescence that flooded the nation at the height of the redress phase.

This study has emphasised the performative role played by the media in developing the Stephen Lawrence story into a transformative moment in British society. It has revealed how the media invested the case with moral charge and invoked moral solidarities—dimensions of media performance that require sustained study if we are to better understand the cultural power of the media whilst also recognising the media's inescapable grounding within society. The use of 'performance' and 'performativity' throughout this study has been deliberate and helps to capture the cultural 'doing' of the media. This performative doing was enacted in different ways, whether through reporting, expressing, commentating, advocating, campaigning, championing or reflexively monitoring. These different levels of performative activity, as we have seen, all informed the public enactment of the Stephen Lawrence case at various times and across different developmental stages. Media performativity was also apparent, for example, in and through the use of linguistic cues, semantic structures, rhetorical parallelisms, declarative headlines, commentaries and editorialising, investigative reports, staged debates, visual iconography, cartoons, page design and juxtaposed layout, and special reports and commissioned programmes—and much, much else besides. Embedded within this mélange of journalism forms and expressions, and granting them a unifying purpose, were appeals to moral solidarities that simultaneously sought to address and summon readerships/audiences as 'publics'. These rhetorical invitations may or may not have been read, felt or accepted by all readers and audiences, but they nonetheless provided a potent means by which they could recognise themselves as part of a wider collectivity, inhabiting the moral constitution of society and participating in its 'serious life'.

There are strong empirical grounds to suggest that these moral appeals did register with many people in Britain and that it was this that animated the mediatised story of Stephen Lawrence and eventually contributed to its instigation of political response, social reforms and wider cultural shifts in multicultural sensibilities. This 'moral summoning' was performed by the media but contrary to much contemporary theory; it is clear that it had a substance beyond the deed of its performative enactment. This substance was society. Structured, conflicted and racially inegalitarian British society, like all such societies, remains capable of generating moral solidarities which, in their performative media enactment, can find collective representation, as well as some degree of emotional and political expression. Such media performativity may even, on occasion, help to unlock social dynamics for change.

Media performativity, then, publicly enacted the Stephen Lawrence case, but it drew its moral force and resonance from wider society. Journalism increasingly acted in a subjunctive mode, notwithstanding journalistic blushes to the contrary, and it needed to if the Stephen Lawrence case was to become a mediatised public crisis capable of releasing transformative energies. The normally buried contradictions and mythic status of civil society became publicly revealed by the mediatised story of Stephen Lawrence, and as each successive form of institutional redress failed, so society's divisions and inequalities were opened up, eventually leading to determined institutional and political efforts to repair society's damaged self-image. The conduct of politics at this point inevitably became morally pressurised; political leaders were obliged to appeal to moral solidarities and comport themselves on a mediatised public terrain high in symbolism and affect. The increased flow of symbols and public performances at this time converged in a key moment of staged symbolic and judicial redress, one that cannot simply be dismissed as a public relations exercise.

Depending on the depth of the crisis exposed and the pent-up social forces that fuel it, so such moments can unleash meaningful and far-reaching changes, even if ultimately these may fall short of a total overhaul of society, its key institutions and inequalities. 'Reform or revolution' is simply too blunt a slogan to meaningfully evaluate the progressive or conservative nature of the political, social and cultural reconfigurations that can be enacted in mediatised public crises. Here civil society may potentially be revitalised and/or progressively moved towards a more socially inclusive and normatively shared vision of how society should be, and insofar as this becomes part of the revised utopian civil society discourse, so it constitutes an important benchmark of use in future struggles for change. The media, as we have seen in this study, performed this process of social imagining and civil society renewal, and, exceptionally, they served to progressively reconfigure the contested terrain of 'race', racism and British identity.

If the media are to be encouraged to play a more progressive role in respect to the continuing injustices and inequalities of 'race' and racism, it is imperative that we better understand their performative and transformative potential as well as the basis of their routine, and often conservative, reporting. This study has hopefully made a small contribution to this most necessary project.

Postscript

Towards the end of this study, I argued that such was the scale and impact of this mediatised public crisis that the name and symbol of Stephen Lawrence had become established as an enduring historical reference in the changing field of British race relations. It also looked set to continue to exert agency as a political benchmark in ongoing antiracist struggles and had become a potent cultural residue within the shifting sensibility of multicultural Britain. Media performance and enactment of the story, I argued, had contributed to this lasting legacy of Stephen Lawrence, and the media remained possible vehicles for its public revitalisation. Towards the end of 2003, just before submitting the manuscript of *The Racist Murder of Stephen Lawrence: Media Performance and Public Transformation,* a further event underlined these conclusions.

The BBC produced and broadcast an investigative exposé programme 'The Secret Policeman' (BBC1, 21.10.2003) in which a BBC reporter, Mark Daly, went undercover as a trainee police recruit and filmed extreme racist attitudes exhibited by a number of fellow police recruits. The liberal press gave advance notice of the programme, prompting a political row between the BBC and David Blunkett, the Labour home secretary, who at first called it 'a stunt' which intended 'to create, not report' the story (*Observer,* 19.10.2003, 2). When broadcast, the programme was watched by five million people, and the extremity of the racist attitudes captured on film were publicly revealed. In one scene, a trainee put on a Klu Klux Klan mask, threatened to beat up an Asian colleague, and said, 'He'll regret the day he was ever born a Paki', then stated that his aim was 'to eradicate the whole fucking country of people like him'. A different recruit claimed that the murdered Stephen Lawrence 'deserved to die' and that his killing 'was a good memory'. These revelations, bad enough in any context, proved incendiary in a climate of expectation that the police, post-Lawrence, post-Macpherson, would by now have put their house in order and ensured that police trainees with such extreme racist attitudes would have been detected and expelled. Indeed, Mark Daly said that the BBC had decided to investigate Greater Manchester police because its chief constable, David Wilmot, had said at the time of the Macpherson inquiry that his force was institutionally racist and that it would strive to eradicate such attitudes (*Guardian*, 21.10.2003, 7). The programme, understandably, produced a media flurry of expressed shock and dismay and, again, flows of moral lava heated up: SHOCK AND SHAME—THE RESPONSE OF POLICE CHIEFS TO THE RACISTS IN THEIR MIDST (*Guardian*, 23.10.2003, 3); THE SHAMING OF BRITAIN'S RACIST POLICEMEN (*Independent*, 23.10.2003, 3); SHOCK AT SECRET VIDEO OF COP'S SICK RANTS (*Sun*, 22.10.2003, 6), RACE HATE 8: TV PROBE NAMES AND SHAMES POLICE BIGOTS (*Daily Mirror*, 22.10.2003, 29). Interestingly, David Blunkett now publicly stated, 'What's been revealed is horrendous' (*Guardian*, 23.10.2003, 1). Ministers and senior police chiefs once again expressed their determination to root out racist behaviour in Britain's police forces, and five of the named racist officers resigned.

This latest incident demonstrated, again, the legacy of Stephen Lawrence as an historical reference point, political benchmark and cultural residue and how it could exert agency in continuing antiracist struggles. It also demonstrates how some sections of the media continue to progressively perform the Stephen Lawrence story and reanimate both its moral charge and momentum for change. The BBC originated this elaborate exposé of continuing racism within the British police, notwithstanding the introduction of new training schemes and high-level commitments made in the aftermath of the Macpherson inquiry. Clearly they were right to do so. The revelations also received wider exposure and critical commentary from Britain's mainstream media. Moral sentiments were once again performatively reanimated and revitalised, and the media were in no doubt that this latest revelation of police racism could only be interpreted in the context of the Macpherson report and its promised reforms. As the *Guardian* editorial, REVOLTING AND RACIST, exclaimed: 'more than 10 years since the death of Stephen Lawrence and more than four since the Macpherson report into his killing charged the Metropolitan police with institutional racism . . . what have we achieved?' (*Guardian*, 23.10.2003, 27). The *Times* was no less obligated to place this latest revelation in the same context: 'The drive to tackle racism has been intensified since the Macpherson report into the death of Stephen Lawrence exposed serious failings in the metropolitan police' (*Times*, 23.10.2003, 5).

This latest, and certainly not the last, controversy in the aftermath of the mediatised public crisis of Stephen Lawrence, then, demonstrates that its political and moral charge have not run their course—and they are unlikely to so long as racial inequality and continuing acts of racist violence stain British society. The moral sentiments and multicultural sensibility of main-stream British society was progressively deepened by the mediatisation of the Stephen Lawrence case, and the media helped to perform these into a mediatised public crisis. In contemporary British society, as in other Western multiethnic societies, however, continuing racist violence and xenophobic reactions to migrants and asylum seekers prove that media performance and performativity are no less necessary in the ongoing and wider struggles to eradicate racism.

Appendix One

Racially Motivated Murders, 1970–2003

This factsheet covers deaths from attacks that appear to have a racial element. It does not include deaths that occurred in police custody or in prison.

1970

April—**Tausir Ali,** east London
December—**Abdul Bari,** Birmingham

1971

January—**Chancal Singh,** West Yorkshire

1973

April—**Velma Murray,** Coventry
June—**Jag Singh Kenth,** Leicester
July—**Jennifer Williams,** Birmingham

1975

January—**Ronald Jones,** south London
February—**Hector Smith,** Glasgow

1976

May—**Ribhi Al-Haddia,** Woodford, Essex
May—**Dinesh Choudhury,** Woodford, Essex
June—**Gurdip Singh Chaggar,** Southall
June—**Emmanuel Allombah,** west London
August—**Mohan Gautam,** Leamington Spa

1978

April—**Kennith Singh,** Plaistow, east London
May—**Altab Ali,** Tower Hamlets, east London
June—**Ishaque Ali,** Hackney, east London
July—**Benjamin Thompson,** northwest London

July—Michael Nathaniel, northwest London

September—Vernon Brown, Birmingham

September—Amber Ali, north London

December—Michael Ferreira, Stoke Newington, east London

1979

January—Abdul Aziz, Peterborough

August—Kayimarz Anklesaria, east London

August—Sawdagar Khan, Birmingham

1980

January—Mohammed Arif, Burnley

January—Sewa Singh Sunder, Windsor

March—Famous Mgutshini, London

June—Palak Majumbar, Greenwich, south London

July—Akhtar Ali Baig, Newham, east London

September—Louston Parry, Manchester

1981

April—Malcolm Chambers, Swindon

May—Mian Azim Khan, found murdered in south London park

April—Satnam Singh Gill, Coventry

June—Amil Dharry, Coventry

June—Fenton Ogbogbo, south London

June—Charan Kaur, Leeds

July—Mrs Parveen Khan and her children, Kharenon, Aqsa and Imran, killed in arson attack, Walthamstow, east London

July—Asif Ahmed Khan Shamsuddin, north London

November—Mohammed Arif, Bradford

1984

July—Peter Burns, stabbed in the eye, Essex

1985

July—Shamira Kassam and her children, Zahir, Rahim and Alim, killed in arson attack in Redbridge, east London

November—Kalbinder Hayre, Kent

1986

April—Sudhir Patel, Wembley

May—Arif Khan, West Bromwich

June—Balbir Chand, Wolverhampton

September—Ahmed Iqbal Ullah, schoolboy, killed by a fellow pupil, Manchester

October—Mohammed Nazir, Halifax

1987

May—Abdus Sattar, Camden, north London

October—Thomas Lee, north London

1988

October—Muhammed Dalibri, south London

1989

January—Ahmed Abukar Shek, Edinburgh

July—Tahir Akram, Oldham

September—Mohammed Musa Saleh, Sheffield

November—Kuldip Singh Sekhon, Southall, west London

1990

December—Tasleem Akhtar (9), abducted and killed in an alley, Birmingham.

1991

February—Rolan Adams (15), stabbed outside Greenwich youth club, by twelve-strong gang shouting 'nigger' in south London. Mark Thornborrow given life sentence for murder, seven others charged with violent disorder (later reduced to minor public order offences and given community service orders).

1992

January—Navid Sadiq (15), shot in shop where he worked, Southwark, south London. Joseph Conroy later said, 'Good I hope they [minorities] die'. He was sentenced to two life sentences for murder and attempted murder.

January—Panchadcharam Sahitharan (28), Tamil refugee, died in gang attack, Newham, east London. Andrew Noble and Gary Hoskin charged with murder and affray. Charges later dropped against Noble, Hoskin acquitted.

January—Mohammed Sarwar (46), taxi driver battered to death, Manchester. Not recorded as racially motivated.

January—Siddik Dada (60), shopkeeper, died from gang attack, Manchester. Not recorded as racially motivated.

March—Donald Palmer (52), stabbed by two men, south London. His two attackers claimed to be from the National Front. George McKay given life sentence for murder and Wayne McGrath given three-and-a-half-years youth custody for manslaughter.

July—Rohit Duggal (16), killed during gang fight in Eltham, south London. Not recorded as racially motivated by police, but CPS made some reference to racial motivation during trial. Peter Thompson given life sentence for murder.

July—Ruhullah Aramesh (24), Afghan refugee, attacked by a gang, Thornton Heath, south London. Barry Hannon, Paul Hannon and Joseph Curtain given life sentences for murder. One other convicted of manslaughter on the grounds of diminished responsibility, and three others were acquitted. Curtain was freed on appeal on a technicality.

September—Ashiq Hussain (21), taxi driver, stabbed after going to aid of driver being racially abused, Birmingham. (Not treated by the police as racially motivated.) Mark Jarvis given five years for manslaughter; two others acquitted of the same charge.

September—Aziz Miah (66), battered to death by racist gang on his way to mosque, Newcastle. Michael Neilson given life for murder.

October—Sher Singh Sagoo, killed by racist gang in Deptford, south London. Prosecution of man charged with manslaughter discontinued after CPS decided there was insufficient evidence.

1993

March—Fiaz Mirza (42), taxi driver, murdered in east London. Mark and Ricky Lee sentenced to life for murder.

April—Stephen Lawrence (18), stabbed to death, Eltham, south London. Charges dropped due to insufficient evidence.

April—Saied Ahmed (68), Somalian refugee, died of burns after an arson attack on his home, Oxford.

November—Ali Ibrahim (21), Sudanese refugee, stabbed to death, Brighton. Ian Leanay sentenced to life for murder. Stephen MacKrill acquitted after jury failed to reach verdict.

1994

July—Donna O'Dwyer (34), African-Caribbean, died after arson attack, east London. Not recorded as racially motivated despite attacker being an ex-member of National Front. Peter Thurston sentenced to life for arson, grievous bodily harm (GBH), and murder.

December—Mohan Singh Kullar (60), shopkeeper, beaten to death with a brick in Neath, South Wales. Grant Watkins sentenced to life for murder, Stephen May to eight years for manslaughter, Ian Thomas to three and a half years for violent disorder. Two others were acquitted.

1995

February—Mushtaq Hussain (49), died of a stroke after being beaten by racist gang in Blackburn. Sean Pilkington and Ryan Baird both charged with manslaughter.

October—Gosar Shah (68), died of a heart attack after suffering racial abuse, Bounds Green, north London.

1996

March—Michael Czytajlo (74), Ukranian Holocaust survivor, died of heart attack after suffering racial abuse at home in Oldham.

March—Daniel Blake (18), died in mysterious circumstances in northwest London. He was found dead on a railway line in Neasden. There was evidence that there had been an argument and a fight before his death. British Transport police arrested eight men and two women in connection with his death, but the CPS decided not to prosecute anyone. In 1999, Daniel's body was exhumed by order of the Racial and Violent Crime Task Unit who reopened the case.

April—John Reid, a white man married to a black woman, beaten to death in his home, following long-running racist harassment against the couple, Plumstead, south London. Three white men were jailed for life for the murder. In October 1998, the three men appealed against their murder convictions but were again found guilty and sentenced to life.

1997

January—Michael Menson (29), set alight in a phone box by white gang, Edmonton, north London. Police initially treated the death as a suicide. Inquest returned a verdict of unlawful killing in September 1998. Two months later, the Racial and Violent Crimes Task Force began to reinvestigate the death. In December 1999, Mario Pereira was found guilty of murder and sentenced to life, Harry Charalambous was jailed for twelve years for manslaughter, and both men were found guilty of conspiracy to pervert the course of justice. The RVCTF also pursued Ozguy Cevat to Northern Cyprus, and he was prosecuted for manslaughter and sentenced to fourteen years.

October—Lakhvinder Reel (20), his body found in River Thames after racial abuse led to fight in Kingston-Upon-Thames. In 1999, an inquest recorded an open verdict, thus refuting police assumptions that Ricky had died while trying to urinate in the river.

1998

February—James Tossell (16), Kenfig Hill, near Bridgend, Wales. James and his friend, Steven Gibbs (both white), were racially abused and attacked by a gang of youths who threw bricks at Steven's home, where they had barricaded themselves. The flat was later set alight and James died. Charges of murder against two youths were dropped because of insufficient evidence. Six men were sentenced for various offences relating to first attack on the property. A police officer also faced unspecified disciplinary charges after a complaint about police handling of the original attack.

April—Akofa Hodasi (24), found hanged, three days after being victim of racial attack by gang of white youths in Frimley, Surrey. An inquest jury in September 1999 rejected a verdict of suicide and recorded a unanimous open verdict. Police are now investigating a possible link between Akofa's death and the McGowan hangings.

September—Remi Surage (56), knifed in back in street in Orpington, Kent. Paul Knight was sent to Broadmoor indefinitely for Remi's manslaughter (through diminished responsibility).

November—Surjit Singh Chokkar (32), attacked with a knife by three white men, all of whom were eventually arrested, but only one stood trial—for assault not murder—and he was later discharged. After a family campaign, the two other men were due to stand trial in connection with Surjit's death but were claiming they would not receive a fair trial due to the publicity that the case has received.

December—Farhan M. Mire (32), kicked to death in street by a white man after an argument with a woman who then shouted for help in Harrow, north London. Man charged with murder in March 1999, but later released after the CPS decided that there was not enough evidence to prosecute. The CPS also queried the racial motivation in the case.

1999

January—Jay Abatan (42), died five days after an attack at the Ocean Rooms nightcub in Brighton after an argument over a minicab. Two men were charged with manslaughter; these charges were later dropped and the men stood trial for actual bodily harm (ABH) on Jay's brother, Michael. The men were acquitted and the jury was not told that Jay had died as a result of the attack.

April—Andrea Dykes (27), John Light (32) and Nicholas Moore (31), killed after bomb planted by a far-right extremist exploded in Admiral Duncan, a gay pub in Soho, central London. Over 129 people were injured in bomb attacks in Soho, Brixton and Brick Lane. In June 2000, 23-year-old David Copeland was sentenced to six life sentences for the bombings after his plea of diminished responsibility was thrown out. He had been a member of the BNP and National Socialist Movement.

May—Stelios Economou, pushed under a train at Hatch End station after helping two black girls being racially abused. 40-year-old Alan Casey was detained indefinitely after pleading guilty to manslaughter on the grounds of diminished responsibility.

July—Joseph Alcendor (62), died after being punched in the head after leaving a party in Kilburn, northwest London. 32-year-old Leo Keaney arrested in connection with the assault.

July—Harold (a.k.a. Errol) McGowan (32), found hanged in suspicious circumstances after suffering a two-year campaign of racist abuse in Telford. Police failed to forensically examine the scene, instead insisting he had committed suicide.

July—Liaquat (a.k.a. Bobby) Ali (30), murdered as he lay sleeping by his racist housemate, 28-year-old Simon Rawcliffe, in Bury near Manchester. His racist record was not fully disclosed in court, but was detained at Ashworth mental hospital for life.

September—Ben Kamanalagi (28), murdered by four men in Salford, Manchester three days after a dispute at a nightclub where he worked. In February 2001, two men were jailed for five and a half years for murder, and another man was cleared.

December—Jason McGowan (20), disappeared minutes before midnight on New Year's Eve, later found hanged. He had been investigating the suspicious death of his uncle (see above, Errol McGowan). Second inquest 02/03 records an open verdict.

December—Hassan Musa (44), died after spending twenty-one years in a vegetative state after a racist attack in 1978. 23-year-old Hassan was kicked unconscious by a gang of white thugs in Sunderland. Three of the men were charged with GBH and public order offences. The inquest recorded a verdict of unlawful killing and the case has been referred back to Sunderland police.

2000

April—Santokh 'Peter' Sandhu, died after being beaten unconscious while on a night out with friends in Port Talbot, south Wales. In January 2001, 57-year-old William Morgan was found not guilty of manslaughter after alleging he punched Peter after an argument over litter.

May—Kombra Divakaren (43), died of head injuries two days after being viciously attacked and abused by a gang of white youths attempting to steal a football from his shop. In January 2001, after pleading guilty to manslaughter charges, a 16-year-old girl and 20-year-old man were sentenced to five years. Two others were found guilty of affray.

June—Jan Marthin Pasalbessi (48), an Indonesian man beaten to death outside the hospital where his 14-year-old stepdaughter was being treated for injuries during a racist gang attack on her. (The same gang attacked Jan.) At the trial the judge rejected any racial motive in the case.

June—Glynne Agard (34), on a night out with his brother Stephen, and friend Gary Belgrave, in Westbury, Wiltshire, they were attacked by a gang of eight who kicked and punched Glynne to death. In July 2001, 20-year-old Wayne King was jailed for four years after pleading guilty to manslaughter charges. 21-year-old Thomas Myers was jailed for two years after admitting ABH and affray. The judge said the murder was not racially motivated.

July—Mohammed Asghar, stabbed to death outside his restaurant in Huddersfield. In May 2001, an all-white jury in Bradford found 34-year-old Jonathan Fairbank not guilty of murder, believing he had acted in self-defence.

November—Tariq Javed (46), murdered by gang of white men who hijacked his cab in Bury, near Manchester. He was beaten, robbed and then run over by his own car. 21-year-old Mark Baxer and 29-year-old Jason Power were convicted of murder and robbery and jailed for life. Police said there was no evidence that the attack was racially motivated.

November—Khaliur Rahman (58), a Birmingham restaurant owner, beaten, robbed and racially abused by two white men in the early hours of 22 October. He died in hospital as a result of his injuries a month later. In June 2002, two men denied charges of murder, one was acquitted and the other, Christopher Cucchiaro, was released on bail to be retried later in the year.

December—Sarfraz Khan (30), Sarfraz was beaten, stabbed five times (once through the heart) and then set alight in his car after picking up a taxi fare in Rotherham. In July 2001, 27-year-old Craig Gilbert pleaded guilty to murder and was sentenced to life. Gilbert claimed he was 'off his head' on drugs.

2001

January—Gian Singh Nagra (37), found with serious head injuries after a suspected racial attack at Elm Park tube station, he later died in Old Church hospital, east London. In August 2001, Matthew Dorrian pleaded guilty to manslaughter charges.

March—Fetah Marku (24), Kosovan asylum seeker stabbed to death in Edgware, London, by a gang of men. In June 2002, 33-year-old Richard Ellis was found guilty of murder. The court heard how a fight broke out at a pub between Ellis and one of Fetah's friends. They were chased out of the pub by a twenty- to thirty-strong gang who caught and beat Fetah in a car park. After the conviction, the judge commented that it was unlikely that Ellis, a black man, was 'solely responsible', and the police offered a £7,500 reward for information on the other gang members.

April—Shiblu Rahman (34), stabbed to death by a gang of white youths in Bow, east London, as he returned home from work. In December 2001, 16-year-old Stephen Hansen was found guilty of murder and sentenced to life. Two others were sentenced to nine years for manslaughter, and a 16-year-old was convicted of perverting the course of justice. Another man was cleared of all charges. Police said the murder was 'purely racial'.

July—Sharon Bubb (30), tortured before having her throat cut at her flat in Bow, east London. Her 26-year-old Scottish boyfriend, George McMaster, confessed to killing her. He was jailed for life after pleading guilty to manslaughter on the grounds of diminished responsibilty. McMaster, an alcoholic and cocaine addict, was found to be suffering from severe personality disorders. When asked by police why he killed her, he replied, 'It was because she was black' and 'I don't care that she is dead'.

August—Firsat Dag (22), a Turkish-Kurd dispersed to the notorious Sighthill estate in Glasgow, stabbed to death by two white men. In December 2001, 26-year-old Scott Burrell found guilty and jailed for life for his murder. Charges of racial motivation were withdrawn halfway through the trial because of insufficent evidence.

2002

August—Peiman Bahmani (28), an Iranian asylum seeker who died after being stabbed in a racist attack in Hendon, Sunderland. Police made arrests soon after the murder, and 18-year-old Steven Roberts from Edinburgh was charged with murder, racially aggravated assault and violent disorder. Two Sunderland men, 22-year-old Joseph Rutherford and 27-year-old Gavin Gash, were also remanded and charged

with racially aggravated assault and violent disorder.

September—Shah Wahab (37), died
two days after suffering serious head
injuries after an unprovoked attack
while waiting for a bus in Southampton.

January—Mohammed Isa Hasan Ali
(22), Afghani asylum seeker who died
a day after being attacked by a gang of
men in Southampton. Alexander Briant
has been charged with manslaughter.

NOTE

Compiled and Copyright by the Institute of Race Relations, 2003.

Appendix Two

Chronology of Stephen Lawrence Case

BREACH

1993

22 April Stephen Lawrence murdered by gang of white youths in an area known for racist violence. Police say racial abuse was shouted prior to attack.

6 May Lawrences meet Nelson Mandela. They criticise police for "patronising" them and for not acting in spite of being given names and addresses of suspects.

7 May Police detain three youths for questioning, then release them.

8 May Antiracism demonstration to protest Stephen's killing turns violent.

14 May One youth is charged in court and remanded in custody.

18 June 800 people attend Stephen's memorial service.

24 June A second youth is charged.

4 July Lawrences bury Stephen's body in Jamaica.

29 July Charges dropped against both suspects for 'insufficient evidence'. Lawrences describe this as 'hurtful and painful'.

CRISIS

13 Sept Vigil held on Stephen's birthday.

21 Dec Inquest adjourned after claims 'dramatic' new evidence had been unearthed.

1994

15 April   Lawrences suggest they may mount a private prosecution against suspects.

1995

22 April   Four suspects arrested for proceedings of private prosecution—suspects named for the first time, now over 18 years of age.

23 April   Memorial plaque unveiled for Stephen Lawrence.

23 Aug   Committal hearing takes place to judge sufficiency of evidence against four suspects.

29 Aug   Fifth suspect, Gary Dobson, is charged.

7, 8 Sept   Jamie Acourt, David Norris discharged due to insufficient evidence.

11 Sept   Remaining three suspects committed for trial.

1996

16 April   Private prosecution begins.

25 April   Private prosecution collapses because of flawed identification evidence by Duwayne Brooks. Content of covert surveillance video showing extreme racial prejudice of suspects is now revealed, which was shown at committal hearing but not at private prosecution.

1997

10 Feb   Inquest reopens. Doreen Lawrence comments on insensitivity of police—presenting officer with list of names which he rolled up into a ball.

11 Feb   Suspects are questioned and stonewall all proceedings by 'claiming privilege'.

12 Feb   Detective in charge of case testifies that within forty-eight hours of the murder police had received tip-offs of names of suspects but did not act on them for two days. In the next few weeks, these same names were given again and again to the police from various sources.

13 Feb   Jury returns verdict of 'unlawful killing from a completely unprovoked racist attack by five white youths'. Lawrences lodge formal complaint against police. Home Secretary Michael Howard says he will consider a public inquiry into the handling of the case.

14 Feb   *Daily Mail* names suspects as 'Murderers'.

4 Jun   New home secretary, Jack Straw, meets Doreen Lawrence.

31 July   Straw announces convening of public inquiry to be headed by William Macpherson.

15 Dec   PCA report published, finding a number of failings on the part of po-
          lice in conduct of case but no finding of racism.

1998

13 Mar   PCA recommends that one police officer face disciplinary charges over
          Lawrence case.

REDRESS

16 Mar   Inquiry begins and is immediately halted due to concerns over chair-
          man, which are assuaged by Straw.

24 Mar   Inquiry reopens with evidence about 'seriously flawed' police behav-
          iour, including failure to make arrests, protect witnesses and collect
          crucial evidence.

25 Mar   Doreen Lawrence testifies about police treatment of family.

30 Mar   Neville Lawrence testifies about informing police of suspects having
          been seen washing blood off themselves.

31 Mar   Hospital staff testify about 'unease' of police approach to black vic-
          tims.

1 April   Police officer testifies about failing to stop racists' car at murder scene.

2 April   Senior officer at scene acknowledges initial suspicion of Duwayne
          Brooks.

8 April   Officer admits police had sufficient information to arrest suspects
          within forty-eight hours.

20 April Police Commissioner Condon says through counsel that inquiry is 'un-
          fair to police'.

21 April Inquiry hears that raid at suspects' home two weeks after murder had
          produced knives and swords.

23 April Inquiry hears from photographer about surveillance, suspects carrying
          bags of clothing and the lack of action taken.

24 April Inquiry hears of failure to challenge Gary Dobson with photographs at
          interview.

27 April Investigating detective tells inquiry that he still thinks murder was not
          racially motivated.

28 April Family liaison officer suggests to inquiry that Lawrences were taken
          over by antiracist causes.

30 April Inquiry hears that vital witness was ignored by police for five years.

8 May   Inquiry hears allegations of possible corruption by a police officer with
          links to the Norris family.

13 May	Detective accepts error in not making arrests sooner.
14 May	Five suspects try to block summons to attend inquiry.
15 May	Duwayne Brooks testifies about murder and police insensitivity. Neville Lawrence collapses from distress.
19 May	Police officers accept that they knew of witness intimidation but took no action.
28 May	Inquiry hears that detective in charge did not meet Lawrence family until one year after the murder.
4 June	Officer admits to inquiry that original 1993 internal police review had omitted police mistakes.
15 June	Videotape showing suspects' extreme racial prejudice is shown to inquiry.
17 June	Metropolitan Police apologise to Lawrences at inquiry.
18 June	High Court rules that suspects must attend inquiry but cannot be asked of guilt or innocence.
30 June	The five suspects testify. Nation of Islam disturbance takes place. Suspects are pelted and verbally abused by protesting crowds as they leave the inquiry.
Early July	Inquiry told of Clifford Norris's power and influence. Police deny corruption claims.
20 July	First stage of inquiry ends. Lawrences call for Condon's resignation.
29 July	Police set up task force to tackle corruption and racism in the ranks.
16 Sept	Inquiry reopens.
1 Oct	Condon testifies—apologises to Lawrences but dismisses racism charges.
13 Oct	Chief Constable of Greater Manchester acknowledges to inquiry that his force is institutionally racist, infuriating his officers.
21 Oct	Deputy Chief Constable of West Yorkshire acknowledges racism in his police force.
13 Nov	Inquiry ends.
25 Dec	Lawrences deliver alternative Christmas message.

1999

| 6 Jan | Tricycle Theatre's 'Colour of Justice', an edited version of the inquiry proceedings, opens to rave reviews. |
| 12 Jan | PCA report announces only one officer to face charges in Lawrence case because all others have retired, finds no evidence of racial discrimination by police in Lawrence case. |

18 Feb	Paul Greengrass's documentary, 'The Murder of Stephen Lawrence', airs on ITV.
19 Feb	Suspects' mothers appear in radio interview proclaiming their sons' innocence. *Daily Mail* invites them to sue for libel.
20 Feb	Government obtains injunction to prevent leaked extracts of inquiry report from publication.
22 Feb	High Court lifts injunction.
24 Feb	Inquiry report is released with key finding of 'institutionalised racism' in police force and seventy extensive recommendations.
26 Feb	Lawrence memorial defaced by white paint.
17 Mar	Lawrences invited to Scotland to back campaign for justice for Surjit Chhokar, the Sikh waiter murdered by three white men—antiracist campaigners call him Scotland's Stephen Lawrence.
18 Mar	New scheme announced for racist criminals in Eltham to be targeted by specialist police officers.

REINTEGRATION/SCHISM

8 April	Suspects interviewed on Granada TV by Martin Bashir—proclaim their innocence much to the anger of the Lawrences.
17 April	Nail bomb explodes in Brixton—suspicion that it was a backlash to Stephen Lawrence inquiry by right-wing groups.
19 April	Two Lawrence suspects are charged with burglary at a drinks depot.
21 April	Lawrences begin process of suing suspects and police.
23 April	Lawrences named Media Personalities of the Year at Race in the Media Awards.
24 April	Second nail bomb explodes in Brick Lane.
25 May	Lawrence suspects fined for depot burglary.
28 May	Lawrences named public figures of the year at Ethnic Multicultural Media Awards.
9 July	Lawrences announce that they have divorced.
13 July	Police tribunal clears only police officer facing serious disciplinary action in Lawrence case of 26 out of 28 charges.
22 July	Police officer receives verbal caution [reprimand] for remaining two charges.
23 Aug	Duwayne Brooks launches suit against police for negligence and discrimination.

13 Sept	Antiracism guidelines announced for British judges in response to Stephen Lawrence inquiry.
17 Sept	Duwayne Brooks is arrested and charged with sexual assault of an eighteen-year-old girl.
3 Oct	Programme of reforms to educate police on ethnic minorities announced in response to Stephen Lawrence inquiry.
11 Oct	Law Commission raises prospect of new Stephen Lawrence trial with proposals to review 'double jeopardy' law. Legal experts doubt suspects could receive a fair trial because of publicity.

2000

7 Jan	Neville Lawrence makes complaint against police after being stopped and questioned.
21 Mar	Police arrest two men in connection to Stephen Lawrence murder—not among original five suspects. Duwayne Brooks is cleared of all charges of sexual assault following a 'series of errors and misjudgements' by the prosecution.
22 Mar	Third man is arrested in connection to the Lawrence murder.
12 May	Art gallery dedicated to Stephen Lawrence opens in University of Greenwich.
14 Oct	Metropolitan Police agree to pay Lawrences £320,000 compensation.
14 Dec	William Hague blames Macpherson report for rise in crime—receives much criticism from other parties and some senior Tories.

EBBING/REVIVIFICATION

2001

12 Feb	Brooks's lawsuit against the Met is thrown out; Brooks appeals.
17 Feb	Two women are arrested and bailed on suspicion of perverting the course of justice in the Stephen Lawrence murder case.
2 Apr	Race Relations (Amendment) Act comes into force, covering all public bodies and bringing them under the accountability of the Commission for Racial Equality (CRE).
13 Sept	The parents of one of the suspects are arrested over allegations of providing a false alibi.
3 Dec	In keeping with Race Relations (Amendment) Act, CRE releases legally binding Code of Practice to 40,000 public bodies to tackle race discrimination and promote equality.

4 Dec   A labourer is arrested and bailed on suspicion of murdering Stephen
             Lawrence.

2002

26 Mar   Brooks appeal to sue the police is upheld.

25 Apr   Jury acquits accused in Damilola Taylor murder trial.

17 July   Criminal Justice Bill proposed by Home Secretary David Blunkett in-
             cludes proposal to abolish double jeopardy rule (receives Royal Assent
             20 November 2003).

18 July   A trial begins on two Lawrence suspects accused of a racist attack on
             an off-duty policeman.

24 July   The two suspects are convicted of the attack.

Aug   Doreen Lawrence expresses hope of a retrial in the Lawrence murder
             if the double jeopardy rule is repealed.

6 Sept   The two Lawrence suspects found guilty of the racist attack on the po-
             liceman are sentenced to eighteen months jail.

31 Dec   The Lawrences are awarded OBEs.

2003

24 Jan   The two Lawrence suspects are released one month early to ease prison
             overcrowding.

22 April   Five hundred people gather in Trafalgar Square for a memorial service
             on the ten-year anniversary of Stephen's murder.

Appendix Three

Average Net Circulation of UK Newspapers, 1993–2003

	1993	1994	1995	1996	1997	1998	1999	2000	2001	2002	2003	1993–2003
Daily Papers												
English												
Sun	3,670,352	4,151,369	4,023,263	3,980,808	3,779,605	3,675,286	3,666,189	3,614,303	3,507,176	3,614,388	3,521,527	3,745,842
Daily Mirror	2,639,131	2,512,687	2,561,831	2,407,561	2,324,109	2,338,049	2,346,970	2,222,811	2,220,996	2,115,289	1,955,315	2,331,341
Daily Mail	1,726,415	1,772,270	1,838,970	2,090,503	2,237,949	2,350,364	2,370,695	2,388,884	2,477,416	2,432,924	2,465,732	2,195,647
Times	388,957	549,770	675,066	790,857	792,151	751,862	724,996	721,506	717,657	692,181	633,067	676,188
Guardian	403,270	400,277	394,810	396,800	403,999	391,919	391,908	397,585	414,425	398,489	385,683	398,106
Financial Times	285,043	287,895	293,161	296,834	328,793	366,969	400,007	474,035	477,476	458,414	437,944	373,325
Independent	333,647	279,468	296,616	265,037	260,223	221,398	224,563	229,863	230,453	225,026	217,474	253,070
UK Other												
Daily Record	750,147	758,459	751,151	716,893	685,039	676,411	637,112	613,099	601,133	546,966	505,249	658,333
Belfast Telegraph	134,640	136,670	136,714	136,787	131,829	124,530	NA	114,961	111,329	111,407	108,651	124,752
Herald	116,045	113,342	108,165	111,542	104,844	101,079	NA	96,855	95,718	91,404	85,932	102,493
Scotsman	85,632	83,553	79,267	77,663	78,762	79,686	77,712	100,147	86,497	75,883	67,591	81,127

Appendix Three (*continued*)

	1993	1994	1995	1996	1997	1998	1999	2000	2001	2002	2003	1993–2003
Sunday/Weekly Papers												
English												
News of the World	4,632,277	4,820,878	4,701,879	4,505,632	4,425,708	4,425,599	4,106,937	4,029,945	4,042,714	3,957,814	3,864,864	4,319,477
Mail on Sunday	1,939,712	1,939,030	2,025,901	2,105,566	2,219,430	2,312,329	2,290,698	2,300,336	2,381,490	2,364,431	2,408,549	2,207,952
Sunday Mirror	2,625,596	2,573,781	2,567,943	2,437,652	2,276,089	1,988,579	1,997,098	1,888,318	1,876,557	1,759,136	1,630,766	2,147,410
Sunday Times	1,224,889	1,232,866	1,257,464	1,325,021	1,343,324	1,349,925	1,343,119	1,382,978	1,383,683	1,389,078	1,322,293	1,323,149
Observer	497,776	486,609	462,185	453,353	439,573	398,983	400,296	443,232	472,711	458,135	441,932	450,435
Independent on Sunday	368,246	317,947	329,712	287,292	287,543	253,907	245,543	249,980	245,250	228,981	214,528	275,357
Voice	50,532	50,147	46,868	41,928	39,146	33,860	34,254	NA	NA	NA	NA	42,391
UK Other												
Sunday Mail (Daily Record)	868,125	852,903	884,279	845,776	821,209	795,952	761,546	722,019	705,540	657,122	614,308	775,344
Scotland on Sunday	84,769	89,745	90,916	92,938	102,917	125,124	113,430	102,703	91,544	82,392	76,692	95,743

Audit Bureau of Circulation (ABC) figures are per issue for the following period of each year unless otherwise specified: May–Oct 1993, May–Oct 1994, Jun–Nov 1995, Jul–Dec 1996, Jul–Dec 1997, Jul–Dec 1998, May–Oct 1999, Jul–Dec 2000, May–Oct 2001, May–Oct 2002, Jun–Jul 2003

Shaded cells signify ABC figures for the period Jan–Jun in these years

Appendix Four

Macpherson Recommendations and Social Reforms

The following Appendix summarises the seventy recommendations of the Stephen Lawrence Inquiry Report by Sir William Macpherson of Cluny, released 24 February 1999. Each category of recommendations is followed by the latest information on institutional reforms stemming from these recommendations that have been implemented, or are scheduled for implementation, as of this book going for publication.

MAIN RECOMMENDATIONS

Openness, Accountability and the Restoration of Confidence

Recommendations 1–11 include:

- That a Ministerial Priority be established for all Police Services: 'To increase trust and confidence in policing amongst minority ethnic communities'
- That Her Majesty's Inspectors of Constabulary (HMIC) be granted full and unfettered powers to inspect all parts of Police Services in order to improve standards of achievement and quality of policing through regular inspection, public reporting and informed independent advice
- That a Freedom of Information Act and the full force of the Race Relations legislation apply to all areas of policing

Status of Reforms

- Ministerial Priority established and HMIC has carried out regular inspections with reports published annually since January 2000

- All police forces have been compliant with new Association of Chief Police Officers (ACPO) Publication Scheme as of June 2003 and will be fully compliant with Freedom of Information legislation by 2005
- Race Relations (Amendment) Act came into force on 2 April 2001, bringing all public functions not previously covered by the Act within its scope and under the accountability of the Commission for Racial Equality (CRE), including the police, hospitals, schools, local councils, customs, licensing, immigration, prison and probation services

Definition, Reporting and Police Investigation of Racist Incidents

Recommendations 12–22 include:

- That the definition to be universally adopted by the police, local government and other relevant agencies should be: 'A racist incident is any incident which is perceived to be racist by the victim or any other person'
- That codes of practice be established to create a comprehensive system of reporting and recording of all racist incidents and crimes and police practices and procedures relating to racist incidents and investigations be openly and thoroughly reviewed

Status of Reforms

- A code of practice on the reporting and recording of racist incidents, promulgating the above definition, was published in May 2000
- The ACPO's "Guide to Identifying and Combating Hate Crime" was updated in April 2002, and critical incident training and diversity strategies have been developed and launched since 1999

Family Liaison, Victims and Witnesses

Recommendations 23–31 include:

- That Police Services ensure that there are readily available designated and trained family liaison officers and that training must include racism awareness and cultural diversity
- That Police Services develop guidelines for the handling of victims and witnesses, particularly in the field of racist incidents and crimes, including proactive use of local contacts within minority ethnic communities and the availability of victim/witness liaison officers

Status of Reforms

- The 'Family Liaison Officers Strategy' and 'National Curriculum for the Training of Family Liaison Officers' have been rolled out to forces

- The Victims of Crime Bill, published in 2003, takes into account the needs of victims and witnesses of racist crimes, and the Witness Service was introduced to all courts in April 2002

Prosecution of Racist Crimes

Recommendations 32–44 include:

- That Police Services and the CPS ensure that particular care is taken at all stages of prosecution to recognise and to include reference to any evidence of racist motivation and that a victim or victim's family shall be consulted and kept informed as to any proposal to discontinue proceedings
- That consideration be given to the court of appeal to permit prosecution after acquittal where fresh and viable evidence is presented
- That consideration be given to amendment of the law to allow prosecution of offences involving racist language or behaviour where such conduct can be proved to have occurred in other than a public place

Status of Reforms

- The CPS has developed a new training programme for all lawyers and caseworkers to complete by the end of 2003 on racially and religiously aggravated crime. The Magistrates New Training Initiative was introduced in 1999, which includes a guide on racial and cultural awareness and compulsory race bias tests. Procedures are also now in place whereby the CPS corresponds directly with the victim on matters relating to the progress of their case
- The Criminal Justice Act received Royal Assent on 20 November 2003, reversing the long held principle of double jeopardy and allowing for retrial following an acquittal in serious cases where new and compelling evidence comes to light

Training

Recommendations 45–54 include:

- That first aid training for all 'public contact' police officers be at once reviewed and revised to ensure that they have basic skills to apply first aid
- That all police officers be trained in racism awareness and valuing cultural diversity, and consideration be given to a review of the provision of such training in local government and other agencies

Status of Reforms

- All police forces now administer first aid training
- Community and race relations training has been ongoing in the police forces since publication of the report. The Institute of Employment Studies was commissioned

to undertake a review of such training in both local and central government with a good practice guide produced based on its findings

Employment, Discipline and Complaints

Recommendations 55–59 include:

- That disciplinary action be available for at least five years after a police officer's retirement and steps be taken to ensure that serious complaints against police officers are independently investigated
- That Police Services, through the implementation of a code of conduct or otherwise, ensure that racist words or acts proved to have been spoken or committed by police officers lead to disciplinary proceedings

Status of Reforms

- The Independent Police Complaints Commission will replace the Police Complaints Authority (PCA) on 1 April 2004, with a wider range of powers than those currently available to the PCA
- A new code of conduct introduced in April 1999 provides for disciplinary proceedings against police officers for any racist language or behaviour

Stop and Search

Recommendations 60–63 include:

- That the home secretary, in consultation with Police Services, ensure that a record is made by police officers of all 'stops' and 'stops and searches' made under any legislative provision with a copy of the record given to the person stopped, and that publicity campaigns be undertaken to ensure that the public is aware of stop and search provisions

Status of Reforms

- A revised Police and Criminal Evidence Act Code A, with new provisions for searches and ethnic monitoring, was implemented on 1 April 2003 together with a phased implementation of the above recommendation. Police authorities have relaunched campaigns to raise people's awareness of their rights when stopped and searched

Recruitment and Retention

Recommendations 64–66 include:

- That the Home Office and Police Services set targets for recruitment, progression and retention of minority ethnic staff and facilitate the development of initiatives to increase the number of qualified minority ethnic recruits

Status of Reforms

- Ten-year targets for recruitment, retention and progression of minority ethnic police officers were set following publication of the inquiry report, and regular reviews are being undertaken to identify and disseminate good practice in this area

- In keeping with its powers under the Race Relations (Amendment) Act, the CRE released a legally binding Code of Practice to 40,000 public bodies on 3 December 2001 to publish and enact race equality schemes, including job training and ethnic recruitment targets

- The Trade Union Congress set up the 'Stephen Lawrence Task Group' and hotline in 2000 for victims of racism in the workplace

- The Commission for Black Staff in Further Education was set up in 1999 to investigate the employment position of black staff and institutional barriers to their career progression in this sector

- The Bar introduced reforms in 2002 to address widespread discrimination experienced by female and ethnic minority lawyers discovered by an investigation into the courts' response to the inquiry report

- The Church of England is considering reforms to increase ethnic minority representation at all levels, including a 1999 amendment to church law allowing services to be conducted in languages other than English

Prevention and the Role of Education

Recommendations 67–70 include:

- That consideration be given to an amendment of the National Curriculum aimed at valuing cultural diversity and preventing racism, and local education authorities and school governors be given the duty to create and implement strategies in their schools to prevent and address racism

- That the Police Services, local government and relevant agencies, in creating strategies under the Crime and Disorder Act or otherwise, specifically consider implementing community and local initiatives aimed at promoting cultural diversity and addressing racism, and the need for focussed, consistent support for such initiatives

Status of Reforms

- The National Curriculum has been revised and a new school inspection framework implemented as of September 2003 to encourage community cohesion and address issues of race and race equality

Bibliography

Alexander, Jeffrey C. (1988). 'Culture and Political Crisis: "Watergate" and Durkheimian Sociology'. In J. C. Alexander (Ed.), *Durkheimian Sociology: Cultural Studies*. New York: Cambridge University Press, 187–224.

Alexander, Jeffrey C., and Jacobs, Ronald N. (1998). 'Mass Communication, Ritual and Civil Society'. In T. Liebes and J. Curran (Eds.), *Media, Ritual and Identity*. London: Routledge, 23–41.

Austin, John L. (1975). *How to Do Things With Words*. Cambridge, MA: Harvard University Press. (Original 1956.)

Bakhtin, Michael. (1986). *Speech Genres and Other Late Essays*. Austin: University of Texas Press.

Barkin, Stephen M., and Gurevitch, Michael. (1987). 'Out of Work and On the Air: Television News and Unemployment'. *Critical Studies in Mass Communication* 4 (4): 1–20.

Barnhurst, Kevin G., and Nerone, John. (2001). *The Form of News: A History*. New York: Guildford Press.

Baudrillard, Jean. (1983). *In the Shadow of the Silent Majorities . . . Or the End of the Social*. New York: Semiotext(e).

Beck, Ulrich. (1992). *Risk Society*. London: Sage.

Becker, Howard. (1967). 'Whose side are we on?'. *Social Problems* 14: 239–47.

Becker, Karen. (1995). 'Media and the ritual process'. *Media, Culture and Society* 17: 629–46.

Bell, Allan, and Garrett, Peter (Eds.). (1998). *Approaches to Media Discourse*. Oxford: Blackwell.

Bendelow, Gillian, and Williams, Simon J. (Eds.). (1998). *Emotions in Social Life: Critical Themes and Contemporary Issues*. London: Routledge.

Benjamin, Walter. (1977). *Illuminations*. London: Fontana/Collins.

Bennett, Lance. (1990). 'Towards a Theory of Press-State Relations in the United States'. *Journal of Communication* 40 (2): 103–25.

Benyon, John (Ed.). (1984). *Scarman and After*. Oxford: Pergamon Press.

Benyon, John, and Solomos, John (Eds.). (1987). *The Roots of Urban Unrest*. Oxford: Pergamon Press.

Bhabha, Homi. (1990). *Nation and Narration*. London: Routledge.

Bird, Elizabeth. (1990). 'Storytelling on the Far Side: Journalism and the Weekly Tabloid'. *Critical Studies in Mass Communication* 7: 377–89.

Blackstone, Tessa, Parekh, Bhikhu and Sanders, Peter (Eds.). (1998). *Race Relations in Britain: A Developing Agenda*. London: Routledge.

Boltanski, Luc. (1999). *Distant Suffering: Morality, Media and Politics*. Cambridge: Cambridge University Press.

Brah, Avatar. (1996). *Cartographies of Diaspora: Contesting Identities*. London: Routledge.

Butler, David. (1995). *The Trouble with Reporting Northern Ireland*. Aldershot: Avebury.

Butler, Judith. (1990). *Gender Trouble: Feminism and the Subversion of Identity*. London: Routledge.

Campbell, Richard. (1987). 'Securing the Middle Ground: Reporter Formulas in 60 Minutes'. *Critical Studies in Mass Communication* 4 (4): 325–50.

Carey, James. (1989). *Communication as Culture*. London: Unwin Hyman.

———. (1998). 'Political Ritual on Television: Episodes in the History of Shame, Degradation and Excommunication'. In T. Liebes and J. Curran (Eds.), *Media, Ritual and Identity*. London: Routledge, 42–70.

Carlson, Marvin. (1996). *Performance: A Critical Introduction*. London: Routledge.

Cashmore, Ellis, and McLauglin, Eugene. (Eds.). (1991). *Out of Order? Policing Black People*. London: Routledge.

Cathcart, Brian. (2000). *The Case of Stephen Lawrence*. London: Penguin Books.

Chaney, David. (1986). 'The Symbolic Form of Ritual in Mass Communication'. In P. Golding, G. Murdock, and P. Schlesinger (Eds.), *Communicating Politics: Mass Communication and Political Process*. Leicester: Leicester University Press, 115–32.

———. (1993). *Fictions of Collective Life: Public Drama in Late Modern Culture*. London: Routledge.

Clifford, James. (1997). *Routes: Travel and Translation in the Late Twentieth Century*. Cambridge, MA: Harvard University Press.

Cohen, Stanley. (1972). *Folk Devils and Moral Panics: The Creation of the Mods and Rockers*. London: MacKibbon and Kee.

Collins, Randal. (2003). 'Stratification, Emotional Energy, and the Transient Emotions'. In M. Emirbayer (Ed.), *Emile Durkheim: Sociologist of Modernity*. Oxford: Blackwell, 129–33.

Commission for Racial Equality. (1999). *Racial Attacks and Harassment*. CRE Factsheets. London: Commission for Racial Equality.

Corner, John. (1991). 'Meaning, Genre and Context: The Problematics of "Public Knowledge" in the New Audience Studies'. In J. Curran and M. Gurevitch (Eds.), *Mass Media and Society*. First edition. London: Edward Arnold, 267–84.

———. (1995). *Television Form and Public Address*. London: Edward Arnold.

Coser, Lewis A. (1977). *Masters of Sociological Thought*. Second edition. New York: Harcourt Brace Jovanovich.

Cottle, Simon. (1992). ' "Race", Racialization and the Media: A Review and Update of Research'. *Sage Race Relations Abstracts* 17 (2): 3–57.

———. (1993). *TV News, Urban Conflict and the Inner City*. Leicester: Leicester University Press.

———. (1998). 'Analysing News Visuals'. In A. Hansen et al., *Mass Communication Research Methods*. Basingstoke: Palgrave.

———. (Ed.). (2000). *Ethnic Minorities and the Media: Changing Cultural Boundaries*. Buckingham: Open University Press.

———. (2002). 'Television Agora and Agoraphobia Post September 11'. In S. Allan and B. Zelizer (Eds.), *Journalism Post September 11*. London: Routledge, 178–98.

———. (Ed.). (2003a). *News, Public Relations and Power*. London: Sage.

———. (Ed.). (2003b). *Media Organization and Production*. London: Sage.

———. (2004). 'Representations'. In E. Cashmore (Ed.), *Encylopedia of Race and Ethnic Studies*. London: Routledge, 368–72.

———. (2005). 'In defence of "Thick" Journalism'. In Stuart Allen (Ed.), *Journalism: Critical Issues*. Maidenhead: Open University Press.

Couldry, Nick. (2003). *Media Rituals: A Critical Approach*. London: Routledge.

Critcher, Chas. (2003). *Moral Panics*. London: Routledge.

Crossly, Nick. (1998). 'Emotion and Communicative Action'. In G. Bendelow and S. J. Williams (Eds.), *Emotions in Social Life: Critical Themes and Contemporary Issues*. London: Routledge, 16–38.

Curran, James. (1991). 'Rethinking the Media as Public Sphere'. In P. Dahlgren and C. Sparks (Eds.), *Communication and Citizenship*. London: Routledge, 27–57.

Dahlgren, Peter. (1995). *Television and the Public Sphere—Citizenship, Democracy and the Media*. London: Sage.

Dahlgren, Peter, and Sparks, Colin. (Eds.). (1992). *Journalism and Popular Culture*. London: Sage.

Dayan, Daniel. (2001). 'The Peculiar Publics of Television'. *Media, Culture and Society* 23 (6): 743–65.

Dayan, Daniel, and Katz, Elihu. (1994). *Media Events: The Live Broadcasting of History*. Cambridge, MA: Harvard University Press.

Debord, Guy. (1983). *Society of the Spectacle*. Detroit: Black and Red.

Durkheim, Émile. (1965). *The Elementary Forms of Religious Life*. New York: Free Press. (Original 1912.)

Edkin, Jenny. (2003). *Trauma and the Memory of Politics*. Cambridge: Cambridge University Press.

Elliott, Philip. (1977). 'Reporting Northern Ireland in London, Dublin and Belfast'. In *Ethnicity and the Media*. Paris: UNESCO, 263–375.

———. (1980). 'Press Performance as Political Ritual'. In H. Christian (Ed.), *The Sociology of Journalism and the Press*. University of Keele: Sociological Review Monograph, no. 29, 141–77.

———. (1986). 'Intellectuals, "the Information Society" and the Disappearance of the Public Sphere'. In R. Collins et al. (Eds.), *Media, Culture and Society— A Critical Reader*. London: Sage, 247–63.

Elliott, Philip, Murdock, Graham, and Schlesinger, Philip. (1986). 'Terrorism and the State: A Case Study of the Discourses of Television'. In R. Collins, J. Curran, N. Garnham, P. Scannell, P. Schlesinger, and C. Sparks (Eds.), *Media, Culture and Society—A Critical Reader*. London: Sage, 264–286.

Emirbayer, Mustapha. (Ed.). (2003). *Emile Durkheim: Sociologist of Modernity*. Oxford: Blackwell.

Ettema, James. (1990). 'Press Rites and Race Relations: A Study of Mass Mediated Ritual'. *Critical Studies in Mass Communication* 7: 309–31.

Faircloth, Norman. (1995). *Media Discourse*. London: Edward Arnold.

Fiske, John. (1994). *Media Matters: Everyday Culture and Political Change*. Minneapolis: University of Minnesota Press.

Fowler, Roger. (1991). *Language in the News: Discourse and Ideology in the Press*. London: Routledge.

Fowler, Roger, Hodge, Bob, Kress, Gunter, and Trew, Tony. (1979). *Language and Control*. London: Routledge and Kegan Paul.

Fraser, Nancy. (1992). 'Rethinking the Public Sphere: A Contribution to the Critique of Actually Existing Democracy'. In C. Calhoun (Ed.), *Habermas and the Public Sphere*. Cambridge, MA: MIT Press, 109–42.

Fryer, Peter. (1984). *Staying Power: The History of Black People in Britain*. London: Pluto Press.

Gabriel, John. (2000). 'Dreaming of a White . . .'. In S. Cottle (Ed.), *Ethnic Minorities and the Media: Changing Cultural Boundaries*. Buckingham: Open University Press, 67–82.

Garnham, Nicholas. (1986). 'The Media as Public Sphere'. In P. Golding, G. Murdock, and P. Schlesinger (Eds.), *Communicating Politics*. Leicester: Leicester University Press, 37–53.

Geertz, Clifford. (1992). 'The Balinese Cockfight as Play'. In J. C. Alexander and S. Seidman (Eds.), *Culture and Society: Contemporary Debates*. Cambridge: Cambridge University Press, 113–21.

Giddens, Anthony. (1971). *Capitalism and Modern Social Theory—An Analysis of the Writings of Marx, Durkheim and Max Weber*. Cambridge: Cambridge University Press.

Gilroy, Paul. (1987). *There Ain't No Black in the Union Jack*. London: Hutchinson.

Glasgow University Media Group. (1976). *Bad News*. London: Routledge & Kegan Paul.

———. (1980). *More Bad News*. London: Routledge & Kegan Paul.

Goffman, Erving. (1959). *The Presentation of Self in Everyday Life*. New York: Doubleday.

———. (1974). *Frame Analysis*. Harmondsworth: Penguin.

Goode, Erich, and Ben-Yehuda, Nacham. (1994). *Moral Panics: The Social Construction of Deviance*. Oxford: Blackwell.

Gordon, Paul, and Rosenberg, David. (1989). *Daily Racism: The Press and Black People in Britain*. London: Runnymede Trust.

Habermas, Jürgen. (1989). *The Structural Transformation of the Public Sphere*. Cambridge: Polity Press.

———. (1996). *Between Facts and Norms*. Cambridge: Polity Press.

Hall, Stuart. (Ed.). (1988). *The Hard Road to Renewal: Thatcherism and the Crisis of the Left*. London: Verso.

———. (1999). 'Interview with Stuart Hall: Culture and Power'. In R. Torres, L. F. Miron, and J. X. Inda (Eds.), *Race, Identity and Citizenship: A Reader*. Oxford: Blackwell, 389–412.

———. (2000). 'The Multicultural Question'. Political Economy Research Centre Annual Lecture, University of Sheffield, at *www.sheff.ac.uk*.

Hall, Stuart, Critcher, Chas, Jefferson, Tony, Clarke, John, and Roberts, Brian. (1978). *Policing the Crisis: Mugging the State and Law and Order*. London: Macmillan.

Hallin, Daniel. (1986). *The 'Uncensored' War: The Media and Vietnam*. Oxford: Oxford University Press.

———. (1994). *We Keep America on Top of the World: Television Journalism and the Public Sphere*. London: Routledge.

Hodge, Bob, and Kress, Gunter. (1979). *Language as Ideology*. Cambridge: Polity.

———. (1998). *Social Semiotics*. Cambridge: Polity.

Hughes-Freeland, Felicia. (Ed.). (1998). *Ritual, Performance, Media*. London: Routledge.

Hunt, Darnell M. (1999). *O. J. Simpson: Fact and Fictions*. Cambridge: Cambridge University Press.

Hymes, Dell. (1975). 'Breakthrough into Performance'. In D. Ben-Amos and K. S. Goldstein (Eds.), *Folklore: Performance and Communication*. The Hague: Mouton.

Institute of Race Relations. (1987). *Policing Against Black People*. London: Institute of Race Relations.

———. (2001). *Counting the Cost: Racial Violence since Macpherson*. London: Institute of Race Relations.

———. (2002a). *Racially Motivated Murders (Known or Suspected) Since 1991*. Factfile. London: Institute of Race Relations.

———. (2002b). *Racial Violence*. Factfile. London: Institute of Race Relations.

———. (2003). *Rising Deaths as a Result of Racial Violence*. London: Institute of Race Relations.

Jacobs, Ronald N. (2000). *Race, Media and the Crisis of Civil Society: From Watts to Rodney King*. Cambridge: Cambridge University Press.

Julien, Isaac, and Mercer, Kobena. (1988). 'Introduction: de Margin and de centre'. *Screen* 29 (4): 2–10.

Kellner, Douglas. (2003). *Media Spectacle*. London: Routledge.

Kerner, Oscar. (1968). *Report of the National Advisory Commission on Civil Disorder*. New York: Bantam Books.

Kertzer, David I. (1988). *Ritual, Politics and Power*. New Haven, CT: Yale University Press.

Kress, Gunter, and Leeuwen, Theo van. (1996). *Reading Images: The Grammar of Visual Design*. London: Routledge.

———. (1998). 'Front Pages: (The Critical) Analysis of Newspaper Layout'. In A. Bell and P. Garrett (Eds.), *Approaches to Media Discourse*. Oxford: Blackwell.

Langer, John. (1997). *Tabloid Television: Popular Journalism and 'Other News'*. London: Routledge.

Larsen, Bent Steeg, and Tufte, Thomas. (2003). 'Rituals in the Modern World: Applying the Concept of Ritual in Media Ethnography'. In P. D. Murphy and M. M. Kraidy (Eds.), *Global Media Studies: Ethnographic Perspectives*. London: Routledge, 90–106.

Law, Ian. (2002). *Race in the News*. Basingstoke: Palgrave.

Lester, Anthony. (1998). 'From Legislation to Integration: Twenty Years of the Race Relations Act'. In T. Blackstone, B. Parekh, and P. Sanders (Eds.), *Race Relations in Britain: A Developing Agenda*. London: Routledge, 22–35.

Livingstone, Sonia, and Lunt, Peter. (1993). *Talk on Television—Audience Participation and Public Debate*. London: Routledge.

Lukes, Stephen. (1973). *Emile Durkheim: His Life and Work*. London: Allen Lane.

———. (1975). 'Political Ritual and Social Integration'. *Sociology* 9 (2): 289–308.

Lull, James, and Hinerman, Stephen (Eds.). (1997). *Media Scandals: Morality and Desire in the Popular Market Place*. Cambridge: Polity Press.

Macpherson, Sir William. (1999). *The Stephen Lawrence Inquiry—Report of an Inquiry by Sir William Macpherson of Cluny*. Cm 4262-I. London: The Stationary Office.

Malik, Kenan. (1996). *The Meaning of Race: Race, History and Culture in Western Society*. Basingstoke: Macmillan.

Malik, Sarita. (2002). *Representing Black Britain: Black and Asian Images on Television*. London: Sage.

Manning, Paul. (2001). *News and News Sources: A Critical Introduction*. London: Sage.

McGuigan, Jim. (2000). 'British Identity and the "People's Princess"'. *The Sociological Review* 50 (1): 1–18.

McRobbie, Angela. (1994). 'The Moral Panic in the Age of the Postmodern Mass Media'. In A. McRobbie (Ed.), *Postmodernism and Popular Culture*. London: Routledge, 198–219.

Media International Australia. (1997). 'Panic: Morality, Media, Culture'. Special Edition, *Media International Australia*, no. 85.

Meštrović, Stjepan G. (1998). *Anthony Giddens: The Last Modernist*. London: Routledge.

Miles, Robert. (1982). *Racism and Migrant Labour*. London: George Allen and Unwin.

Miles, Robert, and Torres, Rodolfo D. (1999). 'Does "Race" Matter? Transatlantic Perspectives on Racism after "Race Relations"'. In R. D. Torres, L. F. Mirón and J. X. Inda (Eds.), *Race, Identity and Citizenship*. Oxford: Blackwell, 17–38.

Mills, C. Wright. (1975). *The Sociological Imagination*. Harmondsworth: Penguin. (Original 1959).

Parekh, Bhikhu. (1998). 'Integrating Minorities'. In T. Blackstone, B. Parekh, and P. Sanders (Eds.), *Race Relations in Britain: A Developing Agenda*. London: Routledge, 1–21.

———. (2000). *Rethinking Multiculturalism: Cultural Diversity and Political Theory*. Basingstoke: Macmillan.

Parekh Report. (2000). *The Future of Multi-Ethnic Britain*. London: Runnymede Trust.

Peters, John Durham. (1993). 'Distrust of Representation: Habermas on the Public Sphere'. *Media, Culture and Society* 15 (4): 541–72.

———. (1999). *Speaking into the Air*. Chicago: Chicago University Press.

Phillips, Mike, and Phillips, Trevor. (1998). *Windrush: The Irresistible Rise of Multi-Racial Britain*. London: HarperCollins.

Rex, John, and Moore, John. (1967). *Community and Conflict*. London: Oxford University Press.

Rex, John, and Tomlinson, Sally. (1979). *Colonial Immigrants in a British City*. London: Routledge and Kegan Paul.

Rojek, Chris. (2003). *Stuart Hall*. Cambridge: Polity.

Rostas, Susanna. (1998). 'From Ritualization to Performativity: The Concheros of Mexico'. In F. Hughes-Freeland (Ed.), *Ritual, Performance, Media*. London: Routledge.

Rothenbuhler, Eric W. (1998). *Ritual Communication: From Everyday Conversation to Mediated Ceremony*. London: Sage.

Ryfe, David Michael. (2001). 'From Media Audience to Media Public: A Study of Letters Written in Reaction to FDR's Fireside Chats'. *Media, Culture and Society* 23 (6): 767–81.

Scannell, Paddy. (2001). 'Media Events'. *Media Culture and Society* 17 (1): 151–57.

Scarman, Lord. (1984). *The Scarman Report: The Brixton disorder 10–12 April 1981*. London: Pelican Books.

Schieffelin, Edward L. (1998). 'Problematizing Performance'. In F. Hughes-Freeland (Ed.), *Ritual, Performance, Media*. London: Routledge.

Schlesinger, Philip, and Tumber, Howard. (1994). *Reporting Crime: The Media Politics of Criminal Justice*. Oxford: Oxford University Press.

Searle, John R. (1969). *Speech Acts: An Essay in the Philosophy of Language*. Cambridge: Cambridge University Press.

Sewell, William H. (2003). 'Historical Events as Transformations of Structures: Inventing Revolution in the Bastille'. In M. Emirbayer (Ed.), *Emile Durkheim: Sociologist of Modernity*. Oxford: Blackwell, 134–38.

Shils, Edward, and Young, Michael. (1956). 'The Meaning of the Coronation'. *Sociological Review* 1 (2): 63–82.

Sivanandan, Ambalavaner. (1990). 'All That Melts into Air is Solid: The Hohum of New Times'. *Race and Class* 31 (3): 1–30.

Silverstone, Roger. (1994). *Television and Everyday Life*. London: Routledge.

Skellington, Richard, and Morris, Pauline. (1992). *'Race' in Britain Today*. London: Sage.

Smith, Susan. (1989). *The Politics of Race and Residence*. Cambridge: Polity.

Solomos, John, and Back, Les. (1996). *Racism and Society*. Basingstoke: Macmillan.

Solomos, John, Findley, Bob, Jones, Simon, and Gilroy, Paul. (1982). 'The Organic Crisis of British Capitalism and Race: The Experience of the Seventies'. In Centre for Contemporary Cultural Studies (Eds.), *The Empire Strikes Back: Race and Racism in 70s Britain*. London: Hutchinson, 9–46.

Sontag, Susan. (2003). *Regarding the Pain of Others*. New York: Farrar, Straus and Giroux.

Tester, Keith. (1994). 'Media and Morality'. Chap. 4 in *Media, Culture and Morality*. London: Routledge.

———. (1995). 'Moral Solidarity and the Technological Reproduction of Images'. *Media, Culture and Society* 17: 469–82.

Thompson, John B. (1995). *The Media and Modernity—A Social Theory of the Media.* Cambridge: Polity Press.

———. (2000). *Political Scandal: Power and Visibility in the Media Age.* Cambridge: Polity Press.

Thompson, Kenneth. (1988). *Emile Durkheim.* London: Tavistock Publications.

———. (1998). *Moral Panics.* London: Routledge.

Tomlinson, John. (1997). ' "And Besides the Wench is Dead": Media Scandals and the Globalization of Communication'. In J. Lull and S. Hinerman (Eds.), *Media Scandals: Morality and Desire in the Popular Market Place.* Cambridge: Polity Press.

Tumber, Howard. (1982). *Television and the Riots.* Broadcasting Research Unit. London: British Film Institute.

Turner, Brian, and Rojek, Chris. (2001). *Society and Culture: Principles of Scarcity and Solidarity.* London: Sage.

Turner, Victor. (1969). *The Ritual Process: Structure and Antistructure.* Ithaca, NY: Cornell University Press.

———. (1974). *Dramas, Fields, and Metaphors: Symbolic Action in Human Society.* Ithaca, NY: Cornell University Press.

———. (1981). 'Social Dramas and Stories about Them'. In W.J.T. Mitchell (Ed.), *On Narrative.* Chicago: University of Chicago Press, 137–64.

———. (1982). *From Ritual to Theatre: The Human Seriousness of Play.* New York: Performing Arts Journal Publication.

Van Dijk, Teun. (1988). *News as Discourse.* Hillsdale, NJ: Lawrence Erlbaum.

———. (1991). *Racism in the Press.* London: Routledge.

———. (2000). 'New(s) Racism: A Discourse Analytical Approach'. In S. Cottle (Ed.), *Ethnic Minorities and the Media.* Buckingham: Open University Press, 33–49.

Volosinov, Valentin N. (1973). *Marxism and the Philosophy of Language.* New York: Seminar Press.

Wagner-Pacifici, Robin E. (1986). *The Moro Morality Play: Terrorism as Social Drama.* Chicago: University of Chicago Press.

Walby, Sylvia. (1991). *Theorizing Patriarchy.* Oxford: Blackwell.

Watney, Simon. (1987). 'Moral Panics'. Chap. 3 in *Policing Desire.* London: Comedia, 38–57.

Williams, Raymond. (1985). *Marxism and Literature.* Oxford: Oxford University Press.

Wolfsfeld, Gadi. (1997). *Media and Political Conflict.* Cambridge: Cambridge University Press.

———. (2003). 'The Political Contest Model'. In S. Cottle (Ed.), *News, Public Relations and Power.* London: Sage, 81–95.

Yuval-Davis, Nira. (1999). 'Ethnicity, Gender Relations and Multiculturalism'. In R. Torres, L. F. Mirón and J. X. Inda (Eds.), *Race, Identity and Citizenship: A Reader.* Oxford: Blackwell, 112–25.

Zelizer, Barbie, and Allan, Stuart (Eds.). (2002). *Journalism After September 11.* London: Routledge.

Index

About the Author

SIMON COTTLE is Director of the Media and Communications Program at the University of Melbourne, Victoria, Australia. He has written extensively on the changing practices and forms of journalism and the mediatisation of conflicts including riots, demonstrations and protests, the environment and 'risk society', war and 9/11, and 'race', racism and ethnicity. His books include *TV News, Urban Conflict and the Inner City* (1993), *Television and Ethnic Minorities: Producers' Perspectives* (1997), *Mass Communication Research Methods* (coauthor 1998), *Ethnic Minorities and the Media: Changing Cultural Boundaries* (editor 2000), *Media Production and Organization* (editor 2003) and *News, Public Relations and Power* (editor 2003). He is currently preparing two new books, *Mediatized Conflicts* (2005) and *Global Crisis, Global Reporting* (2006), and directing an international research study examining the changing forms and flows of terrestrial and satellite television journalism in the US, UK, Australia, India, South Africa and Singapore and how these communicate global crises.